Learn Azure S

Integrate Azure security with artificial intelligence to build secure cloud systems

Richard Diver

Gary Bushey

BIRMINGHAM—MUMBAI

Learn Azure Sentinel

Commissioning Editor: Vijin Boricha

Acquisition Editor: Meeta Rajani

Senior Editor: Arun Nadar

Content Development Editor: Romy Dias

Technical Editor: Mohd Riyan Khan

Copy Editor: Safis Editing

Project Coordinator: Neil D'mello

Proofreader: Safis Editing

Indexer: Rekha Nair

Production Designer: Alishon Mendonca

First published: March 2020

Production reference: 1030420

Published by Packt Publishing Ltd.

Livery Place

35 Livery Street

Birmingham

B3 2PB, UK.

ISBN 978-1-83898-092-4

www.packt.com

Packt.com

Subscribe to our online digital library for full access to over 7,000 books and videos, as well as industry leading tools to help you plan your personal development and advance your career. For more information, please visit our website.

Why subscribe?

- Spend less time learning and more time coding with practical eBooks and Videos from over 4,000 industry professionals

- Improve your learning with Skill Plans built especially for you

- Get a free eBook or video every month

- Fully searchable for easy access to vital information

- Copy and paste, print, and bookmark content

Did you know that Packt offers eBook versions of every book published, with PDF and ePub files available? You can upgrade to the eBook version at packt.com and as a print book customer, you are entitled to a discount on the eBook copy. Get in touch with us at customercare@packtpub.com for more details.

At www.packt.com, you can also read a collection of free technical articles, sign up for a range of free newsletters, and receive exclusive discounts and offers on Packt books and eBooks.

Foreword

It is my great pleasure to contribute the foreword to this piece of work by Gary and Richard. We are in exciting times! Not only is the technology of Azure Sentinel exciting, the opportunity that it presents is exciting as well.

Having been in the technology and security consulting business for around 25 years, I've seen many things that have been called "Next Generation" and "Game Changing" before. But I will say that what is happening right now only happens once in a career. Some would say a statement like this is hyperbole but hear me out. I doubt that we'll have another opportunity in our careers to witness the coming of age of the public cloud, the coming of age of Microsoft's security reference architecture, and the coming of age of cyber security in general...all converging at the same time. What I mean by this convergence is that these things have all hit critical mass in a way that each enables the other, so much so that it will be difficult to tell them apart in a few years.

With this convergence will come change, and disruption as well, which can create a certain amount of chaos and uncertainty. Should we be doing so many things so differently than we have been? Can this newly created technology really be as stable and capable as where we came from? Will we even be able to do things in the same way, and if we can't, who will lead us out of the darkness? To be plain, Microsoft has made the right investments in security. They eat their own dog food in that everything they release is vetted on their own global network. They've quit developing security products as separate components and now focus on the full platform. They recognize that a multi-platform, hybrid infrastructure exists in most environments and they've attacked those problems head on.

Azure Sentinel is capable of bringing Microsoft's own products together, but it additionally brings the capability of being a central component of an organization's security operations center and that is a game changer.

Gary and Richard have embraced the latest tech from Microsoft's security platform and worked with forward-looking clients that have the same vision to assess, architect, and implement this tech even with the (almost weekly) changing capabilities and consoles as Microsoft aggressively integrates and enhances their platform. Whenever there is something new, it takes some brave hearts to invest the time and effort to explore the landscape, make some assumptions, and make it work...and I've watched these guys do just that.

There is a reward for them and for the consumers of this material. For them, they can plant the flag on this hill, congratulate themselves for the discovery thus far, and make preparations for the next leg of the journey. For you, there is a wealth of knowledge compiled here by folks that earned it the old-fashioned way. And knowing what I do about these guys, they are happy to be the Sherpas for you on your Sentinel journey. Enjoy!

Jason S. Rader,

Director of Network and Cloud Security at Insight

Contributors

About the authors

Richard Diver has over 25 years' international experience in technology with a deep technical background in cloud security, identity management, and information security. He works at Insight as the lead for Cloud Security Architecture, working with top partners across the industry to deliver comprehensive cloud security solutions. Any spare time he gets is usually spent with his family.

I would like to thank my loving family for allowing me to take time out to write this book, especially encouraging me during those times of procrastination!

Thank you to Gary for taking on this challenge with enthusiasm and passion, I could not have done this without your expertise. Also, to the experts that have helped to improve this book, including Ashwin Patil, Rod Trent, Dean Gross, Casey Tuohey, and Brandon Huckeba.

Gary Bushey is an Azure security expert with over 25 years of IT experience. He got his start early on when he helped his fifth-grade math teacher with their programming homework and worked all one summer to be able to afford his first computer, a Commodore 64. When he sold his first program, an apartment management system, at 14 he was hooked. During his career, he has worked as a developer, consultant, trainer, and architect. When not spending time in front of a computer, you can find him hiking in the woods, taking pictures, or just picking a direction and finding out what is around the next corner.

First and foremost, I need to thank my parents. They may not understand exactly what I do but they have supported me from allowing me to hook up my Commodore 64 to the color TV to faking interest when I talk about what I do. I'd also like to thank all the people at Microsoft that have helped me. Finally, I need to thank Lora Lake for supporting me through all my crazy decisions that have led to this point and for adopting me as her brother.

About the reviewers

Rod Trent, a community professional, keynoter, and evangelist, is a Cyber PFE for Microsoft and Azure Sentinel SME who spends his entire work life educating customers on how to implement, use, and maintain Azure Sentinel. Rod works with the largest Azure Sentinel implementations in the world. Some may remember Rod from his pre-Microsoft life, where he owned and operated some very significant communities dedicated to IT management and security, ran technology-focused editorial teams, and managed some large and popular technology conferences. When he's not evangelizing Azure Sentinel and digging into KQL queries, he spends time with his wife of 30 years, Megan, and his four wonderful kids, Alex, Rachel, Eric, and Elly.

Ashwin Patil currently works as Senior Program Manager for Microsoft Threat Intelligence Center (MSTIC) and has over 10 years of experience entirely focused on security monitoring and incident response, defending enterprise networks. In his current role, he primarily works on threat hunting, detection research in KQL (Kusto query language) for Azure Sentinel, and developing Jupyter notebooks written in Python/R to do threat hunting and investigation across a variety of cloud and on-premise security event log data sources. He has a bachelor's degree in computer engineering and is also certified with various SANS certifications, such as GCIA, GCFE, and GCIH, in the field of digital forensics and incident response (DFIR).

Packt is searching for authors like you

If you're interested in becoming an author for Packt, please visit `authors.packtpub.com` and apply today. We have worked with thousands of developers and tech professionals, just like you, to help them share their insight with the global tech community. You can make a general application, apply for a specific hot topic that we are recruiting an author for, or submit your own idea.

Table of Contents

2
Azure Monitor – Log Analytics

Section 2:
Data Connectors, Management, and Queries

3
Managing and Collecting Data

4

Integrating Threat Intelligence

5

Using the Kusto Query Language (KQL)

6

Azure Sentinel Logs and Writing Queries

Section 3: Security Threat Hunting

7
Creating Analytic Rules

8
Introducing Workbooks

9
Incident Management

10
Threat Hunting in Azure Sentinel

Section 4: Integration and Automation

11
Creating Playbooks and Logic Apps

12
ServiceNow Integration

Section 5: Operational Guidance

13
Operational Tasks for Azure Sentinel

14
Constant Learning and Community Contribution

Assessments

Other Books You May Enjoy

Preface

Microsoft's launch of Azure Sentinel is a major step forward for **Security Information and Event Management (SIEM)** solutions. As the first completely cloud-first SIEM in the marketplace, Azure Sentinel allows you to collect and query data from Azure, on-premises systems, and other cloud systems.

This book provides you with the guidance you need in order to create, configure, and use Azure Sentinel in your environment.

Who this book is for

This book is for anyone who wants to learn about Azure Sentinel. If you need to install, configure, or use Azure Sentinel, this book is for you.

What this book covers

Chapter 1, Getting Started with Azure Sentinel, will give an overview of Azure Sentinel, including coverage of the current cloud landscape, the cloud security reference framework, **Security Operations Center (SOC)** platform components, and how to map the architecture. You will also learn about integrating on-premises infrastructure into Azure Sentinel as well as how Azure Sentinel is priced.

Chapter 2, Azure Monitor – Log Analytics, will cover Azure Monitor Log Analytics, including planning your Log Analytics instance, how to create a new instance, and how to attach an instance to Azure Sentinel. You will also learn about the advanced settings for Log Analytics and about the Azure Sentinel overview page.

Chapter 3, Data Collection and Management, will explain how to determine what data you need to ingest into Azure Sentinel and how to connect to various data sources to get that information. You will also learn how to adjust data retention plans and how data retention is priced.

Chapter 4, Integrating Threat Intelligence, will introduce you to threat intelligence and how to ingest different threat intelligence feeds into Azure Sentinel.

Chapter 5, Using Kusto Query Language (KQL), will discuss **Kusto Query Language (KQL)** and will explain out how to write your own queries.

Chapter 6, Azure Sentinel Logs and Writing Queries, will introduce you to Azure Sentinel's Logs page and will teach you how to use it to start writing your KQL queries against the data you have ingested.

Chapter 7, Creating Analytic Rules, will teach you how to create analytic rules that will search for anomalies in your environment. It will discuss analytic rule templates and how you can use them to create your own rules as well as how to create them from scratch.

Chapter 8, Introducing Workbooks, will cover Azure Sentinel's workbook page, workbook templates, and how you can create a workbook from a template or from scratch.

Chapter 9, Incident Management, will explain how to manage incidents that your analytic rules create. You will learn about the incident page, how to view an incident's full details, and how to start investigating an incident using Azure Sentinel's Investigate GUI interface.

Chapter 10, Threat Hunting in Azure Sentinel, will introduce you to Azure Sentinel's Hunting page, which will allow you to start your threat hunting activities. It will also briefly discuss Azure Notebook, which is Azure's hosted Jupyter resource. There will also be a discussion of the steps needed to perform your investigation.

Chapter 11, Creating Playbooks and Logic Apps, will introduce you to Azure Sentinel's playbooks and explain how they relate to Logic Apps. You will learn about the logic app Azure Sentinel connector and go through a walk-through about creating your own playbook.

Chapter 12, ServiceNow Integration, will provide an introduction to **Information Technology Service Management (ITSM)**, the ServiceNow application, and how to create a simple Azure Sentinel playbook to create a new ticket in ServiceNow using information from your Azure Sentinel incident.

Chapter 13, Operational Tasks for Azure Sentinel, will cover the steps needed to keep your Azure Sentinel instance running smoothly. The steps will be broken up between your SOC analytics and your SOC engineers, as each have different aspects of Azure Sentinel that they will be responsible for.

Chapter 14, Constant Learning and Community Contributions, contains a list of various places you can go to continuing learning about Azure Sentinel and its supporting resources, including Logic Apps, Jupyter Notebook, KQL, and Fusion.

To get the most out of this book

We recommend that you have access to an Azure environment where you have the rights to create your own Azure Sentinel environment. Prior experience of using the Azure portal would also be beneficial.

Download the color images

We also provide a PDF file that has color images of the screenshots/diagrams used in this book. You can download it here: https://static.packt-cdn.com/downloads/9781838980924_ColorImages.pdf.

Conventions used

There are a number of text conventions used throughout this book.

Code in text: Indicates code words in text, database table names, folder names, filenames, file extensions, pathnames, dummy URLs, user input, and Twitter handles. Here is an example: "Mount the downloaded WebStorm-10* .dmg disk image file as another disk in your system."

A block of code is set as follows:

```
html, body, #map {
  height: 100%;
  margin: 0;
  padding: 0
}
```

When we wish to draw your attention to a particular part of a code block, the relevant lines or items are set in bold:

```
[default]
exten => s,1,Dial(Zap/1|30)
exten => s,2,Voicemail(u100)
exten => s,102,Voicemail(b100)
exten => i,1,Voicemail(s0)
```

Any command-line input or output is written as follows:

```
$ mkdir css
$ cd css
```

Bold: Indicates a new term, an important word, or words that you see onscreen. For example, words in menus or dialog boxes appear in the text like this. Here is an example: "Select **System info** from the **Administration** panel."

> **Tips or important notes**
> Appear like this.

Get in touch

Feedback from our readers is always welcome.

General feedback: If you have questions about any aspect of this book, mention the book title in the subject of your message and email us at customercare@packtpub.com.

Errata: Although we have taken every care to ensure the accuracy of our content, mistakes do happen. If you have found a mistake in this book, we would be grateful if you would report this to us. Please visit www.packtpub.com/support/errata, selecting your book, clicking on the Errata Submission Form link, and entering the details.

Piracy: If you come across any illegal copies of our works in any form on the Internet, we would be grateful if you would provide us with the location address or website name. Please contact us at copyright@packt.com with a link to the material.

If you are interested in becoming an author: If there is a topic that you have expertise in and you are interested in either writing or contributing to a book, please visit authors.packtpub.com.

Reviews

Please leave a review. Once you have read and used this book, why not leave a review on the site that you purchased it from? Potential readers can then see and use your unbiased opinion to make purchase decisions, we at Packt can understand what you think about our products, and our authors can see your feedback on their book. Thank you!

For more information about Packt, please visit packt.com.

Section 1: Design and Implementation

In this section, you will gain an overview of Azure Sentinel, including the current cloud landscape, the cloud security reference framework, **Security Operations Center (SOC)** platform components, and how to map the architecture. You will also learn about Azure Monitor Log Analytics, including how to plan your Log Analytics instance, how to create a new instance, and how to attach an instance to Azure Sentinel.

The following chapters are included in this section:

- *Chapter 1, Getting Started with Azure Sentinel*
- *Chapter 2, Azure Monitor – Log Analytics*

1

Getting Started with Azure Sentinel

Welcome to the first chapter in this book about Azure Sentinel. To understand why this solution was developed, and how best to use it in your organization, we need to explore the cloud security landscape and understand each of the components that may feed data into or extract insights out of this system. We also need to gain a baseline understanding of what a strong **Security Operations Center** (**SOC**) architecture looks like, and how Azure Sentinel is going to help to build the foundations for a cost-effective and highly automated cloud security platform.

In this chapter, we will cover the following topics:

- The current cloud security landscape
- Cloud security reference framework
- SOC platform components
- Mapping the SOC architecture
- Security solution integrations
- Cloud platform integrations
- Private infrastructure integrations

- Service pricing for Azure Sentinel
- Scenario mapping

The current cloud security landscape

To understand your security architecture requirements, you must first ensure you have a solid understanding of the IT environment that you are trying to protect. Before deploying any new security solutions, there is a need to map out the solutions that are currently deployed and how they protect each area of the IT environment. The following list provides the major components of any modern IT environment:

- Identity for authentication and authorization of access to systems.
- Networks to gain access to internal resources and the internet.
- Storage and compute in the data center for internal applications and sensitive information.
- End user devices and the applications they use to interact with the data.
- And in some environments, you can include **Industrial Control Systems (ICS)** and the **(IoT)**.

When we start to look at the threats and vulnerabilities for these components, we quickly find ourselves deep in the alphabet soup of problems and solutions:

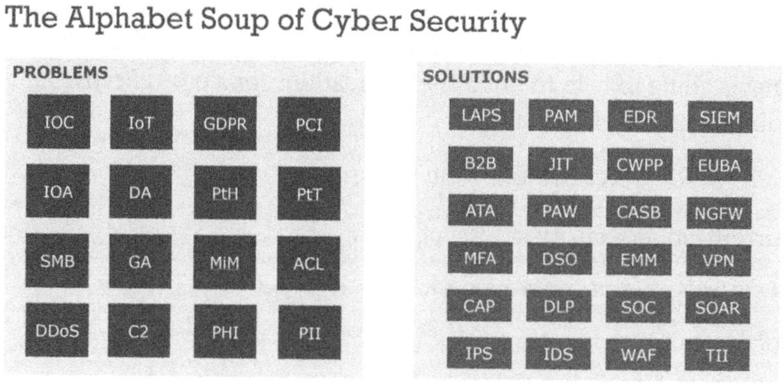

Figure 1.1 – The alphabet soup of cyber security

This is by no means an exhaustive list of the potential acronyms available. Understanding these acronyms is the first hurdle; matching them to the appropriate solutions and ensuring they are well deployed is another challenge all together (a table of these acronyms can be found in the appendix of this book).

Cloud security reference framework

To assist with the discovery and mapping of current security solutions, we developed the cloud security reference framework. The following diagram is a section of this framework that provides the technical mapping components, and you can use this to carry out a mapping of your own environment:

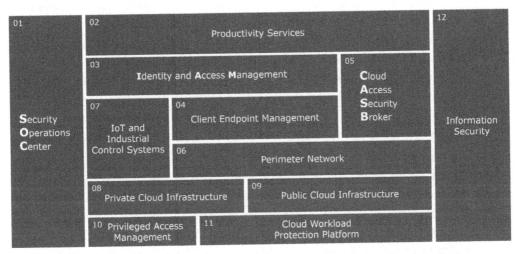

Figure 1.2 – Technical mapping components – cloud security reference framework

Each of these the 12 components is described in the following with some examples of the type of solutions to consider for integration with Azure Sentinel and the rest of your security architecture:

1. **Security Operations Center**: At a high level, it includes the following technologies and procedures: log management and **Security Incident and Event Monitoring (SIEM)**, **Security Orchestration and Automated Response (SOAR)**, vulnerability management, threat intelligence, incident response, and intrusion prevention/ detection. This component is further explored in the, *Mapping the SOC Architecture* section later in this chapter.

2. **Productivity Services**: This component covers any solution currently in use to protect the business productivity services that your end users rely on for their day to day work. This may include email protections, SharePoint Online, OneDrive for Business, Box, Dropbox, Google Apps, and Salesforce. Many more will come in future, and most of these should be managed through the **Cloud Access Security Broker (CASB)** solution

3. **Identity and Access Management**: Identities are one of the most important entities to track. Once an attacker gains access to your environment, their main priority is to find the most sensitive accounts and use them to exploit the systems further. In fact, identity is usually one of the first footholds into your IT environment, usually through a successful phishing attack.

4. **Client Endpoint Management**: This component covers a wide range of endpoints, from desktops and laptops to mobile devices and kiosk systems, all of which should be protected by specialized solutions such as **End Point Detection and Response (EDR)**, **Mobile Device Management (MDM)**, and **Mobile Application Management (MAM)** solutions to ensure protection from advanced and persistent threats against the operating systems and applications. This component also includes secure printing, managing peripherals, and any other device that an end user may interact with, such as the future of virtual reality/augmentation devices.

5. **Cloud Access Security Broker**: This component has been around for several years and is finally becoming a mainstay of the modern cloud security infrastructure due to the increase adoption of cloud services. The CASB is run as a cloud solution that can ingest log data from SaaS applications and firewalls and will apply its own threat detection and prevention solutions. Information coming from the CASB will be consumed by the SIEM solution to add to the overall picture of what is happening across your diverse IT environment.

6. **Perimeter Network**: One of the most advanced components, when it comes to cyber security, must be the perimeter network. This used to be the first line of defense, and for some companies it still is the only line of defense. That is changing now, and we need to be aware of the multitude of options available, from external facing advanced firewalls, web proxy servers, and application gateways to virtual private networking solutions and secure DNS. This component will also include protection services such as DDoS, Web Application Firewall, and Intrusion Protection/Detection services.

7. **IoT and Industrial Control Systems**: **Industrial Control Systems (ICS)** are usually operated and maintained in isolation from the corporate environment, known as the **Information Technology/Operational Technology** divide (**IT/OT** divide). These are highly bespoke and runs systems that may have existed for decades and are not easily updated or replaced.

The **IoT** is different yet similar; in these systems, there are lots of small headless devices that collect data and control critical business functions without working on the same network. Some of these devices can be smart to enable automation; others are single use (vibration and temperature sensors). The volume and velocity of data that can be collected from these systems can be very high. If useful information can be gained from the data, then consider filtering the information before ingesting into Azure Sentinel for analysis and short- or long-term retention.

8. **Private Cloud Infrastructure**: This may be hosted in local server rooms, a specially designed data center, or hosted with a third-party provider. The technologies involved in this component will include storage, networks, internal firewalls, and physical and virtual servers. The data center has been the mainstay of many companies for the last 2-3 decades, but most are now transforming into a hybrid solution, combining the best of cloud (public) and on-premises (private) solutions. The key consideration here is how much of the log data can you collect and transfer to the cloud for Azure Monitor ingestion. We will cover the data connectors more in *Chapter 3, Data Collection and Management.*

   Active Directory is a key solution that should also be included in this component. It will be extended to public cloud infrastructure (component **09**) and addressed in the *Privileged Access Management* section (component **10**). The best defense for Active Directory is to deploy the Azure **Advanced Threat Protection** (Azure **ATP**) solution, which Microsoft has developed to specifically protect Active Directory domain controllers.

9. **Public Cloud Infrastructure**: These solutions are now a mainstay of most modern IT environments, beginning either as an expansion of existing on-premises virtualized server workloads, a disaster recovery solution, or an isolated environment created and maintained by the developers. A mature public cloud deployment will have many layers of governance and security embedded into the full life cycle of creation and operations. This component may include **Infrastructure as a Service (IaaS)**, **Platform as a Service (PaaS)**, and **Software as a Service (SaaS)** services; each public cloud service provider offers their own security protections that can be integrated with Azure Sentinel.

10. **Privileged Access Management**: This is a critical component, not to be overlooked, especially gaining access to the SOC platform and associated tools. The **Privileged Access Management (PAM)** capability ensures all system-level access is highly governed, removing permissioned when not required, and making a record for every request for elevated access. Advanced solutions will ensure password rotation for service accounts, management of shared system accounts (including SaaS services such as Twitter and Facebook), and the rotation of passwords for the local administrator accounts on all computers and servers. For the SOC platform, consider implementing password vaults and session recording for evidence gathering.

11. **Cloud Workload Protection Platform**: This component may also be known as a **Cloud Security Posture Management (CSPM)**, depending on the view of the solution developed. This is a relatively new area for cloud security and is still maturing.

    Whatever they are labelled as, these solutions are addressing the same problem: how do you know that your workloads are configured correctly across a hybrid environment? This component will include any DevOps tools implemented to orchestrate the deployment and ongoing configuration management of solutions deployed to private and public cloud platforms. You can also include solutions that will scan for, and potentially enforce, configuration compliance with multiple regulatory and industry standard frameworks.

12. **Information Security**: This component is critical to securing data at rest and in transit, regardless of the storage: endpoint, portable, or cloud storage. This component is important to cover secure collaboration, digital rights management, securing email (in conjunction with component **02**, **Productivity Services**), scanning for regulated data and other sensitive information.

The Cloud Security Reference Framework is meant to be a guide as to what services are needed to secure your cloud implementation. In the next section, we will look at the SOC in more detail.

SOC platform components

As described earlier, the SOC platform includes a range of technologies to assist with the routine and reactive procedures carried out by various teams. Each of these solutions should help the SOC analysts to perform their duties at the most efficient level to ensure a high degree of protection, detection, and remediation.

The core components of the SOC include log management and **Security Incident and Event Monitoring (SIEM)**, **Security Orchestration and Automated Response (SOAR)**, Vulnerability Management, Threat Intelligence, and Incident Response. All of these components are addressed by the deployment of Azure Sentinel. Additional solutions will be required, and integrated, for other SOC platform capabilities such as Intrusion Prevention/Detection, integrity monitoring, and disaster recovery:

Deploying a SOC using Azure Sentinel comprises the following components:

- **Azure Monitor** for data collection and analysis. This was originally created to ensure a cloud-scale log management solution for both cloud-based and physical data-center-based workloads. Once the data is collected, a range of solutions can then be applied to analyze the data for health, performance, and security considerations. Some solutions were created by Microsoft, and others created by partners.

- **Azure Sentinel** was developed to address the need for a cloud-native solution as an alternative, or as a complimentary solution, to the existing SIEM solutions that have become a mainstay of security and compliance over the last decade. The popularity of cloud services provides some key advantages, including reduced cost of storage, rapid scale compute, automated service maintenance, and continuous improvement as Microsoft creates new capabilities based on customer and partner feedback.

   One of the immediate benefits of deploying Azure Sentinel is the rapid enablement without the need for costly investment in the supporting infrastructure, such as servers, storage, and complex licensing. The Azure Sentinel service is charged based on data consumption, per-gigabyte per month. This allows the initial deployment to start small and grow as needed until full scale deployment and maturity can be achieved.

   Ongoing maintenance is also simplified as there are no servers to maintain or licenses to renew. You will want to ensure regular optimization of the solution by reviewing the data ingestion and retention for relevance and suitability. This will keep costs reasonable and improve the quality of data used for threat hunting.

- **Logic Apps** provides integrations with a vast array of enterprise solutions, ensuring workflows are connected across the multiple cloud platforms and in existing on-premises solutions. While this is initially an optional component, it will become a core part of the integration and automation (SOAR) capabilities of the platform.

   Logic Apps is a standards-based solution that provides a robust set of capabilities, however there are third-party SOAR solutions available if you don't want to engineer your own automation solutions.

Mapping the SOC architecture

To implement a cohesive technical solution for your SOC platform, you need to ensure the following components are reviewed and thoroughly implemented. This is best done on a routine basis and backed up by regularly testing the strength of each capability using penetration testing experts that will provide feedback and guidance to help to improve any weaknesses.

Log management and data sources

The first component of a SOC platform is the gathering and storing of log data from a diverse range of systems and services across your IT environment. This is where you need to have careful planning to ensure you are collecting and retaining the most appropriate data. Some key considerations we can borrow from other big data guidance is listed here:

- **Variety**: You need to ensure you have data feeds from multiple sources to gain visibility across the spectrum of hardware and software solutions across your organization.

- **Volume**: Too large a volume and you could face some hefty fees for the analysis and ongoing storage, too small and you could miss some important events that may lead to a successful breach.

- **Velocity**: Collecting real-time data is critical to reducing response times, but it is also important that the data is being processed and analyzed in real time too.

- **Value/Veracity**: The quality of data is important to understand meaning; too much noise will hamper investigations.

- **Validity**: The accuracy and source of truth must be verified to ensure that the right decisions can be made.

- **Volatility**: How long is the data useful for? Not all data needs to be retained long term; once analyzed, some data can be dropped quickly.

- **Vulnerability**: Some data is more sensitive than others, and when collected and correlated together in one place, can become an extremely valuable data source to a would-be attacker.

- **Visualization**: Human interpretation of data requires some level of visualization. Understanding how you will show this information to the relevant audience is a key requirement for reporting.

Azure Sentinel provides a range of data connectors to ensure all types of data can be ingested and analyzed. Securing Azure Monitor will be covered in *Chapter 2, Azure Monitor – Log Analytics* and connector details will be available in *Chapter 3, Data Collection and Management*.

Operations platforms

Traditionally a SIEM was used to look at all log data and reason over it, looking for any potential threats across a diverse range of technologies. Today there are multiple platforms available that carry out similar functionality to the SIEM, except they are designed with specific focus on a particular area of expertise. Each platform may carry out its own log collection and analysis, provide specific threat intelligence and vulnerability scanning, and make use of machine learning algorithms to detect changes in user and system behavior patterns.

The following solutions each have a range of capabilities built in to collect and analyze logs, carry out immediate remediations, and report their findings to the SIEM solution for further investigation:

- **Identity and Access Management (IAM)**: The IAM solution may be made up of multiple solutions, combined to ensure the full life cycle management of identities from creation to destruction. The IAM system should include governance actions such as approvals, attestation, and automated cleanup of group and permission membership. IAM also covers the capability of implementing multi-factor authentication: a method of challenging the sign-in process to provide more than a simple combination of user ID and password. All actions carried out by administrators, as well as user-driven activities, should be recorded and reported to the SIEM for context.

  Modern IAM solutions will also include built-in user behavior analytics to detect changes in baseline patterns, suspicious activities, and the potential of insider-threat risks. These systems are also integrated with a CASB solution to provide session-based authentication controls, which is the ability to apply further restrictions if the intent changes, or access to higher sensitivity actions are required. Finally, every organization should implement privileged access management solutions to control the access to sensitive systems and services.

- **Endpoint Detection and Response (EDR)**: Going beyond anti-virus and anti-malware, a modern endpoint protection solution will include the ability to detect and respond to advanced threats as they occur. Detection will be based not only on signature-based known threats, but also on patterns of behavior and integrated threat intelligence. Detection expands from a single machine to complete visibility across all endpoints in the organization, both on the network and roaming across the internet.

  Response capabilities will include the ability to isolate the machine from the network, to prevent further spread of malicious activities, while retaining evidence for forensic analysis and provide remote access to the investigators. The response may also trigger other actions across integrated systems, such as mailbox actions to remove threats that executed via email or removing access to specific files on the network to prevent further execution of the malicious code.

- **Cloud Access Security Broker (CASB)**: A CASB is now a critical component in any cloud-based security architecture. With the ability to ingest logs from network firewalls and proxy servers, as well as connecting to multiple cloud services, the CASB has become the first point of collation for many user activities across the network, both on-premises and when directly connected to the internet. This also prevents the need to ingest these logs directly into the SIEM (saving on costs), unless there is a need to directly query these logs instead of taking the information parsed by the CASB.

  A CASB will come with many connectors for deep integration into cloud services, as well as connection to the IAM system to help to govern access to other cloud services (via SSO) acting as a reverse-proxy and enforcing session-based controls. The CASB will also provide many detection rule templates to deploy immediately, as well as providing the ability to define custom rules for an almost infinite set of use cases unique to your organization. The response capabilities of the CASB are dependent on your specific integrations with the relevant cloud services; these can include the ability to restrict or revoke access to cloud services, prevent the upload or download of documents, or hide specific documents from the view of others.

- **Cloud Workload Protection Platform (CWPP)**: The CWPP may also be known as a **Cloud Security Posture Management (CSPM)** solution. Either of these will provide a unique capability of scanning and continually monitoring systems to ensure they meet compliance and governance requirements. This solution provides a centralized method for vulnerability scanning and carrying out continuous audits across multiple cloud services (such as **Amazon Web Services (AWS)** and Azure) while also centralizing the policies and remediation actions.

Today there are several dedicated platforms for CWPP and CSPM, each with their own specialist solutions to the problem, but we predict this will become a capability that merges with the CASB platforms to provide a single solution for this purpose.

When these solutions are deployed, it is one less capability that we need the SIEM to provide; instead, it can take a feed from the service to understand the potential risk and provide an integration point for remediation actions.

- **Next Generation Firewall (NGFW)**: Firewalls have been the backbone of network security since the 1980s and remain a core component for segmentation and isolation of internal networks, as well as acting as the front door for many internet-facing services. With NGFW, not only do you get all of the benefits of previous firewall technologies, but now you can carry out deep packet inspection for the application layer security and integrated intrusion detection/prevention systems. The deployment of NGFW solutions will also assist with the detection and remediation of malware and advanced threats on the network, preventing the spread to more hosts and network-based systems.

As you can see from these examples, the need to deploy a SIEM to do all of the work of centrally collecting and analyzing logs is in the past. With each of these advanced solutions deployed to manage their specific area of expertise, the SIEM focus changes to look for common patterns across the solutions as well as monitoring those systems that are not covered by these individual solutions. With Azure Sentinel as the SIEM, it will also act as the SOAR: enabling a coordinated response to threats across each of these individual solutions, preventing the need to reengineer them all each time there is a change in requirements for alerting, reporting, and response.

Threat intelligence and threat hunting

Threat intelligence adds additional context to the log data collected. Knowing what to look for in the logs and how serious the events may be, requires a combination of skills and the ongoing intelligence feed from a range of experts that are deep in the field of cybercrime research. Much of this work is being augmented by **Artificial Intelligence (AI)** platforms; however, a human touch is always required to add that gut-feeling element that many detectives and police offices will tell you they get from working their own investigations in law enforcement.

SOC mapping summary

The following diagram provides a summary of the multiple components that come together to help to make up the SOC architecture, with some additional thoughts when implementing each one:

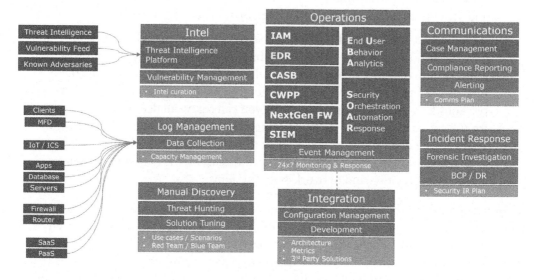

Figure 1.3 – SOC mapping summary

The solution works best when there is a rich source of log data streaming into the log management solution, tied in with data feeds coming from threat intel and vulnerability scans and databases. This information is used for discovery and threat hunting and may indicate any issues with configuration drift. The core solutions of the SOC operations include the SIEM, CASB, and EDR, amongst others; each with their own **End User Behavior Analytics** (**EUBA**) and SOAR capabilities. Integrating these solutions is a critical step in minimizing the noise and working toward improving the speed to response. The outcome should be the ability to report accurately on the current risk profile, compliance status, and clearly communicate in situations that require immediate response and accurate data.

Security solution integrations

Azure Sentinel is designed to work with multiple security solutions, not just those that are developed by Microsoft.

At the most basic level, log collection and analysis are possible from any system that can transmit their logs via the Syslog collectors. More detailed logs are available from those that connect via the CEF standard and servers that share Window Event logs. The preferred method, however, is to have direct integration via APIs to enable a two-way communication and help to manage the integrated solutions. More details of these options and covered in *Chapter 3, Data Collection and Management.*

> **Common Event Format (CEF)**
>
> CEF is an industry standard format applied to Syslog messages, used by most security vendors to ensure commonality between platforms. Azure Sentinel provides integrations to easily run analytics and queries across CEF data.
> For a full list of Azure Sentinel CEF source configurations, review the article at: `https://techcommunity.microsoft.com/t5/Azure-Sentinel/Azure-Sentinel-Syslog-CEF-and-other-3rd-party-connectors-grand/ba-p/803891`.

Microsoft is continually developing the integration options. At the time of writing, the list of integrated third-party solution providers includes the following:

- AWS
- Barracuda
- Checkpoint
- Cisco
- Citrix Systems Inc.
- CyberArk
- ExtraHop Networks
- F5 Networks
- Fortinet
- One Identity LLC.
- Palo Alto Networks
- Symantec
- TrendMicro
- Zscaler

As you can see from this list, there are many of the top security vendors already available directly in the portal. Azure Sentinel provides the ability to connect to a range of security data sources with built-in connectors, ingest the logs data, and display using pre-defined dashboards.

Cloud platform integrations

One of the key reasons you might be planning to deploy Azure Sentinel is to manage the security for your cloud platform deployments. Instead of sending logs from the cloud provider to an on-premises SIEM solution, you will likely want to keep that data off your local network, to save on bandwidth usage and storage costs.

Let's take a look at how some of these platforms can be integrated with Azure Sentinel.

Integrating with AWS

AWS provides API access to most features across the platform, which enables Azure Sentinel a rich integration solution. The following list provides some of the common resources that should be integrated with Azure Sentinel if enabled in the AWS account(s):

- AWS Cloud Trail logs provide insights into AWS user activities, including failed sign-in attempts, IP addresses, regions, user agents, and identity types as well as potential malicious user activities with assumed roles.

- AWS Cloud Trail logs also provide network related resource activities, including the creation, update, and deletions of security groups, network **access control lists (ACLs)** and routes, gateways, elastic load balancers, **Virtual Private Cloud (VPC)**, subnets, and network interfaces.

Some resources deployed within the AWS Account(s) can be configured to send logs directly to Azure Sentinel (such as Windows Event Logs). You may also deploy a log collector (Syslog, CEF, or LogStash) within the AWS Account(s) to centralize the log collection, the same as you would for a private data center.

Integrating with Google Cloud Platform (GCP)

GCP also provides API access to most features; however, there isn't currently an out-of-the-box solution to integrate with Azure Sentinel. If you are managing a GCP instance and want to use Azure Sentinel to secure it, you should consider the following options:

- REST API—this feature is still in development; when released, it will allow you to create your own investigation queries.

- Deploy a CASB solution that can interact with GCP logs, control session access, and forward relevant information to Azure Sentinel.

- Deploy a log collector such as Syslog, CEF, or LogStash. Ensure all deployed resources can forward their logs via the log collector to Azure Sentinel.

Integrating with Microsoft Azure

The **Microsoft Azure** platform provides direct integration with many Microsoft security solutions, and more are being added every month:

- Azure AD, for collecting audit and sign-in logs to gather insights about app usage, conditional access policies, legacy authentication, self-service password reset usage, and management of users, groups, roles, and apps.

- Azure AD Identity Protection, which provides user and sign-in risk events and vulnerabilities, with the ability to remediate risk immediately.

- Azure ATP, for the protection of Active Directory domains and forests.

- Azure Information Protection, to classify and optionally protect sensitive information.

- Azure Security Center, which is a CWPP for Azure and hybrid deployments.

- DNS Analytics, to improve investigations for clients that try to resolve malicious domain names, talkative DNS clients, and other DNS health-related events.

- Microsoft Cloud App Security, to gain visibility into connected cloud apps and analysis of firewall logs

- Microsoft Defender ATP, a security platform designed to prevent, detect, investigate, and respond to advanced threats on Windows, Mac, and Linux computers.

- Microsoft **Web App Firewall (WAF)**, to protect applications from common web vulnerabilities.

- Microsoft Office 365, providing insights into ongoing user activities such as file downloads, access requests, changes to group events, and mailbox activity.

- Microsoft Threat Intelligence Platforms, for integration with the Microsoft Graph Security API data sources: This connector is used to send threat indicators from Microsoft and third-party threat intelligence platforms.

- Windows Firewall, if on your servers and desktop computers (recommended).

Microsoft makes many of these log sources available to Azure Sentinel for no additional log storage charges, which could provide a significant cost saving when considering other SIEM tool options.

Other cloud platforms will provide similar capabilities, so review the options as part of your ongoing due diligence across your infrastructure and security landscape.

Whichever cloud platforms you choose to deploy, we encourage you to consider deploying a suitable CWPP solution to provide additional protections against misconfiguration and compliance violations. The CWPP can then forward events to Azure Sentinel for central reporting, alerting, and remediation.

Private infrastructure integrations

The primary method of integration with your private infrastructure (such as an on-premises data center) is the deployment of Syslog servers as data collectors. While endpoints can be configured to send their data to Azure Sentinel directly, you will likely want to centralize the management of this data flow. The key consideration for this deployment is the management of log data volume; if you are generating a large volume of data for security analytics, you will need to transmit that data over your internet connections (or private connections such as Express Route).

The data collectors can be configured to reduce the load by filtering the data, but a balance must be found between the volume and velocity of data collected in order to have sufficient available bandwidth to send the data to Azure Sentinel. Investment in increased bandwidth should be considered to ensure adequate capacity based on your specific needs.

A second method of integration involves investigation and automation to carry out actions required to understand and remediate any issues found. Automation may include the deployment of Azure Automation to run scripts, or through third-party solution integration, depending on the resources being managed.

Keep in mind that should your private infrastructure lose connectivity to the internet, your systems will not be able to communicate with Azure Sentinel during the outage. Investments in redundancy and fault tolerance should be considered.

Service pricing for Azure Sentinel

There are several components to consider when pricing Azure Sentinel:

- A charge for ingesting data into Log Analytics

- A charge for running the data through Azure Sentinel

- Charges for running Logic Apps for Automation (optional)

- Charges for running your own machine learning models (optional)

- The cost of running any VMs for data collectors (optional)

The cost for Azure Monitor and Azure Sentinel is calculated by how much data is consumed, which is directly impacted by the connectors: which type of information you connect to and the volume of data each node generates. This may vary each day throughout the month as changes in activity occur across your infrastructure and cloud services. Some customers notice a change based on their customer sales fluctuations.

The initial pricing option is to use **Pay As You Go** (**PAYG**). With this option, you pay a fixed price per **gigabyte** (**GB**) used, charged on a per-day basis. Microsoft has provided the option to use discounts based on the larger volumes of data.

It is worth noting that Microsoft has made available some connectors that do not incur a data ingestion cost. The data from these connectors could account for 10-20% of your total data ingestion, which reduces your overall costs. Currently the following data connectors are not charged for ingestion:

- Azure Activity (Activity Logs for Azure Operations)

- Azure Active Directory Identity Protection (for tenants with AAD P2 licenses)

- Azure Information Protection

- Azure Advanced Threat Protection (alerts)

- Azure Security Center (alerts)

- Microsoft Cloud App Security (alerts only)

- Microsoft Defender Advanced Threat Protection (monitoring agent alerts)

- Office 365 (Exchange and SharePoint logs)

The following table is an example of the published pricing for Azure Log Analytics:

Pricing Tier	Price (USD) – per GB/Day	Discount
PAYG	$2.76	0%
100 GB	$1.96	15%
200 GB	$1.84	20%
300 GB	$1.80	22%
400 GB	$1.76	23%
500 GB	$1.73	25%
Above 500 GB	$1.73	25%

The following table is an example of the published pricing for Azure Sentinel:

Pricing Tier	Price (USD) – per GB/Day	Discount
PAYG	$2.00	0%
100 GB	$1.00	50%
200 GB	$0.90	55%
300 GB	$0.87	57%
400 GB	$0.83	58%
500 GB	$0.80	60%
Above 500 GB	$0.80	60%

> **Important note**
>
> In both examples, everything over 500 GB remains at the same price per GB as the 500 GB tier. Pricing also varies depending on the region you choose for the Azure Monitor workspace; these examples are shown based on East US, December 2019. You may receive discounts from Microsoft, depending on individual agreements.

The pricing works by charging a fixed price for the tier (100 GB = $296 per day), and then charges PAYG price for each GB over that tier. When you work out the calculations for the pricing tiers, it makes financial sense to increase to the next tier when you reach the 50% marker. For example, if you are ingesting an average of 130 GB per day, you will pay for the first 100 GB at $2.96 per GB, then pay PAYG price of $4.76 per GB for the additional 30 GB (total per day = $438.80). Now, if you increase your daily usage to 155 GB, you would save money by increasing your plan to the 200 GB option (total per day = $548) and paying for the extra capacity, instead of paying for the 100 GB (fixed) + 55 GB (PAYG) (total per day = $557.80)

When you look at the amount of data you are using, you may see a trend toward more data being consumed each month as you expand the solution to cover more of your security landscape. As you approach the next tier, you should consider changing the pricing model; you have the option to change once every month.

The next area of cost management to consider is retention and long-term storage of the Azure Sentinel data. By default, the preceding pricing includes 90 days of retention. For some companies, this is enough to ensure visibility over the last 3 months of activity across their environment; for others, there will be a need to retain this data for longer, perhaps up to 7 years (depending on regulatory requirements). There are two ways of maintaining the data long term, and both should be considered and chosen based on price and technical requirements:

- **Azure Monitor**: Currently, this is available to store the data for up to 2 years.

  Pro: The data is available online and in Azure Monitor, enabling direct query using KQL searches, and the data can be filtered to only retain essential information.

  Con: This is likely the most expensive option per GB.

- **Other storage options**: Cloud-based or physical-based storage solutions can be used to store the data indefinitely.

  Pro: Cheaper options are available from a variety of partners.

  Con: Additional charges will be made if data is sent outside of Azure, and the data cannot be queried by Azure Monitor or Azure Sentinel. Using this data requires another solution to be implemented for querying the data when required.

The final consideration for cost analysis includes the following:

- Running any physical or virtual machines as Syslog servers for data collection
- Charges for running your own machine learning models, which can be achieved using Azure ML Studio and Azure Databricks
- The cost of running Logic Apps for automation and integration

Each of these components is highly variable across deployments, so you will need to carry out this research as part of your design. Also, research the latest region availability and whether Azure Sentinel is support in the various government clouds, such as China.

Scenario mapping

For the final section of this chapter, we are going to look at an important part of SOC development: scenario mapping. This process is carried out on a regular basis to ensure the tools and procedures are tuned for effective analysis and have the right data flow and responses are well defined to ensure appropriate actions are taken upon detection of potential and actual threats. To make this an effective exercise, we recommend involving a range of different people with diverse skills sets and viewpoints, both technical and non-technical. You can also involve external consultants with specific skills and experience in threat hunting, defense, and attack techniques.

The following process is provided as a starting point; we encourage you to define your own approach to scenario mapping and improve it each time the exercise is carried out.

Step 1 – Define the new scenarios

In this first step, we articulate one scenario at a time; you may want to use a spreadsheet or other documentation method to ensure information is gathered, reviewed, and updated as required:

- **Impact analysis:** This will be the summary of the complete analysis, based on the next components. You may want to provide a scoring system to ensure the implementation of security controls are handled in priority order, based on the severity of the potential impact.

- **Risk versus likelihood:** While some scenarios will have a high risk of catastrophe if they were to occur, we must also balance that risk with the potential that it will occur. Risk calculations help to justify budget and controls required to mitigate the risk, but keep in mind you are unlikely to achieve complete mitigation, and there is always a need to prioritize the resources you have to implement the controls.

- **Cost and value estimate:** Estimate the value of the resource to your organization and cost to protect it. This may be a monetary value or percentage of the IT security budget, or it could be some other definable metric such as time and effort. If the cost outweighs the value, you may need to find a more affordable way to protect the resource.

- **Systems impacted:** Create a list of the systems that are most likely to be targeted to get to the resources and information in one or many scenarios (primary systems) and a list of the other systems that could be used or impacted when attacking the primary systems (these are secondary systems). By understanding the potential attack vectors, we can make a map of the targets and ensure they are being monitored and protected.

- **People impacted:** For each scenario list, the relevant business groups, stakeholders, and support personnel that would be involved or impacted by a successful attack. Ensure all business groups have the opportunity to contribute to this process and articulate their specific scenarios. Work with the stakeholders and support personnel to ensure clear documentation for escalation and resolution.

- **Customer impacted:** For some scenarios, we must also consider the customer impact for the loss or compromise of their data or an outage caused to services provided to them. Make notes about the severity of the customer impact, and any mitigations that should be considered.

Step 2 – Explain the purpose

For each scenario, we recommend providing a high-level category to help to group similar scenarios together. Some categories that may be used include the following:

- **System Health:** This is the scenario focused on ensuring the operational health of a system or service required to keep the business running.

- **Compliance:** This is the consideration due to compliance requirements specific to your business, industry, or geographical region.

- **Vulnerability:** Is this a known system or process vulnerability that needs mitigation to protect it from?

- **Threat:** This is any scenario that articulates a potential threat, but may not have a specific vulnerability associated.

- **Breach:** These are scenarios that explore the impact of a successful breach.

Step 3 – The kill-chain stage

The **Kill Chain** is a well-known construct that originated in the military and later developed as a framework by Lockheed Martin (see here for more details: `https://en.wikipedia.org/wiki/Kill_chain`). Other frameworks are available, or you can develop your own.

Use the following list as headers to articulate the potential ways resources can become compromised in each scenario and at each stage of the kill chain:

- Reconnaissance

- Weaponization

- Delivery

- Exploitation

- Installation
- Command and control
- Actions on objectives

Step 4 – Which solution will do detection?

Review the information from earlier in this chapter to map which component of your security solutions architecture will be able to detect the threats for each scenario:

- SIEM
- CASB
- DLP
- IAM
- EDR
- CWPP

Step 5 – What actions will occur instantly?

As we aim to maximize the automation of detection and response, consider what actions should be carried out immediately, then focus on enabling the automation of these actions.

Actions may include the following:

- Logging and alerting.
- Notify/warn the end user.
- Block the action.
- Offer alternative options/actions.
- Trigger workflow.

Step 6 – Severity and output

At this step, you should be able to assign a number to associate with the severity level, based on the impact analysis in the previous steps. For each severity level, define the appropriate output required:

- **Level 0** – Logs and reports
- **Level 1** – Dashboard notifications
- **Level 2** – Generate event in ticketing system
- **Level 3** – Alerts sent to groups/individuals
- **Level 4** – Automatic escalation to the senior management team (sirens and flashing lights are optional!)

Step 7 – What action should the analyst take?

Where the *Step 5 - What actions will occur instantly?* section was an automated action, this step is a definition of what the security analysts should do. For each scenario, define what actions should be taken to ensure an appropriate response, remediation, and recovery.

The following diagram is a simple reference chart that can be used during the scenario-mapping exercise:

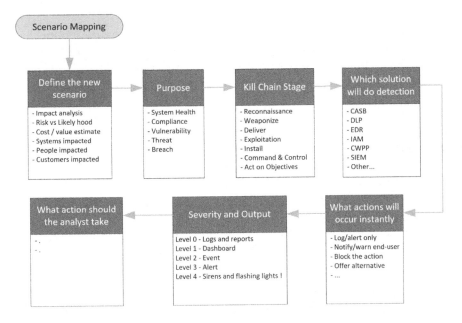

Figure 1.4 – Scenario-mapping process

By following this seven-step process, your team can better prepare for any eventuality. By following a repeatable process, and improving that process each time, your team can share knowledge with each other, and carry out testing to ensure protections and detections are efficient and effective as well as to identify new gaps in solutions that must be prioritized.

You should commit to take time away from the computer and start to develop this type of table-top exercise on a regular basis. Some organizations only do this once per year while others will do it on a weekly basis or as needed based on the demands they see in their own systems and company culture.

Summary

In this chapter, we introduced Azure Sentinel and how it fits into the cloud security landscape. We explored some of the widely used acronyms for both problems and solutions, then provided a useful method of mapping these technical controls to the wide array of options available from many security platform providers today. We also looked at the future state of SOC architecture to ensure you can gain visibility and control across your entire infrastructure: physical, virtual, and cloud-hosted.

Finally, we looked at the potential cost of running Azure Sentinel as a core component of your security architecture and how to carry out the scenario-mapping exercise to ensure you are constantly reviewing the detections, the usefulness of the data, and your ability to detect and respond to current threats.

In the next chapter, we will take the first steps toward deploying Azure Sentinel by configuring an Azure Monitor workspace. Azure Monitor is the bedrock of Azure Sentinel for storing and searching log data. By understanding this data collection and analysis engine, you will gain a deeper understanding of the potential benefits of deploying Azure Sentinel in your environment.

Questions

1. What is the purpose of the cyber security reference framework?

2. What are the three main components when deploying a SOC based on Azure Sentinel?

3. What are some of the main operations platforms that integrate with a SIEM?

4. Can you name five of the third-party (non-Microsoft) solutions that can be connected to Azure Sentinel?

5. How many steps are in the scenario-mapping exercise?

Further reading

You can refer to the following URLs for more information on topics covered in this chapter:

- Lessons learned from the Microsoft SOC – Part 1: Organization , at `https://www.microsoft.com/security/blog/2019/02/21/lessons-learned-from-the-microsoft-soc-part-1-organization/`

- Lessons learned from the Microsoft SOC – Part 2a: Organizing People, at `https://www.microsoft.com/security/blog/2019/04/23/lessons-learned-microsoft-soc-part-2-organizing-people/`

- Lessons learned from the Microsoft SOC – Part 2b: Career paths and readiness, at `https://www.microsoft.com/security/blog/2019/06/06/lessons-learned-from-the-microsoft-soc-part-2b-career-paths-and-readiness/`

- The Microsoft Security Blog, at `https://www.microsoft.com/security/blog/`

2

Azure Monitor – Log Analytics

In this chapter, we will explore the Azure Monitor Log Analytics platform, which is used to store all the log data that will be analyzed by Azure Sentinel. This is the first component that needs to be designed and configured when implementing Azure Sentinel, and will require some ongoing maintenance to configure the data storage options and control costs of the solution.

This chapter will also explain how to create a new workspace using the Azure portal, PowerShell, and the CLI. Once a workspace has been created, we will learn how to attach various resources to it so that information can be gathered, and we will explore the other navigation menu options.

By the end of this chapter you will know how to set up a new workspace, connect to resources to gather data, enable Azure Sentinel for data analysis, and configure some of the advanced features to ensure security and cost management.

We will cover the following topics in this chapter:

- Introduction to Azure Monitor Log Analytics
- Planning a workspace
- Creating a workspace
- Managing permissions of the workspace
- Enabling Azure Sentinel
- Exploring the Azure Sentinel Overview page
- Connecting your first data source
- Advanced settings for Log Analytics

Technical requirements

Before you start creating Log Analytics workspaces and using Azure Sentinel, you will need to set up an Azure tenant and subscription. It does not matter what type of Azure tenant you have, just as long as you have one that you can use. If you do not have access to an Azure tenant, you can set up a free trial by following the instructions at `https://azure.microsoft.com/en-us/free/`.

Once you have a tenant, you will need a subscription as well, if there is not one that you can use already. Depending on the type of Azure tenant you have access to, you may need to contact someone else to create the subscription. If you need help creating a new subscription, go to `https://docs.microsoft.com/en-us/azure/active-directory/fundamentals/active-directory-how-subscriptions-associated-directory`.

Introduction to Azure Monitor Log Analytics

Azure Monitor is the name of a suite of solutions built within the Azure platform to collect logs and metrics, then use that information to create insights, visualizations, and automated responses. Log Analytics is one of the main services, created to analyze the logs gathered. The platform supports near real-time scenarios, is automatically scaled, and is available to multiple services across Azure (including Azure Sentinel). Using a version of the **Kusto Query Language** (**KQL**), the query language used to obtain information from logs, complex information can be queried quickly and the queries are saved for future use. In this book, we will refer to this service simply as Log Analytics.

In order to create a Log Analytics workspace, you must first have an Azure subscription. Each subscription is based on a specific geographic location that ties the data storage to that region. The region selection is decided based on where you want your data to be stored; consider the distance between the source data and the Azure data center (region), alongside the legal requirements for data sovereignty requirements for your organization. The selection of the region will also impact the costs associated with both Log Analytics and Azure Sentinel.

Each workspace has its own separate data repository, and each can be configured uniquely to meet the business and technical requirements for security, governance, and cost management. Azure Sentinel can only be enabled to use a single Log Analytics workspace; we therefore recommend that you centralize all your security logs to a dedicated central workspace. If your organization requires you to create more than one location for your data for the legal or technical requirements mentioned before, then you will need to run multiple instances of Azure Sentinel (one per Log Analytics workspace), and each instance would need to be monitored, in which case you should consider the deployment of Azure Lighthouse.

> **Azure Lighthouse**
>
> Microsoft has addressed the need to manage multiple Azure subscriptions and resources in a centralized console. This is usually deployed by managed service providers who have multiple customers, although it may also be used by organizations with complex requirements and who have deployed multiple Azure subscriptions. Azure Sentinel is now a supported resource for this portal, and more features are expected to be added in time to ensure strong parity for directly interacting with Azure Sentinel.

The following diagram shows how Log Analytics workspaces relate to the rest of Azure. Each workspace resides in a single resource group, although there can be multiple workspaces in a single resource group and most likely other Azure resources. Each resource group belongs to a single subscription, and each subscription belongs to a single Azure Tenant. There can be, and usually are, multiple resource groups in a subscription, and many companies will have multiple subscriptions in a tenant:

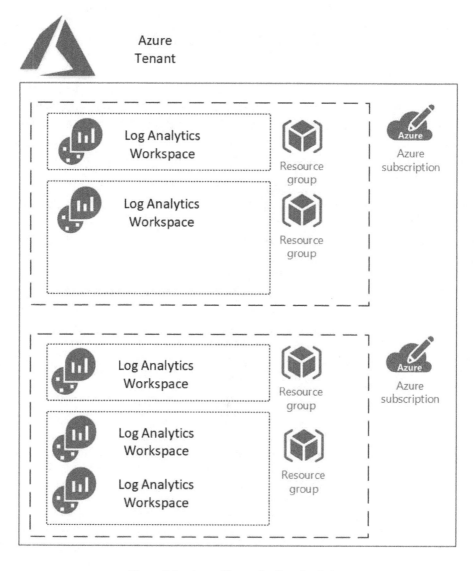

Figure 2.1 – Azure Tenant for Log Analytics

Once created, a workspace can be used to gather information from many different sources, including the following:

- Azure resources in the same subscription

- Azure resources in different subscriptions

- Data from other cloud services (such as Amazon Web Services, and Google Cloud Platform)

- Data from your private data center (on-premises or third-party hosted)

- Data from on-premises resources (via secure internet connections)

- Data from IoT and industrial control systems

To protect the data collected, security and compliance standards are built into this solution; the Log Analytics service manages your data in a secure cloud data repository and ensures the data is secured with multiple layers of protection, including the following:

- Data segregation and isolation, with geographic sovereignty

- Data retention and deletion policies, per data source type

- Internationally certified standards for physical security, inherited from the Azure subscription (commercial and government)

- Microsoft-managed incident management processes

- Certified conformity to multiple compliance and regulatory standards

- Secure channels for sending data to Log Analytics; certificate-based authentication, and SSL via port 443

- Workspace and role-based access permissions, managed by the customer; more details later in this chapter

For more information on the way data is secured, we recommend reading the official Microsoft documentation: `https://docs.microsoft.com/en-us/azure/azure-monitor/platform/data-security`.

Planning a workspace

While it is easy to just go and create a workspace, it is better to plan out the workspace configuration beforehand to avoid having to perform rework later. Some of the aspects to take into account include the following:

- **The name of the workspace**: This must be unique across all of Azure. It should be descriptive enough to show what service this workspace provides just by looking at the name. It is recommended that your company and the word **Sentinel** are used in the name.

  If this raises concerns that the name will make it a bigger target for bad actors, use whatever naming convention makes sense and meets corporate standards. Just remember that it must be unique across all of Azure. That name must also be between 4 and 64 letters, digits, and - should not be the first or last character.

- **The subscription the workspace belongs to**: It is recommended that a separate subscription is created just for Azure Sentinel use in order to limit access to it. If this is not feasible, choose an appropriate subscription to use.

- **The location of the workspace**: The workspace should reside in the same location as the resources feeding it in order to prevent egress charges that would occur if you send the data from one location to another. Large companies will most likely have resources in many different locations, in which case it would make sense to use the location that has the most resources and has the lowest price for the workspace. Keep in mind that there may be laws in place that denote where the data must reside.

  For more information on Log Analytics pricing, see `https://azure.microsoft.com/en-us/pricing/details/monitor`.

- **Which resource group will the workspace reside in**: It is recommended that all the Azure Sentinel resources reside in the same resource group, although that is not a hard and fast rule. If it makes more sense to have all your workspaces in one resource group, Azure Sentinel in another, and the workbooks in a third resource group, then do that. It will not affect the performance of Azure Sentinel at all.

- **Which pricing tier to use**: If the subscription being used to house the workspace has had a workspace created in it before April 2, 2018, or if the subscription is part of an Enterprise Agreement that was in place prior to February 1, 2019, it will continue to be able to access the legacy pricing tiers. Otherwise, only **Per GB (2018)** is allowed and data is charged for ingestion and retention per GB. The legacy options are:

    a) **Free**: There is no charge for the data being ingested, although there is a 500 MB daily limit and the data is retained for only 7 days. This can only be used for lab and research purposes.

    b) **Standalone (Per GB)**: This is the same as **Per GB (2018)**.

    c) **Per Node (OMS)**: Use this one if OMS E1 Suite, OMS E2 Suite, or OMS Add-On for System Center has been purchased to use the authorization that came from those purchases.

Planning your workspace before you create it is very important. Making sure to select a unique and meaningful name, the proper location to avoid egress charges, the correct resource group, and other decisions before deploying will save you frustration or complete rework later.

Creating a workspace using the portal

This section will describe how to create the Log Analytics workspace using the Azure portal website. This is a graphical representation of the PowerShell and CLI commands discussed later, and as such may be the easiest way to start working with workspaces:

1. In the Azure portal, enter `Log Analytics workspaces` into the search bar at the top of the screen. This will show a list of services that are related to the search term entered. Locate and click on the **Log Analytics workspaces** link.

2. Click the **Add** button to create a new workspace:

Figure 2.2 – Create a new Log Analytics workspace

3. Enter the required values in the new blade:

    a) Enter the name for the workspace.

    b) Select a **Subscription** where this will reside.

    c) Choose the **Resource group** for this workspace.

    d) Select the **Location** where this workspace will reside.

    e) For the **Pricing tier**, **Per GB (2018)** will automatically be selected.

    The blade will look something like this:

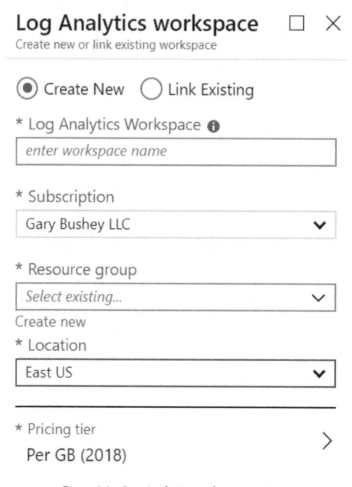

Figure 2.3 – Log Analytics workspace options

4. When all the values have been filled in, click the **OK** button at the bottom of the screen to continue. Even though the button will change to say **Validating**, it is also creating the workspace in the background.

5. Once the workspace has been created, you will be taken back to the listing of all the workspaces. You may need to refresh this listing to see your new workspace.

That is all there is to creating a workspace using the Azure portal. While this is very easy to do, there may be times when you will want to perform these same actions using command-line actions, and that will be described next.

Creating a workspace using PowerShell or the CLI

There are times when you need to be able to consistently recreate an Azure Sentinel environment. Perhaps you are just testing all the various configuration options, creating environments for many different subscriptions for an international company, or creating instances for customers. No matter the reason, if you need to create many Azure Sentinel environments that are all the same, using PowerShell or the **Command-Line Interface (CLI)** is a better option than doing it in the Azure portal.

Creating an Azure Resource Management template

When creating a new Log Analytics workspace using PowerShell in this lab, you will use an **Azure Resource Management (ARM)** template to perform the actual configuration. While you can create the workspace directly using either technology, using an ARM template provides additional benefits, including being able to easily recreate the workspace, using the ARM template in a DevOps workflow, or using it in Azure Blueprints.

> **Note**
>
> A complete discussion of ARM templates is beyond the scope of this lab, but briefly, an ARM template is a JSON file that describes what needs to be created in Azure. It contains parameters, which are the values that a user will provide to determine items such as name, location, and pricing tier. It can also have variables, which are internal values that can be used to determine other values. It will also have a list of one or more resources, which are the Azure resources to create.

Go to `https://docs.microsoft.com/en-us/azure/azure-monitor/ platform/template-workspace-configuration` and copy the JSON text. You will be pasting this into a file that you create later.

In this example, you will be prompted for the workspace name and the location, but the pricing tier will default to `pergb2018` due to the presence of a `defaultValue` entry. If you do not wish to have those defaults, you can either change the values shown or remove the entire `defaultValue` line, including the comma at the end, in which case you will be prompted for the values when executing the command.

While JSON is just text, so you can use a program such as Notepad to view it, it is recommended that you use something like Visual Studio or Visual Studio Code, which provides options including color coding and showing available commands. We will be using a version of Visual Studio Code in the Azure portal for this lab.

In your Azure portal, click on the Cloud Shell icon in the top right-hand corner of the screen:

Figure 2.4 – Launching the Cloud Shell

If prompted, select the subscription you are currently using for Azure Sentinel and then click **Create Storage**. This will only have to be done once, so if you have used the Cloud Shell before you will not be prompted for this.

At the bottom of the screen will be the Cloud Shell, which should look like the following screenshot. The text may not match exactly what is shown:

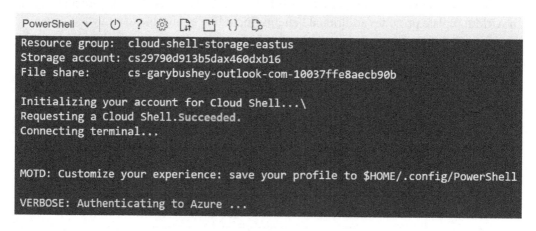

Figure 2.5 – Cloud Shell setup

If in the top left-hand corner it says **Bash** rather than **PowerShell**, use the dropdown to change it to **PowerShell**, as that will have the command we need for this lab.

Once the Cloud Shell has finished loading, enter the following:

```
code deployworkspacetemplate.json
```

This will start a version of Visual Studio code that you can use in the Cloud Shell. Type the code from the preceding example. On the right side of the screen, click on the context menu and click **Save**. You can then either click the **X** to close the editor or click on the context menu and click on **Close Editor**:

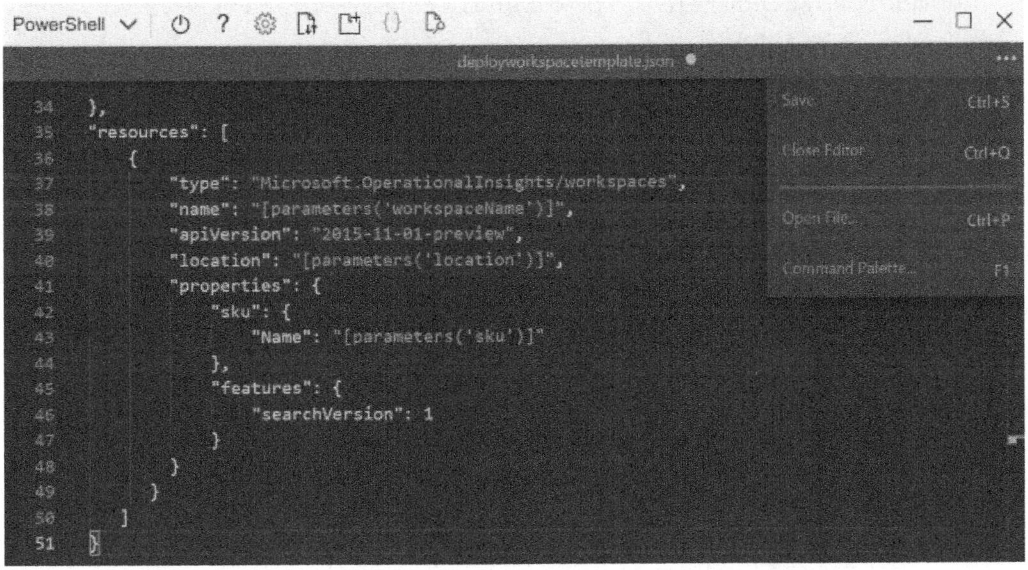

Figure 2.6 – PowerShell deployment using a JSON template

> **Note**
>
> If you want to run this on your own computer rather than via the Azure portal, go to `https://docs.microsoft.com/en-us/powershell/azure/install-az-ps?view=azps-3.2.0` to learn how to install the Azure PowerShell module, or `https://docs.microsoft.com/en-us/cli/azure/install-azure-cli?view=azure-cli-latest` to install the Azure CLI module.

That is how you can use the CLI to create a new Log Analytics ARM template. This is the external file that we will be using in the following sections to create the new workspace.

Using PowerShell

PowerShell is a scripting language that can be used across various machines, including Windows and Linux computers, that was built on top of .NET. Because of this, it can accept .NET objects, making it incredibly powerful. PowerShell has many different commands, including some specifically created for working with Azure, which will be used here.

> **Note**
>
> You may not have the Azure PowerShell module loaded on your local computer. To install it, follow the instructions located at `https://docs.microsoft.com/en-us/powershell/azure/install-az-ps?view=azps-3.5.0`

Follow these steps to create a new workspace using PowerShell:

1. Determine in which resource group the workspace will reside. If you have one already created, skip to step 3.

2. To create a new resource group, run this command:

   ```
   New-AzResourceGroup -Name <resource-group-name> -Location <location>
   ```

   Replace `<resource-group-name>` with the name of the new resource group and `<location>` with the location where the resource group will reside, such as `EastUS` or `WestUS`. If you do not know what to use for your location, run this command:

   ```
   Get-AzLocation
   ```

   Find the location you want and use the value listed under `Location`.

3. Enter the following command:

   ```
   New-AzResourceGroupDeployment -Name <deployment-name>
   -ResourceGroupName <resource-group-name> -TemplateFile
   $HOME/deployworkspacetemplate.json
   ```

Replace <deployment-name> with the name of this deployment. You can use something like <labworkspace>. It is not important what you enter, as this is just a placeholder name so that if you look at the resource group you can see the various deployments. Replace <resource-group-name> with the name of the resource group where the workspace will reside.

4. You will be prompted for the Log Analytics workspace name as well. Enter a valid name and press *Enter* to continue.

5. Once the command has finished running, it will show a success screen with a summary of the values used as follows:

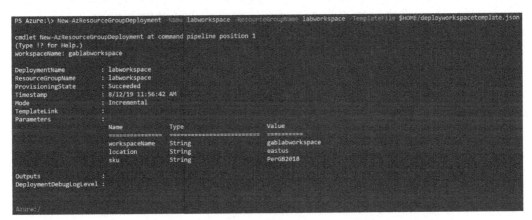

Figure 2.7 – Running New-AzResourceGroupDeployment in PowerShell

If you get an error screen, read the message, as the messages are usually quite specific as to what caused the error.

6. Close the Cloud Shell session.

That is how you can create a new Log Analytics workspace using an ARM template and PowerShell. This can be preferable to using the Azure portal as it is repeatable. Next, we will look at using the Azure CLI and see how to create a new workspace without using the ARM template.

Using CLI

The Azure CLI is also a cross-platform scripting tool developed by Microsoft. Initially, it was the only tool that was cross-platform, so if you were working on a computer that was not running Windows, it was your only option. PowerShell is now cross-platform as well, so the main difference between the two is that Azure CLI can create Azure resources directly without using an ARM template.

> **Note**
>
> The following steps describe how to run the CLI from the Azure portal. If you want to run this on your local computer, you will need to make sure you have the CLI installed. Go to `https://docs.microsoft.com/en-us/cli/azure/install-azure-cli?view=azure-cli-latest` for instructions on how to perform the installation:

1. Determine which resource group the workspace will reside in. If you have already created one, skip to step 3.

2. To create a new resource group, run this command:

    ```
    az group create --name <resource-group-name> --location
    <location>
    ```

3. Replace `<resource-group-name>` with the name of the new resource group and `<location>` with the location where the resource group will reside, such as `EastUS` or `WestUS`. If you do not know what to use for your location, run this command:

    ```
    az account list-location
    ```

4. Find the location you want and use the value listed under `name`.

5. Enter the following command:

    ```
    az group deployment create --resource-group <my-resource-
    group> --name <my-deployment-name> --template-file
    deploylaworkspacetemplate.json
    ```

6. Replace `<deployment-name>` with the name of this deployment. You can use something like `<labworkspace>`. It is not important what you enter, as this is just a placeholder name so that if you look at the resource group you can see the various deployments. Replace `<resource-group-name>` with the name of the resource group where the workspace will reside.

You will be prompted for the Log Analytics workspace name as well. Enter a valid name and press *Enter* to continue.

Once the command has finished running, it will show either the JSON values for this workspace as shown in the following screenshot or an error message. Note that not all the JSON is shown for brevity:

```
PS Azure:\> az group deployment create --resource-group labworkspace --name labworkspace --template-file deploywork
Please provide string value for 'workspaceName' (? for help): gablabworkspace
{
  "id": "/subscriptions/                                    /resourceGroups/labworkspace/providers/Microsoft.Resour
  "location": null,
  "name": "labworkspace",
  "properties": {
    "correlationId": "777341ca-14d8-446e-8f0a-c850713245aa",
    "debugSetting": null,
    "dependencies": [],
    "duration": "PT19.6849936S",
    "mode": "Incremental",
    "onErrorDeployment": null,
    "outputResources": [
      {
        "id": "/subscriptions/                               /resourceGroups/labworkspace/providers/Microsoft.
        "resourceGroup": "labworkspace"
      }
    ],
    "outputs": null,
    "parameters": {
      "location": {
        "type": "String",
        "value": "eastus"
      },
      "sku": {
        "type": "String",
        "value": "PerGB2018"
```

Figure 2.8 – Running az group deployment in CLI

Note that as stated earlier, you can use the Azure CLI to create the Log Analytics workspace directly using the `az monitor log-analytics workspace create` command. Go to `https://docs.microsoft.com/en-us/cli/azure/monitor/log-analytics/workspace?view=azure-cli-latest#az-monitor-log-analytics-workspace-create` for more information on this command.

7. Close the Cloud Shell session.

Exploring the Overview page

No matter how you created your Log Analytics workspace, the rest of the work in this lab will be done using the Azure Portal:

1. Open the portal and go to the Log Analytics solution page.

2. Find your new Log Analytics workspace for Azure Sentinel and click on it. This will take you to the **Overview** screen, as shown in the following screenshot:

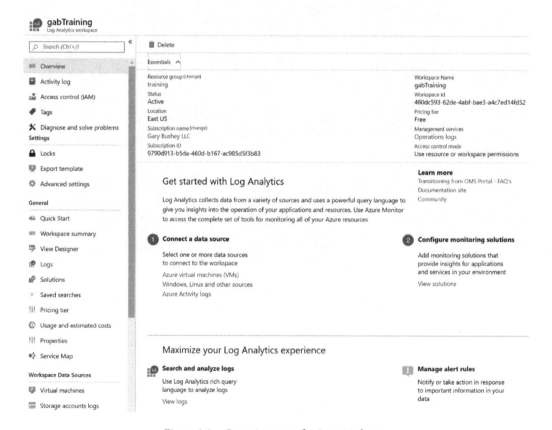

Figure 2.9 – Overview page for Log Analytics

Note that this is just a partial screen shown due to the amount of information on this page.

3. Starting with the **Essentials** listing at the top of the page, we can review the following items:

    a) **Resource group**: The resource group where the workspace resides. Selecting [**change**] will allow you to move to another resource group.

b) **Status**: The status of the workspace should show **Active**.

c) **Location**: The Azure location where the workspace resides.

d) **Subscription name**: The subscription this resource is associated with. Selecting [**change**] will allow you to move to another subscription.

e) **Subscription ID**: The unique GUID for the preceding subscription, which is useful when calling Microsoft for technical support.

f) **Workspace name**: The name of the Log Analytics workspace.

g) **Workspace ID**: The GUID for the workspace, which is also useful when calling Microsoft for technical support.

h) **Pricing tier**: The pricing tier for the workspace.

i) **Management services**: View the activity log for the workspace.

j) **Access control mode**: How users are granted permission to access the information in this workspace. See the following section for more information.

The previous sections described the various ways that you can create a new Log Analytics workspace to use with Azure Sentinel. This can be done either through the Azure portal or programmatically using either PowerShell or CLI commands. Once the workspace has been created, we next need to ensure access is restricted to only those users that need to access it.

Managing the permissions of the workspace

Before we connect and store data in the workspace and enable Azure Sentinel to carry out analytics on the data, let's review the options to secure access to this new resource. Azure provides three main levels of access to resources:

- **Owner**: Highest level of access to resources
- **Contributor**: Can create and modify resources, but cannot grant or revoke access
- **Reader**: Can view all resources

These permissions can be granted at four different levels:

- **Subscription**: Highest level of access, applies to all resources within the subscription
- **Resource group**: Applies to the specific resource group, which may contain multiple workspaces
- **Workspace**: Applies only to the specific workspace

- **Table level RBAC**: Applies to individual tables within the log

> **Table Level RBAC**
>
> While there is no user interface available to set permissions on individual tables within the log, you can create Azure custom roles to set these permissions. See `https://docs.microsoft.com/en-us/azure/azure-monitor/platform/manage-access#table-level-rbac` for more information on how to do this.

Permissions can be applied using built-in roles, or you can make a custom role for specific access if you need to be more granular. To make this simpler, there are several built-in user roles we recommend you use to manage access to Log Analytics for the purpose of using Azure Sentinel, and we recommend you apply these to the specific resource group used for Azure Sentinel:

- Engineers developing new queries and data connectors:

  a) **Azure Sentinel Contributor**: Provides the ability to create and edit dashboards, analytics rules, and other Azure Sentinel resources

  b) **Log Analytics Reader**: Provides read-only visibility to all Azure resources and Azure Sentinel logs

- Analysts running daily operations:

  a) **Azure Sentinel Responder**: Provides the ability to manage incidents, view data, workbooks, and other Azure Sentinel resources

  b) **Log Analytics Reader**: Provides read-only visibility to all Azure resources and Azure Sentinel logs

If additional permissions are required, keep to the idea of providing the minimal permissions and applying only to the specific resources required. It may take some trial and error to get the right outcome, but it is a safer option than providing broad and excessive permissions. For further information, please take a look at the following article: `https://docs.microsoft.com/en-us/azure/azure-monitor/platform/manage-access`.

Enabling Azure Sentinel

Once you have created a Log Analytics workspace that you want to use with Azure Sentinel, it is very easy to attach it to Azure Sentinel:

1. If you do not have Azure Sentinel enabled for your tenant, sign into the Azure portal, enter Azure Sentinel in the search box, and select the **Azure Sentinel** entry, as shown here:

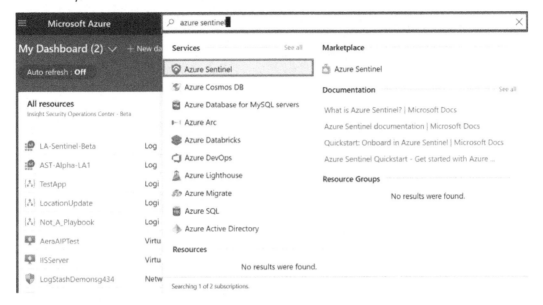

Figure 2.10 – Launch Azure Sentinel

2. Click the **Add** button to add a workspace to Azure Sentinel:

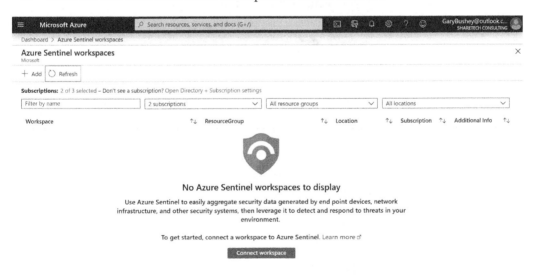

Figure 2.11 – Add workspace to Azure Sentinel

3. Select the workspace from the list provided, or click **Create a new workspace** to add a new workspace using the instructions listed previously and then select it. Click the **Add Azure Sentinel** button at the bottom of the screen to continue:

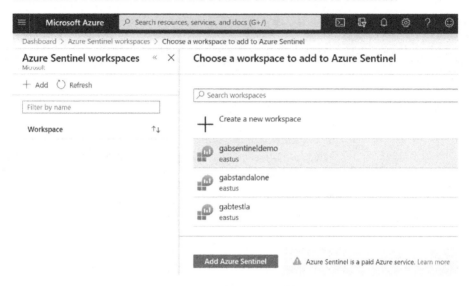

Figure 2.12 – Choose a workspace

4. Once the workspace has been created, you will be taken to the **News & guides** page of Azure Sentinel. This page will show some simple instructions on how to set up the workspace. See the following section next for more information:

Figure 2.13 – Azure Sentinel News & guides page

Congratulations! You now have your Azure Sentinel environment created and ready to go. While the **News & guides** page is where you will go automatically after attaching a Log Analytics workspace to Azure Sentinel, if you leave Azure Sentinel and go back to it, you will automatically go to the Azure Sentinel Overview page which is described next.

Exploring the Azure Sentinel Overview page

The Azure Sentinel **Overview** page is the page that you will automatically go to when entering Azure Sentinel after you have associated the Log Analytics workspace with it. This page provides a general overview of the information in your Azure Sentinel environment and will look like the following screenshot. The actual numbers and data being shown will vary depending on your environment, of course:

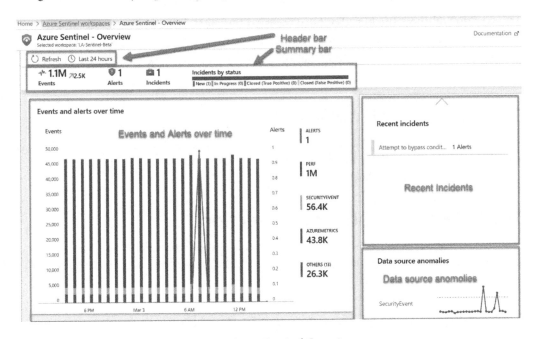

Figure 2.14 – Azure Sentinel Overview page

The page is broken up into various sections and each of these is described in the following sections.

The header bar

The header bar allows you to refresh the screen to see any updates, as well as to select how far back in time to look for the data. You can select the icon that looks like a clock to change how far back you want to look.

The summary bar

The summary bar will show you how much data has been ingested in the selected time period as well as how many alerts were raised, and the number of incidents those alerts created. In addition, the incidents are broken down by their status.

The Events and alerts over time section

This section will show the logs that have ingested the most data and the number of incidents created in the selected time frame. This is an interactive chart, so when you mouse over a specific time, the information will be filtered to show what happened at that time.

The Recent incidents section

This section will show up to the last five created incidents as well as the number of alerts that have generated the incident. You can click on the incident name to get more information about the incident.

The Data source anomalies section

This section will show up to two different data sources that Azure Sentinel's Machine Learning has determined contain anomalies. You can click on the log name to get more information about the anomaly.

The Potential malicious events section

This section, not shown, will show an interactive map where any potential malicious events will be highlighted. You can zoom into the map to get a very precise indication of where the event occurred.

The Democratize ML for your SecOps section

This section, not shown, provides some general information on Azure Sentinel's use of Machine Learning and provides a link where you can obtain more information.

That is the Azure Sentinel **Overview** page. It is a great place to go to get an overview of what is going on in your Azure Sentinel environment and is the landing page of Azure Sentinel. While Figure 2.14 shows lots of data, when you first create a Log Analytics workspace, it will be empty. The next section will explain how to start getting data into your workspace.

Connecting your first data source

Before we dig into the details of the Azure Sentinel data connectors (see *Chapter 3*, *Data Collection and Management*), we will review how Log Analytics enables connectivity to a range of different sources in order to receive data to store and analyze. Some of the data source options include the following:

- Application and operating system diagnostics
- Virtual machine log data
- Azure storage account logs
- Azure Activity log
- Other Azure resources

In this section, we will show you how you can enable log collection from Azure virtual machines.

Obtaining information from Azure virtual machines

To have the **virtual machines** (**VMs**) populate a Log Analytics workspace, they need to be connected to it. This is done from the Log Analytics workspace **Overview** page.

There are two different ways to get to this page. First, you can select **Log Analytics** in the Azure portal navigation menu and then select the appropriate workspace. The second, and perhaps easier, way is to select **Settings** from the Azure Sentinel navigation menu and then select **Workspace settings** from the menus at the top of the page, as shown in the following screenshot:

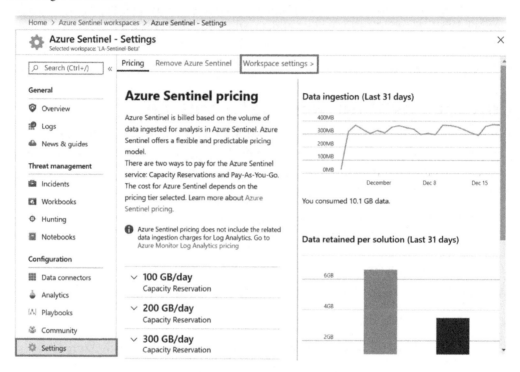

Figure 2.15 – Azure Sentinel Settings

No matter which method you use to get to the page, it will look similar to the following screenshot:

Figure 2.16 – Log Analytics Overview Page

Under **Connect a data source** in the **Get started with Log Analytics** section, select **Azure virtual machines (VMs)**. This will take you to the **Virtual machines** page, which lists each VM and shows whether it is connected, as well as the OS, subscription GUID, the resource group, and the location it belongs to. The following screenshot is an example of what this page looks like:

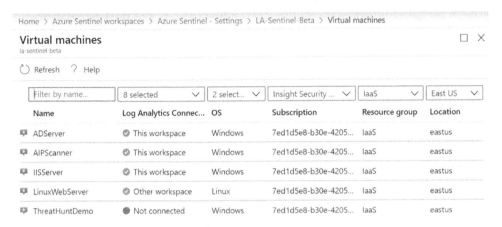

Figure 2.17 – Log Analytics – Azure Virtual machines page

You can see that the first three VMs are connected to this workspace, the fourth one, called **LinuxWebServer**, is connected to another workspace, and the final one, **ThreatHuntDemo**, is not connected to any workspace.

To change the connection status of any of the VMs, click on the row containing it. This will open a new blade, where you can either connect or disconnect the VM:

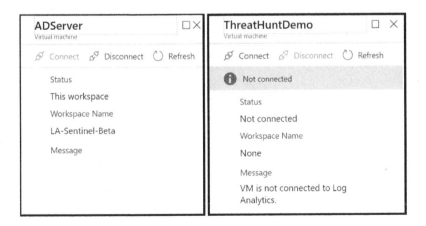

Figure 2.18 – Azure virtual machine log data connection

Select either the **Disconnect** or **Connect** link to perform the action you desire.

Connecting a VM to a Log Analytics workspace downloads and installs the Microsoft Monitoring Agent to the VM, so this step can be performed automatically when provisioning the VM using tools such as PowerShell Desired State Configuration. However, the actual steps to perform this task are beyond the scope of this book.

In a large-scale deployment, especially with VMs that are not hosted in Azure, you may not want each individual server directly sending their logs to the Log Analytics workspace. Instead, you may consider deploying the Syslog/CEF connector to centralize log collection and data ingestion. Each VM would then point towards the CEF collector server instead of Log Analytics.

Advanced settings for Log Analytics

The advanced settings for Log Analytics allow you to perform actions such as connecting on-premises and other non-Azure Windows and Linux servers, Azure Storage, and System Center Management groups. You can also set what information to import from Windows and Linux servers, import IIS Logs and Syslog events, and add custom logs and fields. Finally, you can create groups of computers, or use groups already created in Active Directory, **Windows Server Update Service** (**WSUS**), and SCCM, which can be used in your queries.

To get to the **Advanced settings** page, follow the instructions to get the Log Analytics Overview page in the previous section and instead of selecting **Azure virtual machines (VMs)**, select **Windows, Linux and other sources**. This will open a new page as shown in the following screenshot:

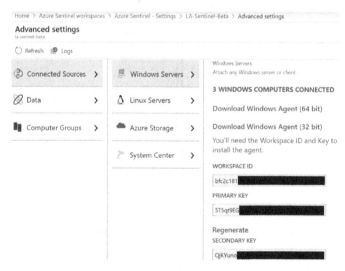

Figure 2.19 – Azure Sentinel Advanced Settings – Connected Sources

As you can see, there are various menu options that will allow you to connect to various servers, determine what data to ingest, and help with querying the data that these servers provide. Each one will be discussed in the next section.

Connected Sources

This area allows you to attach non-Azure Windows and Linux servers, Azure Storage, and System Center Operations Manager:

- **Windows Servers**: This section allows you to attach a non-Azure Windows based VM to the workspace. Click on either **Download Windows Agent (64bit)** or **Download Windows Agent (32bit)** to match the Windows version you are using and run the program on the server. Copy the Workspace ID and either the Primary or Secondary key and fill them in when asked.

- **Linux Servers**: This works the same as the Windows Server, except there is also a listing for a wget command that will download and install the application without needing any user interaction.

> **Note**
>
> While this can be used to connect Azure VMs, it is far easier to use the steps in the previous section to do so.

- **Azure Storage**: This will list the number of Azure Storage accounts connected and provides a link to documentation explaining how to connect to the Storage account. This will need to be performed from the Storage account and cannot be done here.

- **System Center**: This allows us to connect System Center Operations Manager management groups or the entire deployment to your workspace with a few clicks rather than having to connect each server individually.

The **Connected Sources** area shows you how to connect to on-premises servers as well as Azure Storage and System Center Manager groups. Next, we will look at the **Data** menu, which will tell Azure Sentinel what information from those servers to ingest.

The Data option

This area allows you to determine which data from connected servers will be imported. Selecting the **Data** option will show you the following page:

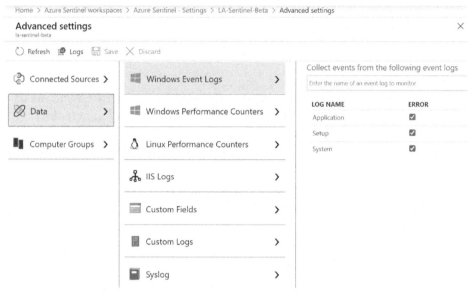

Figure 2.20 – Azure Sentinel Advanced Settings – Data

Let's take a look at the different fields under the **Data** option:

- **Windows Event Logs**: This allows you to search for all the various logs that show up in the Windows Event viewer, including items such as the **Application**, **Setup**, and **System** logs, to have them included in the Log Analytics workspace. While having all this data can be handy, if there are a lot of Windows servers connected, it can lead to a large amount of data being imported. Note that the Windows Security log is not available since it will always be imported from any connected Windows server.

- **Windows Performance Counters**: This will show a listing of all the performance counters that will be included by default and the polling interview. From here, you can change the interview or remove the counter completely. You can also add other counters to monitor.

- **Linux Performance Counters**: This will show a listing of all the Linux performance counters that will be included by default and the polling interval for those counters that use a polling interval. From here, you can change the interview or remove the counter completely. You can also add other counters to monitor.

- **IIS Logs**: This determines if the W3C format IIS log files will be ingested from Windows web servers or not.

- **Custom Fields**: This shows a listing of all the custom fields that have been added, as well as the logs they belong to and their data types. Clicking on the **Go to** button will take you to the **Log** page, where a query will be shown, giving you an overview of the field. You can also remove the custom field from here.

- **Custom Logs**: This page allows you to add custom logs that you cannot, or do not want to, add using other data sources. An example of this is the web logs from a Linux-based web server. Go to `https://docs.microsoft.com/en-us/azure/azure-monitor/platform/data-sources-custom-logs` for more information on adding a custom log.

As you can see, there are a lot of ways you can configure the data to import. This will always be a tradeoff between what data you need or want and the cost of ingesting and storing the data. In the next section, we will look at **Computer Groups**, which can help you with your queries.

Computer Groups

This section will show all the custom computer groups that have been created and provide a way to create your own. These groups can then be used in queries. You can use these groups to create queries that reference a specific set of servers that can then be easily changed without having to change the query itself.

Selecting the **Computer Groups** option will show you the following screen:

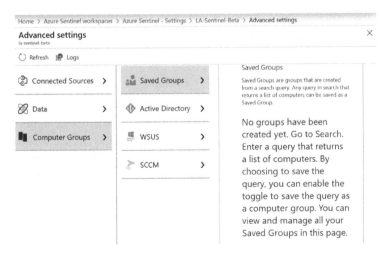

Figure 2.21 – Azure Sentinel Advanced Settings – Computer Groups

Let's discuss the different fields under **Computer Groups**:

- **Saved Groups**: This page will show all the custom groups that have been added. It also provides instructions on creating a computer group from a query. An example of how to do this will be provided at the end of this section.

- **Active Directory**: Select the **Import Active Directory group memberships from computers** checkbox to allow groups from Active Directory to be imported. After this is enabled, it may take a few minutes before any groups show up.

- **WSUS**: Select the **Import WSUS group memberships** checkbox to allow groups from the Windows Server Update Service to be imported. After this is enabled, it may take a few minutes before any groups show up.

- **SCCM**: Select the **Import Configuration Manager collection memberships** checkbox to allow groups from SCCM to be imported. After this is enabled, it may take a few minutes before any groups show up.

There are various ways to create computer groups to help you with your queries. Each of these will be discussed in more detail in the following sections.

Adding a computer group from a query

Adding a computer group using a query involves running a query that will return a list of computers and then save that information as a computer group:

1. In the **Saved Groups** section under **Computer Groups**, click on the **Go to Search** link to go the **Logs** page. Enter any query that will generate a listing of computers. Here's an example:

```
Heartbeat
| where TimeGenerated > ago(30m)
| distinct Computer
```

    Don't worry about what the query means, it will be explained in *Chapter 5, Using the Kusto Query Language (KQL)*. For now, this will return a listing of all the computers who have sent a heartbeat to the workspace in the last 30 minutes. Note that you will need to have a server connected to Azure (see the *Obtaining information from Azure Virtual Machines* and the *Connected Sources* sections) to get any information from this query.

2. Click on the **Run** button to get a list of computers. If you do not get any computers returned, change 30 to a larger value until you do.

3. Once you have a list, click on the **Save** button to save this query:

Figure 2.22 – Computer heartbeat query

This will bring up a new blade where you can enter the query information.

4. Enter a descriptive name.

5. Change the **Save as** dropdown to **Function**, as shown in the following screenshot:

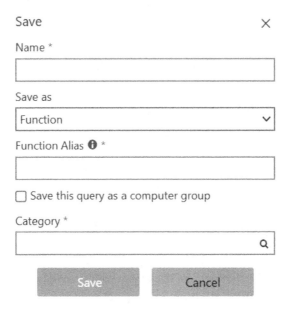

Figure 2.23 – Save query options

6. Add a **Function Alias**, which will be used in the queries later. Make sure to check the **Save this query as a computer group** option, otherwise it will just save as a query that can be the same as the **Name**.

7. Finally, add a **Category**, which is just used to group the computer groups together.

8. Click the **Save** button.

When you go back to the **Saved Groups** page, you will see your saved group, which will look similar to what is shown in the following screenshot:

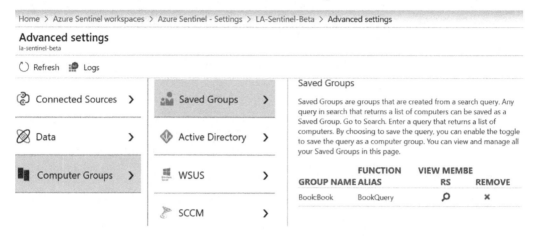

Figure 2.24 – Saved Groups

9. Click on the **View Members** icon, which looks like a magnifying glass, to view the members of the group. It is worth noting that this group is dynamic, so based on the query in this section, the number and names of the computers that show up in the query can change.

10. Click on the **Remove** icon, which looks like an **X**, to remove a saved group. You will be prompted to verify that you want to remove the saved group before the action occurs.

To use a saved group, enter a query like this:

```
Perf
| where Computer in (BookQuery)
```

Substitute BookQuery for the name of the query you just created. Again, do not worry about what this query means, it is just an example of how to use a saved group. It will make more sense after reading *Chapter 5, Using the Kusto Query Language (KQL)*.

Summary

In this chapter, we explored the Azure Monitor Log Analytics solution, including how to create a new workspace using the Azure portal, PowerShell, or CLI, and how to configure the security options to ensure each user has the appropriate level of access. We also looked at how to connect a data source and configure some of the advanced settings. This information is very useful when you need to first configure Azure Sentinel, and in future if you need to make any changes to the Log Analytics platform supporting your operations and business needs.

In the next chapter, we will look at how to select data that is most useful for security threat hunting, which connectors to use to gather the data from any system, and the options available to enable long-term data retention while keeping costs under control.

Questions

Answer these questions to test your knowledge of this chapter:

1. What is the name of the query language used in Azure Monitor Log Analytics?
2. What is the purpose of Azure Lighthouse?
3. Can you list three ways the data is protected in Log Analytics?
4. What are the three ways to create a new Log Analytics workspace?
5. What are the recommended permissions for an Engineer role?

Further reading

- *Agent data sources in Azure Monitor*: https://docs.microsoft.com/en-us/azure/azure-monitor/platform/agent-data-sources

- *Manage access to log data and workspaces in Azure Monitor*: https://docs.microsoft.com/en-us/azure/azure-monitor/platform/manage-access

- *Log Analytics agent overview*: https://docs.microsoft.com/en-us/azure/azure-monitor/platform/log-analytics-agent

Section 2:
Data Connectors, Management, and Queries

In this section, you will learn how to collect data, manage data to prevent overspending, and query data for useful information as part of threat hunting and other security-related activities.

The following chapters are included in this section:

- *Chapter 3, Data Collection and Management*
- *Chapter 4, Integrating Threat Intelligence*
- *Chapter 5, Using Kusto Query Language (KQL)*
- *Chapter 6, Azure Sentinel Logs and Writing Queries*

3
Managing and Collecting Data

One of the primary purposes of a **Security Information and Event Management (SIEM)** solution is to centralize the storage and analysis of security events across a diverse range of products that provide protection across your organization's IT infrastructure. To do this, the solution needs to connect to those data sources, pull the data into a central store, and manage the life cycle of that data to ensure it is available for analysis and ongoing investigations.

In this chapter, we will review the types of data that are most interesting and useful for security operations, and then explore the functionality available to connect to multiple data sources and ingest that data into Azure Sentinel, by storing it in the Log Analytics workspace. Once the data is ingested, we need to ensure the appropriate configuration for data retention to maximize the ability to hunt for events and other security information, while also ensuring the cost of the solution is maintained at a reasonable level.

We will cover the following areas specific to data collection:

- Choosing data that matters
- Understanding connectors
- Configuring Azure Sentinel connectors

Then, we will cover these areas to ensure appropriate data management:

- Configuring Log Analytics storage options
- Calculating the cost of data ingestion and retention
- Reviewing alternative storage options

Choosing data that matters

Quality data management is critical to the success of big data analytics, which is the core basis of how a SIEM solution works. Gathering data for analysis is required in order to find security threats and unusual behavior across a vast array of infrastructure and applications. However, there needs to be a balance between capturing every possible event from all available logs and not having enough data to really find the correlating activities. Too much data will increase the signal noise associated with alert fatigue and will increase the cost of the security solution to store and analyze the information, which, in this case, is Azure Log Analytics and Azure Sentinel, but also applies to other SIEM solutions.

One of the recent shifts in the security data landscape is the introduction of multiple platforms that carry out log analysis locally and only forward relevant events on to the SIEM solution. Instead of duplicating the logs, hoping to fish relevant information from it by using a single security analysis tool (such as a SIEM solution), new security products are focused on gathering specific data and resolving threats within their own boundaries; examples include the following:

- **Identity and Access Management (IAM)** for continuous analysis and condition-based access, per session
- **Endpoint Detection and Response (EDR)** for detailed analysis on every host, with centralized analytics across devices for threat mapping and remediation
- **A cloud-access security broker (CASB)** for use-behavior analytics across firewalls and external cloud-based solutions
- **A next-generation firewall (NGFW)** for monitoring and responding to dynamic changes in behavior across internal- and external-facing networks

> **Note**
> Refer to *Chapter 1, Getting Started with Azure Sentinel,* for further details about each of these solutions.

Each of these solutions already gather large volumes of data from their respective data sources; therefore, there is no need to duplicate the data in the SIEM log storage. Instead, these solutions can be integrated with the SIEM solution to only send relevant and actionable information, to enable the SIEM to act as the central point of communication for analysis, alerting, and ticketing. The net result is a reduction in duplication and overall solution cost. This idea is summarized in the following screenshot:

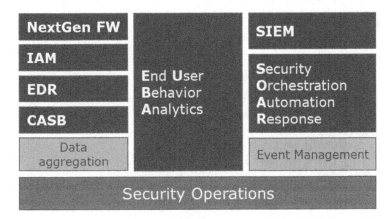

Figure 3.1 – Data for security operations

When dealing with large data volumes, we can use the 7 Vs of Big Data to guide our decisions on what is the right data to collect, based on the priorities assigned:

- **Volume**: This directly impacts the cost of moving and storing the data.
- **Velocity**: This impacts the time to respond to an event.
- **Variety**: Are we including every aspect of apps and infrastructure? Where are the blackspots?
- **Variability**: Is the information easy to understand and act upon?
- **Veracity**: Do we trust the source and accuracy of the data?
- **Visualization**: Can we use this data to create visualizations and comparisons?
- **Value**: Consistently review the value of the data, reduce waste, and retain value.

Here is an example of how to use each of these values to prioritize and justify the data— for volume, instead of focusing on the volume of data, we need to focus on the quality and variety of the data to provide accurate and actionable information across multiple systems.

A summary of this topic is shown in the following screenshot:

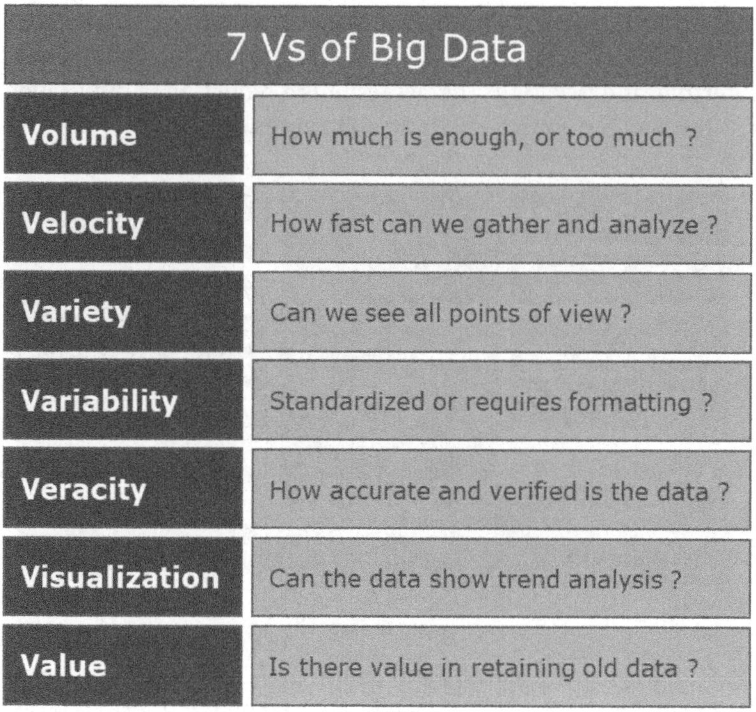

7 Vs of Big Data	
Volume	How much is enough, or too much ?
Velocity	How fast can we gather and analyze ?
Variety	Can we see all points of view ?
Variability	Standardized or requires formatting ?
Veracity	How accurate and verified is the data ?
Visualization	Can the data show trend analysis ?
Value	Is there value in retaining old data ?

Figure 3.2 – The 7 Vs of Big Data

You can use the chart shown in the preceding screenshot to make your initial assessment of the types of data you need to ingest into Azure Sentinel and that which can be excluded. We recommend you also review this periodically to ensure you are maintaining a healthy dataset, either by adding more data sources or tuning out some of the data that no longer meets the requirements (but which costs to store and process).

Understanding connectors

Azure Sentinel relies on Log Analytics to store large volumes of data, in order to process that data and find useful information about potential risks and security threats. The data required may be located in many different types of resources across many different platforms, which is why we need many different options for connecting to those data sources. Understanding the options available, and how to configure them, is key to developing a strong data architecture to support the Azure Sentinel solution.

A summary of the connectors is shown in the following screenshot:

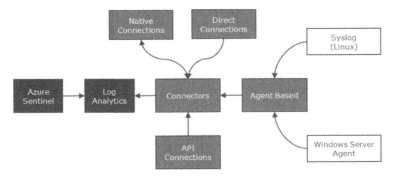

Figure 3.3 – Azure Sentinel connector flow

Connectors can be categorized based on the method used to ingest data from source. Currently, there are four major types:

- Native connections
- Direct connections
- API connections
- Agent-based (Windows Server Agent and Syslog)

Let's explore each of these types in more detail.

Native connections – service to service

Azure Sentinel has been developed to integrate directly with several resources across the Microsoft security product range, including (but not limited to) the following:

- **Azure Active Directory** (**Azure AD**), including the advanced Identity Protection solution
- Office 365, including Exchange Online, Teams, and OneDrive for Business
- Cloud App Security, the CASB and **cloud workload protection platform** (**CWPP**) solution
- Azure Security Center, including Microsoft Defender **Advanced Threat Protection** (**ATP**)
- Azure ATP

This is the preferred method for connecting to resources, if the option is available. Let's take a look at direct connectors.

Direct connections – service to service

Some connectors available in Azure Sentinel need to be configured from the source location. The connector will usually provide the information required and a link to the appropriate location. Examples of these connectors include the following:

- **Amazon Web Services** (**AWS**), for AWS CloudTrail

- Azure Firewall

- Azure Front Door

- Azure **network security groups** (**NSGs**); flow logs and rule activations

- Microsoft Intune; audit logs and operational logs

Now, let's look at API connections.

API connections

Several security providers have API options that allow connections to be made to their solutions in order to extract the logs and bring the data in to Azure Sentinel. This is the preferred method for connecting to third-party solutions that support it, and you have the option to create your own connectors. For further information on creating API-based connectors, see this article: `https://techcommunity.microsoft.com/t5/azure-sentinel/azure-sentinel-creating-custom-connectors/ba-p/864060`.

Examples of API-based data connectors include the following:

- **Azure Information Protection** (**AIP**)

- Barracuda Web Application Firewall

- Microsoft Web Application Firewall

- Symantec **Integrated Cyber Defense Exchange** (**ICDx**)

- Symantec Cloud Workload Protection

The next type of connection is required for services that do not support any of the preceding options; usually for virtual or physical servers, firewalls, proxy, and other network-based devices.

Agent-based

This connector type will allow for the widest range of data connection and is an industry-standard method of shipping logs between resources and SIEM solutions. There are three types of connectors to consider; you may deploy one or more depending on your needs, and you may deploy multiple of the same type too. Let's discuss them in detail.

Windows Server Agent

Any server running Microsoft Windows can forward logs for **Domain Name System (DNS)**, security events, Windows Firewall, and AD.

Syslog server

This is an agent deployed to a Linux host that can act as a concentrator for many resources to send logs to, which are then forwarded on to Log Analytics for central storage. For detailed guidance on implementing a Syslog server, please see this article: `https://docs.microsoft.com/en-us/azure/sentinel/connect-syslog`. Examples of third-party solutions that support this method include (but are certainly not limited to) the following:

- Carbon Black
- Cisco (IronPort Web Security, Meraki, and others)
- Citrix
- F5 BIG-IP
- McAfee **ePolicy Orchestrator (ePO)**
- NetApp
- Palo Alto Cortex
- Trend Micro

While these options provide a wide range of options for data sources to gather, there is another method that, if available from the service provider, will give a richer dataset. Let's take a look at the **Common Event Format (CEF)** option next.

Syslog server with CEF

This is very similar to the Syslog server deployment mentioned previously. For more detailed information, see this article: `https://docs.microsoft.com/en-us/azure/sentinel/connect-common-event-format`. The difference is that the source supports the CEF for logs. Examples of solutions that support this method include the following:

- Cisco (Umbrella, Cloud Security Gateway, and others)
- CyberArk
- F5 Firewall
- McAfee Web Gateway
- Palo Alto Networks Firewall
- Varonis
- Zscaler

With this range of connectors available, it is possible to connect to and gather information from multiple resources across all your operating environments, including on-premises, a hosted service, the public cloud, and even industrial operations environments or the **Internet of Things (IoT)**.

Configuring Azure Sentinel connectors

The **Azure Sentinel - Data connectors** page shows the total number of connectors, how many are currently connected, and how many are in development. An example of the **Data connectors** page is shown in the following screenshot:

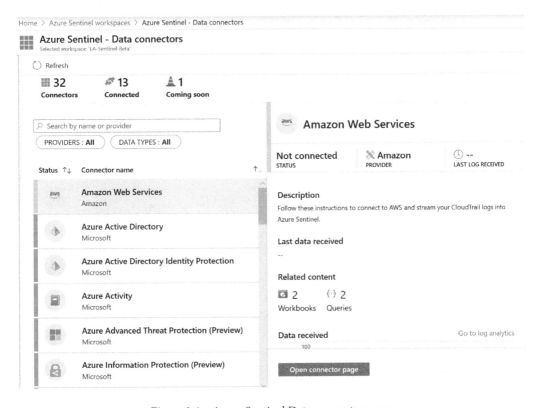

Figure 3.4 – Azure Sentinel Data connectors page

As you can see in the preceding screenshot, there are currently **32** connectors available to implement in this Azure Sentinel workspace. The list is likely to grow over time as more solutions become natively integrated, which is why you can see the ability to filter the list and search for specific data connectors. By selecting the connector on the left-hand side, we can view the connector details on the right-hand side. For this example, we will use the data connector for AWS, as shown in the following screenshot:

Figure 3.5 – Data connector details

At the top of the page in the preceding screenshot, we can see the **STATUS** of the connector (**Not connected**), the provider (**Amazon**), and the **LAST LOG RECEIVED** date/timestamp (empty due to a disconnected state).

The next section provides a description and further details about the connector, including a graph that will show the last few days of active log ingestion rate (when connected).

At the bottom of the page, we can see the **Data types** that are included in this connector; in this example, we are expecting to retrieve the AWS CloudTrail logs, when enabled.

Click on the **Open connector page** button to go to the next screen and start the configuration process, as shown in the following screenshot:

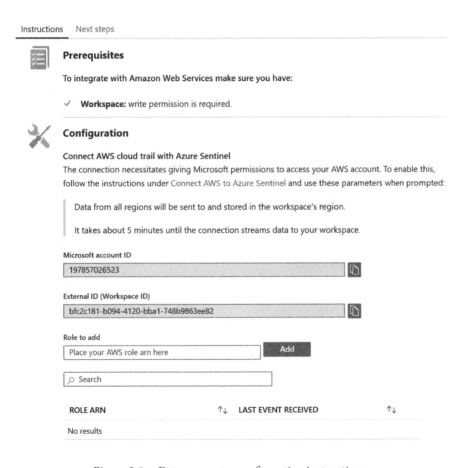

Figure 3.6 – Data connector configuration instructions

Each connector will show a slightly different screen, depending on the type of connector (native, direct, API, or agent) and the steps required to complete the configuration. In this example, the AWS connector is an API-based connector, and instructions are provided on how to set up the required permissions for Azure Sentinel to access the AWS account via the API. Once completed, you can select the **Next steps** tab to view the available workbooks and other resources available for this data connector, as shown in the following screenshot:

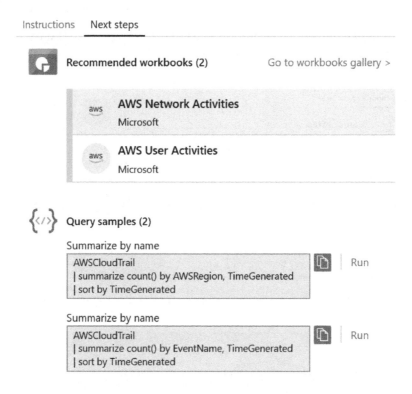

Figure 3.7 – Data connector configuration instructions

As we can see in the preceding screenshot, the AWS connector has the following two workbooks associated:

- **AWS Network Activities**
- **AWS User Activities**

Each of these workbooks is configured based on the information available in the AWS CloudTrail logs. The page also provides example queries you can use to get started with interrogating the logs for your own requirements. Further information about how to use workbooks can be found in *Chapter 8, Introducing Workbooks*.

Now, when we look at a data connector that has been successfully configured, we can view the same pages and see the differences, as shown in the following screenshot:

Figure 3.8 – Azure AD connector

We can see in the data connector page for Azure AD that this data source is connected and has received logs **4 minutes ago**. We can see that **3** workbooks and **2** queries are using this data connector, and a regular flow of data has occurred over the last 3 weeks (**December 8** to **December 29**). By selecting the **Open connector page** button, we get a view of the details of this connector, as shown in the following screenshot:

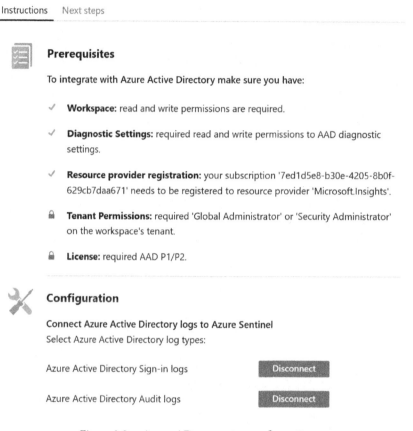

Instructions   Next steps

Prerequisites

To integrate with Azure Active Directory make sure you have:

✓ **Workspace:** read and write permissions are required.

✓ **Diagnostic Settings:** required read and write permissions to AAD diagnostic settings.

✓ **Resource provider registration:** your subscription '7ed1d5e8-b30e-4205-8b0f-629cb7daa671' needs to be registered to resource provider 'Microsoft.Insights'.

🔒 **Tenant Permissions:** required 'Global Administrator' or 'Security Administrator' on the workspace's tenant.

🔒 **License:** required AAD P1/P2.

Configuration

Connect Azure Active Directory logs to Azure Sentinel
Select Azure Active Directory log types:

Azure Active Directory Sign-in logs   Disconnect

Azure Active Directory Audit logs   Disconnect

Figure 3.9 – Azure AD connector configuration

On the **Instructions** page, we see check marks to indicate the successful configuration of each element, with some padlocks to indicate other aspects that are also required. In the **Configuration** section, both the **Azure Active Directory Sign-in logs** and the **Azure Active Directory Audit logs** are connected. If you click on either of the blue buttons for **Disconnect**, this will stop the logs from being ingested to Azure Sentinel. Selecting the **Next steps** tab will show more information about what we can do with this connector, as shown in the following screenshot:

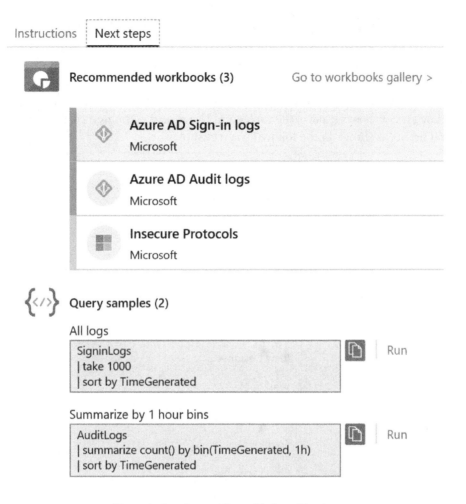

Figure 3.10 – Azure AD-enabled workbooks

On the **Next steps** page, we can see three recommended workbooks. Two of them have been enabled, shown by the bar on the left-hand side, and one of them is available but not yet enabled.

In this section, we walked through the setup of the data connectors to enable data ingestion. In the next section, we will move on to look at how we manage that data to ensure we retain enough information to be useful, without storing so much that it becomes expensive.

Configuring Log Analytics storage options

Once you have completed the configuration of a few data connectors, you will begin to see how much data you will ingest and store in Log Analytics on a daily basis. The amount of data you store and retain directly impacts the costs—see *Chapter 1, Getting Started with Azure Sentinel* for further details. You can view the current usage and costs by navigating to the Log Analytics workspace, then selecting **Usage and estimated costs** from the **General** menu, as shown in the following screenshot:

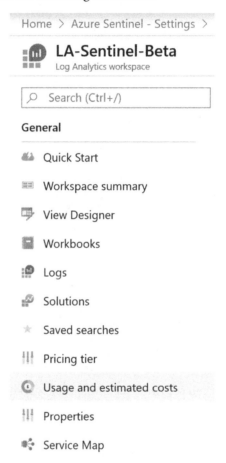

Figure 3.11 – Log Analytics navigation menu

Once selected, you are then presented with a dashboard of information that will show the pricing tier and current costs on the left-hand side and graphs on the right-hand side, to show the variation in consumption on a daily basis for the last 31 days. A second graph shows the total size of retained data, per solution. An example of the dashboard is shown in the following screenshot:

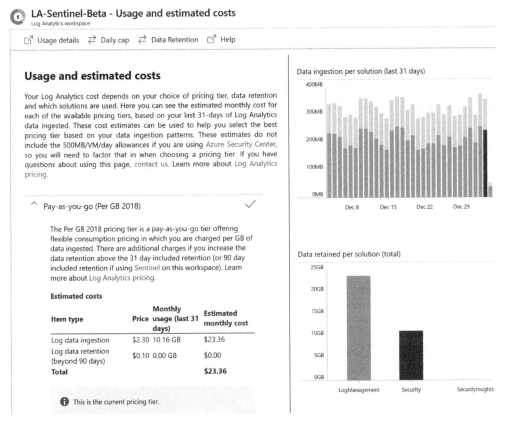

Figure 3.12 – Log Analytics usage and cost dashboard

From this page, explore two of the options available along the top menu bar:

- **Daily cap**: With this option, you can enable or disable the ability to limit how much data is ingested into the Log Analytics workspace on a per-day basis. While this is a useful control to have to limit costs, there is a risk that the capped data will result in a loss of security information valuable for detecting threats across your environment. We recommend only using this for non-production environments.

- **Data Retention**: This option allows you to configure the number of days data should be retained in the Log Analytics workspace. The default for Log Analytics is 31 days; however, when Azure Sentinel is also enabled on the Log Analytics workspace, the default free amount is 90 days. If you choose to increase beyond 90 days, you will be charged a set fee per gigabyte (GB) per month.

In the next section, we will look at how we calculate the costs involved in data ingestion and retention for Azure Sentinel and Log Analytics.

Calculating the cost of data ingestion and retention

Many organizations have a need to retain security log data for longer than 90 days, and budget to ensure they have enough capacity based on business needs. For example, if we consider the need to keep data for 2 years, with an average daily ingestion rate of 10 GB, then we can calculate the cost of the initial ingestion and analysis, then compare to the cost of retention. This will provide an annual cost estimate for both aspects.

The following table shows the cost for ingesting data into Log Analytics and analyzing that data in Azure Sentinel. This price includes 90 days of free retention:

	Per day	Per month	Per year total	2 year total
Azure Sentinel	$20	$600	$7,200	$14,600
Log Analytics	$23	$690	$8,280	$16,790
Total	$43	$1,290	$15,480	$30,960

The following table shows the amount of data being retained past the free 90 days included in the preceding pricing, based on ingesting 10 GB per day:

	Day 91	Day 120	Day 270	Day 330	Day 365	Day 730
Total Data Size (GB)	910	1,200	2,700	3,300	3,650	7,300
Retention Costs (per month)	$91	$120	$270	$330	$365	$730

Now, if we add these together, we can see the total cost of the solution over a 12-month period, shown in the following table:

	Data Size (GB)	Log Analytics	Azure Sentinel	Data Retention	Total Cost (per month)
Month 1	300	$690	$600	$0	$1,290
Month 2	600	$690	$600	$0	$1,290
Month 3	900	$690	$600	$0	$1,290
Month 4	1,200	$690	$600	$120	$1,410
Month 5	1,500	$690	$600	$150	$1,440
Month 6	1,800	$690	$600	$180	$1,470
Month 7	2,100	$690	$600	$210	$1,500
Month 8	2,400	$690	$600	$240	$1,530
Month 9	2,700	$690	$600	$270	$1,560
Month 10	3,000	$690	$600	$300	$1,590
Month 11	3,300	$690	$600	$330	$1,620
Month 12	3,600	$690	$600	$360	$1,650
Annual Totals	3.6 TB	$8,280	$7,200	$2,160	$17,645
Two Year Total	7.2TB	$16,560	$14,400	$8,820	$39,780

> **Note**
>
> These prices are based on the current rates applicable to the US East Azure region, and figures are rounded to simplify. Actual data usage may fluctuate each month.

Based on these examples, the total cost for running Azure Sentinel, ingesting 10 GB per day and retaining data for 2 years, would be **$39,780**. Data retention accounts for 22% of the cost.

Because the charges are based on the volume of data (in GB), one way of maintaining reasonable costs is to carefully select which data is initially gathered, and which data is kept long term. If you plan to investigate events that occurred more than 90 days ago, then you should plan to retain that data. Useful log types for long-term retention include the following:

- IAM events such as authentication requests, password changes, new and modified accounts, group membership changes, and more

- Configuration and change management to core platforms, network configuration, and access controls across boundaries

- Creation, modification, and deletion of resources such as virtual machines, databases, and cloud applications **(Platform- as- a- Service (PaaS)** and **Software- as- a- Service (SaaS)** resources)

Other data types can be extremely useful for initial analysis and investigation; however, they do not hold as much value when the relevance of their data reduces. They include the following:

- Information from industrial control solutions

- Events streamed from IoT devices

Also, consider that some platforms sending data to Azure Sentinel may also be configured to retain the original copies of the log data for longer periods of time, potentially without additional excessive costs. An example would be your firewall and CASB solutions.

Reviewing alternative storage options

The benefit of retaining data within Log Analytics is the speed of access to search the data when needed, without having to write new queries. However, many organizations require specific log data to be retained for long periods of time, usually to meet internal governance controls, external compliance requirements, or local laws. Currently, there is a limitation, as Log Analytics only supports storage for up to 2 years.

The following solutions may be considered as an alternative for long-term storage, outside of Log Analytics:

- **Azure Blob Storage**: You can create a query in Azure Monitor to select the data you want to move from the Log Analytics workspace and point it to the appropriate Azure Storage account. This allows for filtering of the information by type (or select everything), and only moving data that is about to come to the end of its life, which is the limit you have set for data retention in the Log Analytics workspace. Once you have the query defined, you can use Azure Automation to run PowerShell and load the results as a CSV file, then copy to Azure Blob Storage. With this solution, data can be stored for up to 400 years! For further information, see this article: `https://docs.microsoft.com/en-us/azure/azure-monitor/platform/powershell-quickstart-samples`.

- **Azure SQL**: Data that is stored in Azure Blob Storage can be then be ingested into Azure SQL (Database or Data Warehouse), which enables another method for searching and analyzing the data. This process utilizes Azure Data Factory to connect the Azure Blob Storage location to Azure SQL Database/Data Warehouse, automating the ingestion of any new data. For further information, see this article: `https://azure.microsoft.com/en-us/documentation/articles/data-factory-copy-data-wizard-tutorial/`.

- **Azure Data Lake Storage Gen2**: As an alternative to Azure Blob Storage, this option enables access to the data via open source platforms such as HDInsight, Hadoop, Cloudera, Azure Databricks, and Hortonworks. The data does not need to be transferred (as with Azure SQL), and this solution provides easier management and increased performance and is more cost-effective. For further information, see this article: `https://docs.microsoft.com/en-us/azure/storage/blobs/data-lake-storage-introduction`.

As you can see, there are plenty of options available to store the data in alternative locations, both for extended archive/retention and for additional analysis with alternative tools. We expect Microsoft will increase the number of options available.

Summary

In this chapter, we reviewed the importance of data quality, using the 7 Vs of Big Data as a guide to selecting the right data. We also looked at the various data connectors available to retrieve logs from a wide variety of sources, and the importance of constantly reviewing the connectors for updates and additional resources, such as workbooks. You now have the skills required to set up data connectors to begin ingesting data for later use in analysis and threat hunting.

Ongoing data management plays a key part of this solution, ensuring you maintain cost efficiency of the solution without losing valuable information that can help identify risk and mitigate potential loss. Use the information in this chapter to apply to your own environment, and review regularly.

In the next chapter, you will learn how to integrate threat intelligence feeds into Azure Sentinel, in order to enrich your data with insights from security experts and make your investigations more effective.

Questions

Use these questions to test your knowledge of this chapter:

1. Can you list the 7 Vs of Big Data?
2. What are the four different types of data connectors?
3. What is the purpose of a Syslog server?
4. How long is data stored in Azure Sentinel without extra cost?
5. What are the alternative storage options for log retention?

Further reading

The following resources can be used to further explore some of the topics covered in this chapter:

- Azure Sentinel: Creating Custom Connectors
  https://techcommunity.microsoft.com/t5/azure-sentinel/
  azure-sentinel-creating-custom-connectors/ba-p/864060

- Connect your external solution using Syslog
  https://docs.microsoft.com/en-us/azure/sentinel/connect-
  syslog

- Connect your external solution using CEF
  https://docs.microsoft.com/en-us/azure/sentinel/connect-
  common-event-format

- Azure Monitor PowerShell quick start samples
  https://docs.microsoft.com/en-us/azure/azure-monitor/
  platform/powershell-quickstart-samples

- Tutorial: Create a pipeline with Copy Activity using Data Factory Copy Wizard
  https://azure.microsoft.com/en-us/documentation/articles/
  data-factory-copy-data-wizard-tutorial/

- Introduction to Azure Data Lake Storage Gen2
  https://docs.microsoft.com/en-us/azure/storage/blobs/data-
  lake-storage-introduction

4

Integrating Threat Intelligence

This chapter will explore the options available for adding **Threat Intelligence (TI)** feeds into Azure Sentinelt to enable the security team to have a greater understanding of the potential threats against their environment. We will explore the available TI feeds from Microsoft and other trusted industry sources, then learn how to choose the most appropriate feeds for your organization based on geography, industry, and other risk factors.

This chapter will also introduce several new topics you may not be familiar with, but we encourage you to further research to add to your **SOC** capabilities, including the collaborative efforts of **STIX** and **TAXII**, a TI framework and set of standards that will help organizations to contribute and benefit from the knowledge of others.

By the end of this chapter, you will know how to implement several TI feeds.

This chapter will cover the following topics:

- Introduction to TI

- Understanding STIX and TAXII

- Choosing the right intel feeds for your needs

- Implementing TI connectors

Introduction to TI

Due to the complex nature of cybersecurity and the sophistication of modern attacks, it is difficult for any organization to keep track of the vulnerabilities and multiple ways that an attacker may compromise a system, especially if cybersecurity is not the focus of the organization. Understanding what to look for and deciding what to do when you see a system anomaly or an other potential threat is complex and time-consuming. This is where TI comes in useful.

TI is critical in fighting against adversaries and is now integrated with most security products; it provides the ability to set a list of indicators for detection and blocking malicious activities. You can subscribe to TI feeds to gain knowledge from other security professionals in the industry and create your own indicators that are specific to the environment you are operating.

If you are new to this topic, there are some new keywords and abbreviations to learn:

- **Threat Indicators**: This is a list of suspicious or known malicious entities, such as IP addresses, URLs, and files. They are used to alert when usage is discovered in your environment.

- **Indicators of Compromise (IoC)**: This indicates uniquely known behaviors and activities that show signs of potential malicious intent or an actual breach. These are available as open source and some paid-for services.

- **Alert definitions:** By combining multiple TIs and IoCs, you can build an alert definition that only trigger in the right context. This will reduce alert fatigue from overloading the SOC with too many false-positives.

- **Malware Information Sharing Project (MISP)**: This is an open source **Threat Intelligence Platform (TIP)** and a set of open standards for threat information sharing. MISP covers malware indicators, fraud, and vulnerability information. Read more here: `https://www.misp-project.org/`.

- **Adversarial Tactics, Techniques and Common Knowledge (ATT&CK)**: This is a knowledge base providing a list of the known adversary tactics and techniques, collated from real-world observations. Microsoft has integrated this framework into the Azure Sentinel platform. Read more here: `https://attack.mitre.org/`.

- **Structured Threat Information eXpression (STIX)**: STIX is a standardized XML-based language, developed for the purpose of conveying cybersecurity threat data in a standard format.

- **Trusted Automated eXchange of Indicator Information (TAXII)**: TAXII is an application layer protocol for the communication of cybersecurity threat intelligence over HTTP.

- **MineMeld threat intelligence sharing**: MineMeld is an open source TI processing tool that extracts indicators from various sources and compiles them into compatible formats for ingestion into Azure Sentinel.

- **ThreatConnect**: This is a third-party solution that has built an integration with Microsoft Graph Security threat indicators. This is one example of a **TIP** that can provide a comprehensive offering, for an additional cost.

> **Note**
>
> ATT&CK™, TAXII™, and STIX™ are trademarks of The MITRE Corporation. MineMeld™ is a trademark of Palo Alto Networks.

Microsoft provides access to its own TI feeds via the **tiIndicators API**, and has built connectors for integration with feeds from Palo Alto Networks (MineMeld), ThreatConnect, MISP, and TAXII. You can also build your own integration to submit custom threat indicators to Azure Sentinel and Microsoft Defender ATP. For further details, review this information: `https://github.com/microsoftgraph/security-api-solutions/tree/master/QuickStarts`.

Once your TI sources are connected, you can create rules to generate alerts and incidents when events match threat indicators or use built-in analytics, enriched with TI. You can also correlate TI with event data via hunting queries to add contextual insights to investigations.

In the next section, we will look at the specifics of one of these recommended approaches: STIX and TAXII, which is important to understand and consider implementing within your SOC as part of designing Azure Sentinel.

Understanding STIX and TAXII

The MITRE Corporation is a not-for-profit company that provides guidance in the form of frameworks and standards to assist with the development of stronger cybersecurity controls; the STIX language and TAXII protocol are some examples of this development effort.

These two standards were developed by an open community effort, sponsored by the U.S. **Department of Homeland Security (DHS)**, in partnership with the MITRE Corporation. These are not software products, but the standards that products can use to enable automation and compatibility when sharing TI information with your security community and business partners.

As per the description provided by MITRE: *STIX is a collaborative community-driven effort to define and develop a standardized language to represent structured cyber threat information.* The STIX language was developed to ensure threat information can be shared, stored, and used in a consistent manner to facilitate automation and human-assisted analysis. You can read more about the STIX standard here: `https://stixproject.github.io/`.

The TAXII protocol was developed to provide support for TI feeds from **Open Source Intelligence (OSINT)** and TIP supporting this standard protocol and STIX data format. You can read more details about the TAXII protocol here: `https://www.mitre.org/sites/default/files/publications/taxii.pdf`.

Microsoft has developed a connector to enable integration with services using the TAXII protocol, enabling the ingestion of STIX 2.0 Threat Indicators for use in Azure Sentinel.

Public previews

Due to the nature of agile development and an ever-green cloud environment, Microsoft makes new features available first through private previews to a select few reviewers, and then releases the feature to public preview to allow wider audience participation for feedback. Your organization needs to determine whether it is acceptable to use preview features in your production tenants or restrict access to only a development/testing environment. At the time of writing, the TAXII data connector is in public preview with an expected release date of April 2020. You can check the list of available Data Connectors in your Azure Sentinel tenant to see whether it is currently available.

In the next chapter, we will review the options for intel feeds and choose which ones are right for your organization's needs.

Choosing the right intel feeds for your needs

With Azure Sentinel, you can import TIs from multiple sources to enhance the security analysts' ability to detect and prioritize known threats and IOCs. When configured, several optional features become available within the following Azure Sentinel tools:

- **Analytics**: It includes a set of scheduled rule templates you can enable to generate alerts and incidents based on matches of log events.

- **Workbooks**: It provides summarized information about the TI imported into Azure Sentinel and any alerts generated from analytics rules that match your threat indicators.

- **Hunting**: Hunting queries allow security investigators to use threat indicators within the context of common hunting scenarios.

- **Notebooks**: Notebooks can use threat indicators to assist with the investigation of anomalies and to hunt for malicious behaviors.

There are several options available to gain access to TI feeds and you may choose to generate your own indicators based on specific information gathered through internal IT investigations; this allows you to develop a unique list of indicators that are known to be specific to your organization. Depending on your industry and region, you may choose to share these with partner organizations and communities to gain specific information related to healthcare, government, energy, and so on.

You can choose to leverage direct integration with the Microsoft Graph Security tiIndicators API, which contains Microsoft's own TI, gathered across their vast internet services landscape (such as Azure, Office 365, Xbox, and Outlook). This feature also allows you to upload your own threat indicators and to send to other Microsoft security tools for the actions of allowing, blocking, or alerting on activities, based on the signals received from the intel.

It is recommended that you also obtain TI feeds from open source platforms, such as the following:

- MISP Open Source TIP
- MineMeld by Palo Alto Networks
- Any that are based on the MITRE STIX/TAXII standards

Optionally, you can also choose to purchase additional TI feeds from solution providers. Azure Sentinel currently offers the capability to integrate with the ThreatConnect Platform, which is a TIP you can purchase separately. Other platforms are expected to be integrated in the near future; review the data connector for TIPs for any updates.

Implementing TI connectors

Azure Sentinel provides a data connector specifically for the integration with TIP solutions (both commercial and open source). This section will provide walk-through guidance for the steps required to ingest TI data into Azure Sentinel, using MineMeld as an example:

1. Enabling the data connector for TIPs

2. Registering app permission in Azure AD

3. Configuring the TI feed (MineMeld)

4. Confirming that the TI feed data is visible

> **Note**
> At the time of writing, this feature is still in public preview. You can enable this solution in your Azure Sentinel workspace to gain access to these features; however, you should expect it to change as it is developed.

Let's discuss each of these steps in detail in the following sections.

Enabling the data connector

Use the following steps to enable the data connector for TIPs within the Azure Sentinel:

1. Navigate to the Azure Sentinel portal and go to the **Data connectors** page, as shown in the following screenshot:

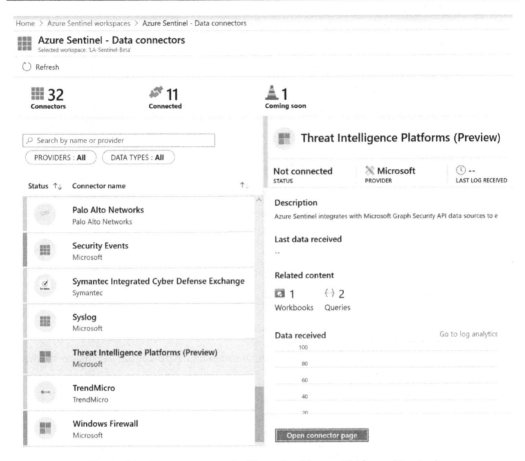

Figure 4.1 – Data connector for Threat Intelligence Platforms (Preview)

2. Select the data connector for **Threat Intelligence Platforms (Preview)**.

3. Click on the **Open connector page** button.

4. At the top of the page, you will see the **Prerequisites** for the data connector. Review these to ensure you have properly configured the workspace and tenant permissions, as shown in the following screenshot:

Figure 4.2 – Data connector prerequisites

5.   Next, you will see the configuration steps required to ensure the data connector will function correctly (which is what we did in the previous step). Click on the **Connect** button at the bottom of the page.

You should now have a working connector waiting for the TI feed data to flow in. Next, we will configure the app registration in Azure AD, which is necessary to then set up the MineMeld server.

Registering an app in Azure AD

In this section, we will create an app registration in Azure AD. This will be used by the TI server/service to run and send information to Azure Sentinel.

> **Note**
>
> You will need to repeat this process for each TI server/service you intend to integrate with Azure Sentinel.

Use the following steps to create an app registration in Azure AD:

1.   In the Azure portal, navigate to Azure AD and select **App registrations**, as shown in the following screenshot:

Figure 4.3 – Azure AD app registrations

2.   In the toolbar, select **+ New registration**, as shown in the following screenshot:

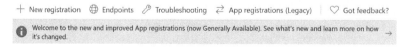

Figure 4.4 – Create a new app registration

3. On the next screen, provide a unique name for the specific TI connector. In this example, we are creating one for the MineMeld server, so we'll name it as shown in the following screenshot. Choose the default option for **Who can use this application or access this API?**, then select **Register**, as shown in the following screenshot:

Register an application
* Name
The user-facing display name for this application (this can be changed later).
Threat Intel - MineMeld Server
Supported account types
Who can use this application or access this API?
Accounts in this organizational directory only ( ) only - Single tenant)
Accounts in any organizational directory (Any Azure AD directory - Multitenant)
Accounts in any organizational directory (Any Azure AD directory - Multitenant) and personal Microsoft accounts (e.g. Skype, Xbox)
Help me choose...
Redirect URI (optional)
We'll return the authentication response to this URI after successfully authenticating the user. Providing this now is optional and it can be changed later, but a value is required for most authentication scenarios.
Web
e.g. https://myapp.com/auth
By proceeding, you agree to the Microsoft Platform Policies
Register

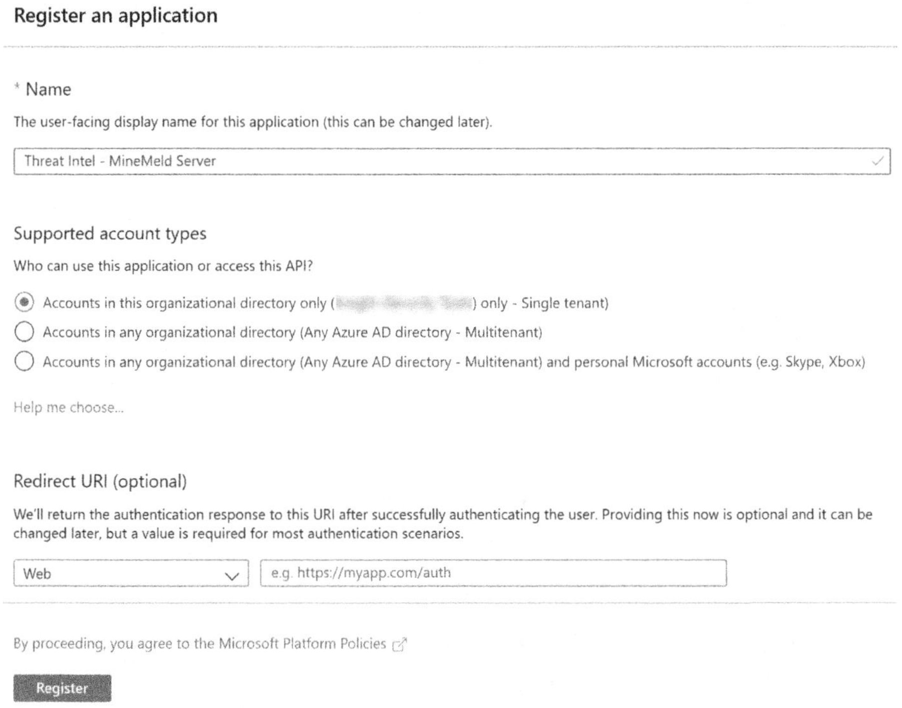

Figure 4.5 – Creating a new app registration

4. When registration is complete, you will be presented with the **Overview** page, as shown in the following screenshot:

Threat Intel - MineMeld Server
Search (Ctrl+/)
Delete
Endpoints
Got a second? We would love your feedback on Microsoft identity platform (previously Azure AD for developer). →
Overview
Quickstart
Manage
Branding
Display name : Threat Intel - MineMeld Server
Application (client) ID : ee46252f-2a91-448f-
Directory (tenant) ID : b258f8fa-6403-455d-
Object ID : f72768e4-df95-48d5-
Supported account types : My organization only
Redirect URIs : Add a Redirect URI
Application ID URI : Add an Application ID URI
Managed application in ... : Threat Intel - MineMeld Server

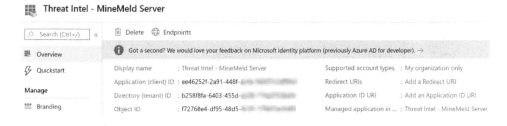

Figure 4.6 – New app registration details

5. You will need to refer to these ID values when you configure your integrated TIP product or an app that uses direct integration with the Microsoft Graph Security API.

6. Next, we will configure API permissions for the registered application. To do this, go to the menu on the left and select **API Permissions**, as shown in the following screenshot:

Figure 4.7 – API permissions menu option

7. When first created, there will be a default permission of **User.Read**. Select **+ Add a permission**.

8. On the next screen, select the **Microsoft Graph** API, as shown in the following screenshot:

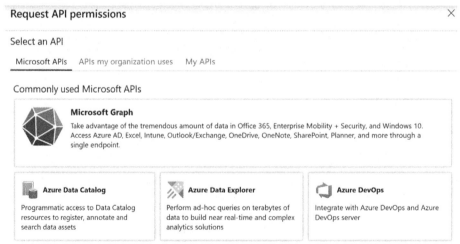

Figure 4.8 – Selecting an API

9. Then, select **Application permissions**, as shown in the following screenshot:

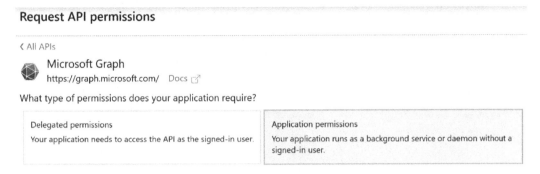

Request API permissions

< All APIs

Microsoft Graph
https://graph.microsoft.com/   Docs 🗗

What type of permissions does your application require?

Delegated permissions	Application permissions
Your application needs to access the API as the signed-in user.	Your application runs as a background service or daemon without a signed-in user.

Figure 4.9 – Application permissions

10. In the search bar, enter `ThreatIndicators`, then select the **ThreatIndicators.
    ReadWrite.OwnedBy** option, as shown in the following screenshot:

Select permissions   expand all

ThreatIndicators   ✓

Permission	Admin Consent Required
⌄ **ThreatIndicators (1)**	
☐ ThreatIndicators.Read.All Read all threat indicators ⓘ	Yes
☑ ThreatIndicators.ReadWrite.OwnedBy Manage threat indicators this app creates or owns ⓘ	Yes

Figure 4.10 – Searching for permissions

11. Click on **Add permissions**. On the next screen, select the **Grant admin consent
    for <tenant name>** button.

> **Note**
>
> You can also get to this screen from the Azure portal: navigate to **Azure Active
> Directory** | **App registrations** | `<app name>` | **View API Permissions** |
> **Grant admin consent for <tenant name>**.

12. You will be prompted with a screen requesting permissions consent, on which you
    will need to click the **Accept** button.

13. You will now be able to confirm the permissions are successfully granted by viewing the permissions and looking for the green checkmark, similar to the following screenshot:

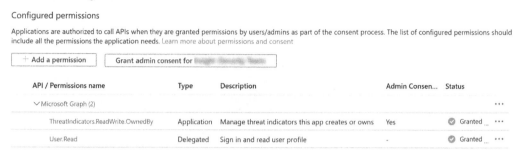

Figure 4.11 – Confirming permissions have been granted

Now the app is registered in Azure AD, we can start to configure the MineMeld server, which involves setting up a new **virtual machine** (**VM**) to collect and forward the TI feeds.

Configuring the MineMeld threat intelligence feed

With the previous steps complete, you are ready to configure the services that will send TI data to Azure Sentinel. This section will walk you through the configuration of the MineMeld threat intelligence sharing solution.

> **Note**
>
> If this service is not already running in your environment, you will need to configure the TIP product; this guidance is only for the Azure Sentinel connectors.

There are three steps to this process:

1. Building the VM and installing MineMeld
2. Installing the Microsoft Graph Security API extension in MineMeld
3. Configuring the extension to connect to the Microsoft Graph via the Security API

To carry out this procedure, you will need administrative access to the Azure Tenant and the MineMeld service.

Building the VM and installing MineMeld

Ideally you will already have the MineMeld VM configured and running in your environment; however, if you do not, you can find configuration instructions online via the official Palo Alto Networks website: `https://live.paloaltonetworks.com/t5/MineMeld-Articles/Manually-Install-MineMeld-on-Ubuntu-16-04/ta-p/253336`.

> **Note**
>
> Ensure you use Ubuntu version 16.04 only; other versions may not be compatible.

Installing the Microsoft Graph Security API extension in MineMeld

The following are the steps to install the API extension:

1. Log in to the MineMeld web portal and go to **SYSTEM** then **EXTENTIONS**.

2. Click on the Git icon, and enter the following address: `https://github.com/PaloAltoNetworks/minemeld-msgraph-secapi.git`.

3. Click **RETRIEVE** then choose **master** from the drop-down list and click **INSTALL**, as shown in the following screenshot:

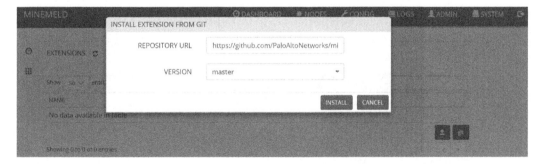

Figure 4.12 – Install the extension from Git

4. Confirm the installation has completed, then select the **Activate** button beside the cross. To confirm activation, the API extension should show a white background instead of the gray-hashed background, as shown in the following screenshot:

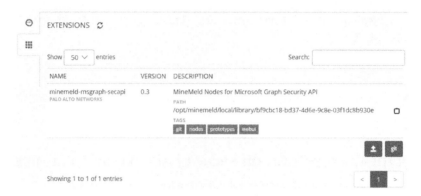

Figure 4.13 – Confirming installation of the API extension

Now that the Microsoft Graph Security API extension has been set up on the MineMeld server, we can configure the Azure Sentinel connector.

Configuring the Azure Sentinel connector

The following are the steps to configure the API extension:

1. Log in to the MineMeld web portal. Go to **CONFIG**, then select the prototypes icon at the bottom of the page with three horizontal lines, as shown in the following screenshot:

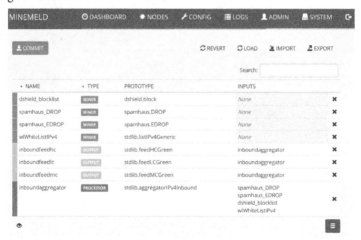

Figure 4.14 – MineMeld config page

2. As you will see, there are many options to choose from. Review the list for additional TI feeds you may want to implement, then search for `Microsoft` and review the results. Select the prototype named **microsoft_graph_secapi_output**:

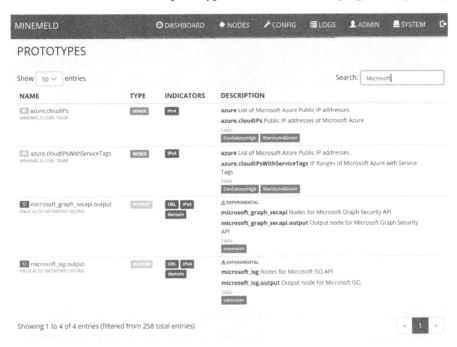

Figure 4.15 – Microsoft prototypes

3. On the next page, select **CLONE** in the top-right corner:

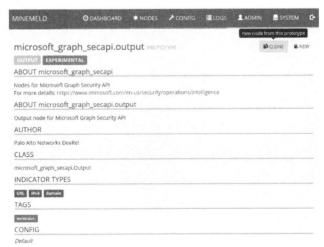

Figure 4.16 – Creating a new node from a prototype

4. On the next page, provide a name for the node, then select **inboundaggregator** for the **INPUTS** field:

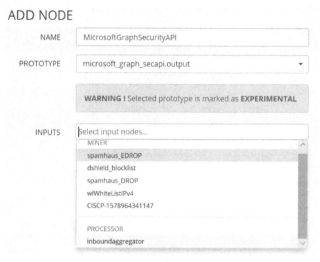

Figure 4.17 – Configuring a new node

5. Confirm the new node is active by viewing the list of nodes as shown in the following screenshot. Select the **COMMIT** button at the top of the page. This will save the changes and restart the process to enable the new functionality:

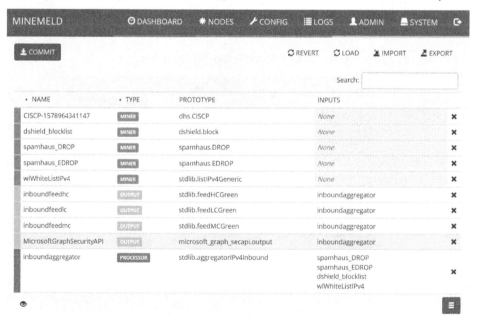

Figure 4.18 – Confirming the new node is added

6. Now go to the **NODES** tab and select the new API extension, then enter the relevant details from the previously registered app in Azure AD (see *figure 4.6*):

Figure 4.19 – Configuring the API extension for Azure Sentinel

7. For the **CLIENT SECRET** field, you need to generate a new secret in the Azure AD App: Go to the Azure AD App created earlier and select **Certificates & secrets**, then select **+ New client secret** and follow the steps that will appear to create a new secret:

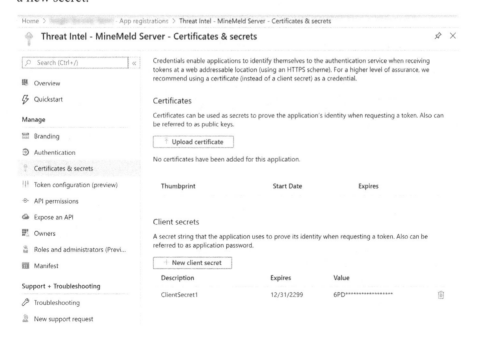

Figure 4.20 – Create a new client secret

8. With this new secret added to the settings, you should see the following completed screen:

Figure 4.21 – Completed configuration

This concludes the configuration requirements for the MineMeld service. TI feeds should now be sent to your Azure Sentinel instance.

Confirming the data is being ingested for use by Azure Sentinel

To confirm the data is being sent to Azure Sentinel, follow these steps:

1. Go to the Azure portal, then Azure Sentinel.

2. Select **Logs**, then expand **SecurityInsights**.

3. Type the following command into the command window and select **Run**:

```
ThreatIntelligenceIndicator
| take 100
```

4. You should see the following screen with the results:

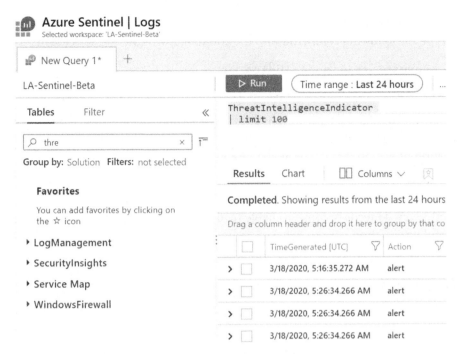

Figure 4.22 – Checking for TI feed activity

5. The following screenshot shows an example of the details for one of the events:

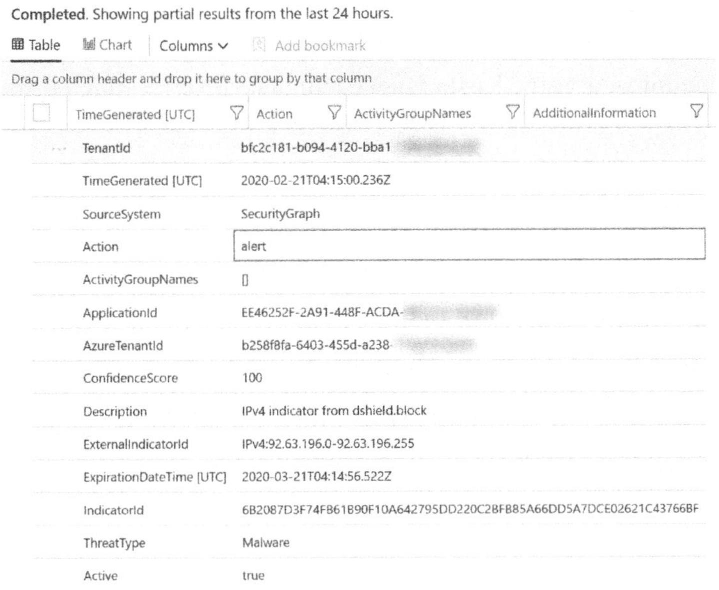

Figure 4.23 – TI data feed details

6. The following command can be used to show which TIs are enabled and delivering. Type the following command into the command window and select **Run**:

```
ThreatIntelligenceIndicator
  | distinct SourceSystem
```

You have now configured and connected the MineMeld server to your Azure Sentinel workspace and can see the TI data feeds appearing in the logs. You can now use this information to help to create new analytics and hunting queries, notebooks, and workbooks in Azure Sentinel.

We recommended regular reviews to ensure this information is both relevant and updated frequently. New TI feeds become available regularly and you don't want to miss out on that useful information if it can help you to find new and advanced threats.

Summary

In this chapter, we explored the concept of TI, new terminology and solutions options available, and the concept of creating and sharing TI feeds as a community effort.

There are several options available for adding TI feeds into Azure Sentinel, and we know Microsoft is working to develop this even further. TI feeds will assist with the analysis and detection of unwanted behavior and potentially malicious activities. With many options to choose from, selecting the right feeds for your organization is an important part of configuring Azure Sentinel.

The next chapter introduces the **Kusto Query Language** (**KQL**), which is the powerful means to search all data collected for Azure Sentinel, including the TI data we just added.

Questions

1. Name three examples of threat indicator types.

2. Name three examples of threat indicator types.

3. What is the full name of the ATT&CK framework?

4. Which Azure Sentinel components can utilize threat intelligence feeds?

5. Who developed the STIX language and the TAXII protocol?

Further reading

The following resources can be used to further explore some of the topics covered in this chapter:

- Malware Information Sharing Project:
  `https://www.misp-project.org/`

- Mitre ATT&CK framework: `https://attack.mitre.org/`

- Microsoft Security Graph API: `https://github.com/microsoftgraph/security-api-solutions/tree/master/QuickStarts`

- STIX standard: `https://stixproject.github.io/`

- TAXII protocol: `https://www.mitre.org/sites/default/files/publications/taxii.pdf`

- Build a MineMeld server: `https://live.paloaltonetworks.com/t5/MineMeld-Articles/Manually-Install-MineMeld-on-Ubuntu-16-04/ta-p/253336`

- The Microsoft Graph Security API extension in MineMeld: `https://github.com/PaloAltoNetworks/minemeld-msgraph-secapi.git`

5
Using the Kusto Query Language (KQL)

The **Kusto Query Language** (**KQL**) is a plain-text, read-only language that is used to query data stored in Azure Log Analytics workspaces. Much like SQL, it utilizes a hierarchy of entities that starts with databases, then tables, and finally columns. In this chapter, we will only concern ourselves with the table and column levels.

In this chapter, you will learn about a few of the many KQL commands that you can use to query your logs.

In this chapter, we will cover the following topics:

- How to test your KQL queries
- How to query a table
- How to limit how many rows are returned
- How to limit how many columns are returned
- How to perform a query across multiple tables
- How to graphically view the results

Running KQL queries

For the purpose of this chapter, we will be using the sample data available in the **Azure Data Explorer** (**ADE**). This is a very useful tool for trying simple KQL commands. Feel free to use it to try the various commands in this chapter. All the information used in the queries comes from the sample data provided at `https://dataexplorer.azure.com/clusters/help/databases/Samples`.

If prompted, use the login credentials you would use to log in to the Azure portal. When you log in for the first time, you will see the following screen. Note that your login name may show up on the right-hand side of the header:

Figure 5.1 – Azure Data Explorer

In order to run the samples for this chapter, you will need to expand the **Samples** logs on the left-hand side of the screen and then select **StormEvents**. You can expand **StormEvents** to see a listing of fields if you want to. If you do so, your screen should look similar to the following:

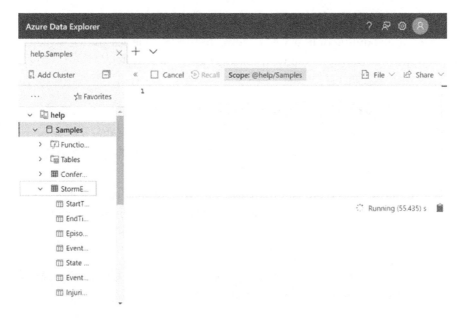

Figure 5.2 – StormEvents

To run a query, either type or paste the command into the query window at the top of the page, just to the right of the line numbered **1** in the preceding screenshot. Once the query has been entered, click on the **Run** button to run the query. The output will be shown in the results window at the bottom of the page.

In the following screenshot, a simple query was entered and run. The query was entered in the query window and you can see that the results are shown below it:

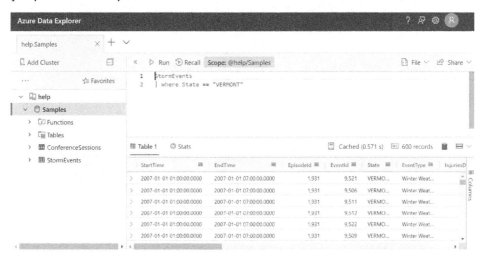

Figure 5.3 – Executed Query

There is a lot more you can do with the ADE, so feel free to play around with it. Now that you have an understanding of how we are going to run the queries and view the results, let's take a look at some of the various commands KQL has to offer.

Introduction to KQL commands

Unlike SQL, the query starts with the data source, which can be either a table or an operator that produces a table, followed by commands that transform the data into what is needed. Each command will be separated using the pipe (|) delimiter.

What does this mean? If you are familiar with SQL, you would write a statement such as `Select * from table` to get the values. The same query in KQL would just be `table`, where table refers to the name of the log. It is implied that you want all the columns and rows. Later, we will discuss how to minimize what information is returned.

We will only be scratching the surface of what KQL can do here, but it will be enough to get you started writing your own queries so that you can develop queries for Azure Sentinel.

The following table provides an overview of the commands, functions, and operators we will be covering in the rest of this chapter:

Type	Name	Description
Tabular Operators	`print`	Prints the results of a query.
	`search`	Searches for specific data throughout the logs.
	`where`	Filters a table to the subset of rows that satisfy a comparison.
	`take/limit`	Returns up to the specified number of rows.
	`count()`	Returns the number of records in the input record set.
	`summarize`	Produces a table that summarizes the content of the selected columns.
	`extend`	Creates calculated columns and appends them to the result set.
	`project`	Selects the columns to include.
	`distinct`	Produces a table with the distinct combination of the provided columns of the input table.
	`sort/order`	Sorts the rows of the input table into order by one or more columns.
	`join`	Merges the rows of two tables to form a new table by matching the values of the specified column(s) from each table.
	`union`	Takes two or more tables and returns the rows of all of them.
	`render`	Displays the output in a chart, including pie, bar, and line charts, among others.

Type	Name	Description
Query Statements	`let`	Creates variables.
Scalar Functions	`ago()`	Subtracts the given timespan from the current UTC clock time.
	`bin()`	Rounds values down to an integer of a given size.
String Operators	`Operators`	Not a command but a discussion of operators to use with the `where` command.

> **Note**
>
> For a complete list of all the KQL commands and more examples, go to `https://docs.microsoft.com/en-us/azure/kusto/query/index`.

Tabular operators

A tabular operator in KQL is one that can produce data in a mixture of tables and rows. Each tabular operator can pass its results from one command to another using the pipe delimiter. You will see many examples of this throughout this chapter.

The print command

The `print` command will print the results of a simple query. You will not be using this in your KQL queries, but it is useful for trying to figure out how commands work and what output to expect.

A simple print command such as `print "test"` will return a single row with the text **test** on it. You will see this command being used in the *The bin () function* section later.

The search command

As we stated earlier, to search using KQL, you just need to look at the table in the log. This will return all the columns and all the rows of the table, up to the maximum your application will return.

So, in the ADE, if you enter `StormEvents` into the search window and click **Run**, you will see a window similar to what is shown in the following screenshot. Note that there are a lot more rows available; the following screenshot just shows a small sample:

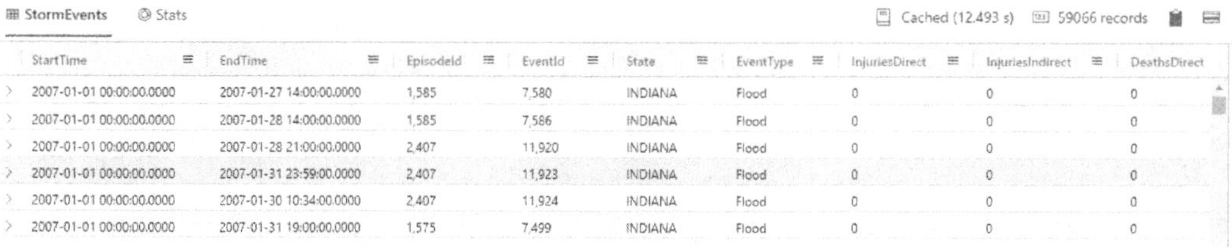
StormEvents Stats Cached (12.493 s) 59066 records

StartTime	EndTime	EpisodeId	EventId	State	EventType	InjuriesDirect	InjuriesIndirect	DeathsDirect
2007-01-01 00:00:00.0000	2007-01-27 14:00:00.0000	1,585	7,580	INDIANA	Flood	0	0	0
2007-01-01 00:00:00.0000	2007-01-28 14:00:00.0000	1,585	7,586	INDIANA	Flood	0	0	0
2007-01-01 00:00:00.0000	2007-01-28 21:00:00.0000	2,407	11,920	INDIANA	Flood	0	0	0
2007-01-01 00:00:00.0000	2007-01-31 23:59:00.0000	2,407	11,923	INDIANA	Flood	0	0	0
2007-01-01 00:00:00.0000	2007-01-30 10:34:00.0000	2,407	11,924	INDIANA	Flood	0	0	0
2007-01-01 00:00:00.0000	2007-01-31 19:00:00.0000	1,575	7,499	INDIANA	Flood	0	0	0

Figure 5.4 – Sampling the rows of StormEvents

If you need to search for a specific term in all the columns in all the logs in your workspace, the `search` command will do that for you.

If you need to find all the occurrences of `York`, you can use the following command:

```
search "York"
```

This will return results like what is shown in the following screenshot. Note that I have hidden some of the columns to make it easier to see that `York` is shown in more columns than just `State`:

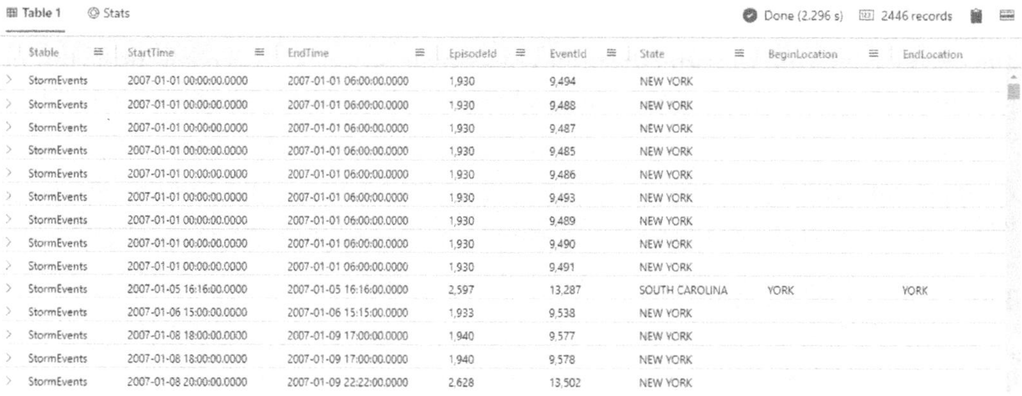
Table 1 Stats Done (2.296 s) 2446 records

$table	StartTime	EndTime	EpisodeId	EventId	State	BeginLocation	EndLocation
StormEvents	2007-01-01 00:00:00.0000	2007-01-01 06:00:00.0000	1,930	9,494	NEW YORK		
StormEvents	2007-01-01 00:00:00.0000	2007-01-01 06:00:00.0000	1,930	9,488	NEW YORK		
StormEvents	2007-01-01 00:00:00.0000	2007-01-01 06:00:00.0000	1,930	9,487	NEW YORK		
StormEvents	2007-01-01 00:00:00.0000	2007-01-01 06:00:00.0000	1,930	9,485	NEW YORK		
StormEvents	2007-01-01 00:00:00.0000	2007-01-01 06:00:00.0000	1,930	9,486	NEW YORK		
StormEvents	2007-01-01 00:00:00.0000	2007-01-01 06:00:00.0000	1,930	9,493	NEW YORK		
StormEvents	2007-01-01 00:00:00.0000	2007-01-01 06:00:00.0000	1,930	9,489	NEW YORK		
StormEvents	2007-01-01 00:00:00.0000	2007-01-01 06:00:00.0000	1,930	9,490	NEW YORK		
StormEvents	2007-01-01 00:00:00.0000	2007-01-01 06:00:00.0000	1,930	9,491	NEW YORK		
StormEvents	2007-01-05 16:16:00.0000	2007-01-05 16:16:00.0000	2,597	13,287	SOUTH CAROLINA	YORK	YORK
StormEvents	2007-01-06 15:00:00.0000	2007-01-06 15:15:00.0000	1,933	9,538	NEW YORK		
StormEvents	2007-01-08 18:00:00.0000	2007-01-09 17:00:00.0000	1,940	9,577	NEW YORK		
StormEvents	2007-01-08 18:00:00.0000	2007-01-09 17:00:00.0000	1,940	9,578	NEW YORK		
StormEvents	2007-01-08 20:00:00.0000	2007-01-09 22:22:00.0000	2,628	13,502	NEW YORK		

Figure 5.5 – Search command

Be warned that using the `search` command can take a significant amount of time to perform the query.

The where command

Recall from the screenshot from the *The search command* section that you get all the rows in the table when you just enter the table name, up to the maximum number of rows allowed to be returned. 99% of the time, this is not what you want to do. You will only want a subset of the rows in the table. That is when the where operator is useful. This allows you to filter the rows that are returned based on a condition.

If you want to see just those storm events that happened in North Carolina, you can enter the following:

```
StormEvents
| where State == "NORTH CAROLINA"
```

This will return all the rows where the column called State exactly equals NORTH CAROLINA. Note that == is case-sensitive, so if there was a row that had North Carolina in the State column, it would not be returned. Later, in the *String operators* section, we will go into more depth about case-sensitive and case-insensitive commands.

The take/limit command

There may be times when you just need a random sample of the data to be returned. This is usually so you can get an idea of what the data will look like before running a larger data query.

The take command does just that. It will return a specified number of rows; however, there is no guarantee which rows will be returned so that you can get a better sampling.

The following command will return five random rows from the StormEvents table:

```
StormEvents
| take 5
```

Note that limit is just an alias for take so that the following command is the same as the preceding command. However, it's likely that different rows will be returned since the sampling is random:

```
StormEvents
| limit 5
```

While you may not use the limit or take commands much in your actual queries, these commands are very useful when you're working to define your queries. You can use them to get a sense of the data that each table contains.

The count command

There may be times when you just need to know how many rows your query will return. A lot of times, this is done to get an idea of the data size you will be working with or just to see if your query returns any data without seeing the return value.

count will return the number of rows in the query. So, if we want to see the number of rows in the StormEvents table, we can enter the following:

```
StormEvents
| count
```

This will return just one column with 59,066 as the answer. Note how much faster this was than just showing all the rows in StormEvents using a basic search command and looking at the information bar to get the total. It can take around 12 seconds to process and show all the rows compared to around 0.2 seconds to get the answer when using count. The time that will be taken to perform the query may vary, but in all cases, it will be significantly faster to just get a count of the number of rows than to look at all the rows.

The summarize command

There will be times when you just need to know the total values for a specific grouping of rows. Suppose you just need to know how many StormEvents occurred for each location. The following command will show that:

```
StormEvents
| summarize count() by BeginLocation
```

This will return values like the ones shown in the following screenshot:

BeginLocation	count_
MELBOURNE BEACH	1
ORMOND BEACH	1
EUSTIS	12
LOTTS	1
CRANFIELD	1
SERVICE	1
BROOKHAVEN	3
FRENCH CAMP	2
PAGO PAGO	6
VANCEBURG	3
COLDWATER	11
WAPAKONETA	6
LOCKINGTON	1
DE GRAFF	1
EASTON	8
HOMEWOOD	3

Figure 5.6 – Summarize by BeginLocation

Note that this screenshot is only showing a partial listing of the results.

You may have noticed that `count`, in this case, has parentheses after it. That is because `count`, as used here, is a function rather than an operator and, as a function, requires parentheses after the name. For a complete list of aggregate functions that can be used, go to `https://docs.microsoft.com/en-us/azure/kusto/query/summarizeoperator#list-of-aggregation-functions`.

The by keyword is telling the command that everything that follows are the columns that are being used in the query to perform the summary.

You can also list multiple columns if you want to have more detailed information. For instance, the following command will summarize `StormEvents` by `State` and then `BeginLocation`:

```
StormEvents
| summarize count() by State, BeginLocation
```

If there is more than one `BeginLocation` in a state, the state will be listed multiple times, as shown in the following screenshot:

State	BeginLocation	count_
ATLANTIC SOUTH	MELBOURNE BEACH	1
FLORIDA	ORMOND BEACH	1
FLORIDA	EUSTIS	1
GEORGIA	LOTTS	1
MISSISSIPPI	CRANFIELD	1
MISSISSIPPI	SERVICE	1
MISSISSIPPI	BROOKHAVEN	3
MISSISSIPPI	FRENCH CAMP	2
AMERICAN SAMOA	PAGO PAGO	6
KENTUCKY	VANCEBURG	3
OHIO	COLDWATER	2
OHIO	WAPAKONETA	6
OHIO	LOCKINGTON	1
OHIO	DE GRAFF	1
KANSAS	EASTON	2
MISSISSIPPI	HOMEWOOD	3

Figure 5.7 – Summarize by State and BeginLocation

Again, this screenshot is only showing a partial list of the results.

The extend command

There may be times when you need information that the table does not provide but can be generated from the data that has been provided. For example, the `StormEvents` table provides a start time and an end time for the event but does not provide the actual duration of the event. We know we can get the duration by subtracting the start time from the end time, but how can we tell KQL to do this?

The `extend` command does this. It allows you to create new columns from existing columns, or other data, such as hardcoded values. The following command will create a new column called `Duration` that will then be populated by the difference between the `EndTime` and the `StartTime` in each row of the `StormEvents` table:

```
StormEvents
| extend Duration = EndTime - StartTime
```

The following screenshot shows a sample of the output. It may not be obvious from this screenshot, but it should be noted that any column that's created using `extend` will always be shown as the last column in the list, unless specifically told otherwise (more on that later):

EventNarrative	StormSummary	Duration
At the Petersburg river gage, th...	{"TotalDamages":0,"StartTime":"...	26.14:00:00
At the Hazleton river gage, the ...	{"TotalDamages":0,"StartTime":"...	27.14:00:00
The Wabash River in Vermillion ...	{"TotalDamages":10000,"StartTi...	27.21:00:00
The Wabash in Sullivan County ...	{"TotalDamages":10000,"StartTi...	30.23:59:00
The Wabash River at Vincennes...	{"TotalDamages":10000,"StartTi...	29.10:34:00
At New Harmony, moderate flo...	{"TotalDamages":0,"StartTime":"...	30.19:00:00
Moderate flooding occurred al...	{"TotalDamages":0,"StartTime":"...	30.10:00:00
At Mount Carmel, moderate flo...	{"TotalDamages":0,"StartTime":"...	29.18:00:00
Save for brief drops below floo...	{"TotalDamages":10000,"StartTi...	19.10:24:00
The White River in Daviess Cou...	{"TotalDamages":10000,"StartTi...	23.18:47:00
The White River in Knox Count...	{"TotalDamages":10000,"StartTi...	26.10:27:00
At Mount Carmel, moderate flo...	{"TotalDamages":0,"StartTime":"...	29.19:00:00
The White River in Greene Cou...	{"TotalDamages":10000,"StartTi...	21.18:49:00

Figure 5.8 – The extend command

As we stated previously, the `extend` command does not need to use other columns as it can use hardcoded values as well, so the following command is perfectly valid:

```
StormEvents
| extend  Test = strcat("KQL"," rocks")
```

Note that the `strcat` function concatenates two or more strings into one. The output will look like the following screenshot. Since we are not taking any values from the rows via a column reference, the value will always be the same, in this case, **KQL rocks**:

EventNarrative	≡	StormSummary	≡	Test	≡
At the Petersburg river gage, th...		{"TotalDamages":0,"StartTime":"...		KQL rocks	
At the Hazleton river gage, the ...		{"TotalDamages":0,"StartTime":"...		KQL rocks	
The Wabash River in Vermillion ...		{"TotalDamages":10000,"StartTi...		KQL rocks	
The Wabash in Sullivan County ...		{"TotalDamages":10000,"StartTi...		KQL rocks	
The Wabash River at Vincennes...		{"TotalDamages":10000,"StartTi...		KQL rocks	
At New Harmony, moderate flo...		{"TotalDamages":0,"StartTime":"...		KQL rocks	
Moderate flooding occurred al...		{"TotalDamages":0,"StartTime":"...		KQL rocks	
At Mount Carmel, moderate flo...		{"TotalDamages":0,"StartTime":"...		KQL rocks	
Save for brief drops below floo...		{"TotalDamages":10000,"StartTi...		KQL rocks	
The White River in Daviess Cou...		{"TotalDamages":10000,"StartTi...		KQL rocks	
The White River in Knox Count...		{"TotalDamages":10000,"StartTi...		KQL rocks	

Figure 5.9 – The extend command with hardcoded values

This command will be very useful when outputting information that may exist in multiple columns but you want it to be shown in a single column.

The project command

If you don't need to see all the columns that a query would normally show, `project` is used to determine what columns to show. In the following query, only `StartTime`, `EndTime`, and `EventId` will be shown:

```
StormEvents
| project StartTime, EndTime, EventId
```

The output is shown in the following screenshot. One item of interest is that the query took significantly less time to run than when showing all the columns:

StartTime	EndTime	EventId
2007-01-01 00:00:00.0000	2007-01-27 14:00:00.0000	7,580
2007-01-01 00:00:00.0000	2007-01-28 14:00:00.0000	7,586
2007-01-01 00:00:00.0000	2007-01-28 21:00:00.0000	11,920
2007-01-01 00:00:00.0000	2007-01-31 23:59:00.0000	11,923
2007-01-01 00:00:00.0000	2007-01-30 10:34:00.0000	11,924
2007-01-01 00:00:00.0000	2007-01-31 19:00:00.0000	7,499
2007-01-01 00:00:00.0000	2007-01-31 10:00:00.0000	7,506
2007-01-01 00:00:00.0000	2007-01-30 18:00:00.0000	7,505
2007-01-01 00:00:00.0000	2007-01-20 10:24:00.0000	11,914
2007-01-01 00:00:00.0000	2007-01-24 18:47:00.0000	11,930
2007-01-01 00:00:00.0000	2007-01-27 10:27:00.0000	11,931
2007-01-01 00:00:00.0000	2007-01-30 19:00:00.0000	7,498
2007-01-01 00:00:00.0000	2007-01-22 18:49:00.0000	11,929

Figure 5.10 – Project command

project is like extend in that they can both create new columns. The main difference is that the extend command creates a new column at the end of the result set, while the project command creates the column wherever it is in the list of variables. It's good practice to use the extend command for anything other than the simplest of computations to make it easier to read the query. There are two commands that produce the same results. The first command is as follows:

```
StormEvents
| extend Duration = EndTime - StartTime
| project StartTime, EndTime, EventId, Duration
```

The other command is as follows:

```
StormEvents
| project StartTime, EndTime, EventId, Duration = EndTime -
StartTime
```

Here, you can see that the project command is quite useful for cleaning up the results by removing those columns you don't care about.

The distinct command

There may be times where you get multiple instances of the same value returned but you only need to see one of them. That is where `distinct` comes in. It will return only the first instance of a collection of the specified column(s) and ignore all the rest.

If I run the following command, I will get a value back for all 59,066 rows and it will include many duplicates:

```
StormEvents
| project State
```

The output is shown in the following screenshot. Note the multiple occurrences of **FLORIDA**, **MISSISSIPPI**, and **OHIO**:

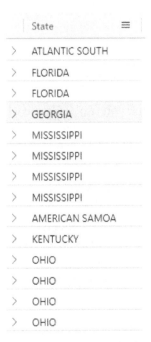

Figure 5.11 – Rows with multiple states

If we need to see just one instance of each state, we can use the following command and only get 67 rows returned to us:

```
StormEvents
| distinct State
```

This still returns the states but only one instance of each state will be returned, as shown here:

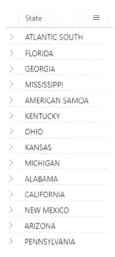

Figure 5.12 – The distinct command

By using the `distinct` command, you can easily see which values are in a column. This can be quite useful when building up your query. In the preceding example, you can see which states are represented in the dataset without having to scroll through all the rows if you didn't use **distinct**.

The sort/order command

When you run a query, by default, the rows will be returned in whatever order they were saved into the table you are querying. If we look at the results from running the last command in the *The distinct command* section, the states are returned in the order the first occurrence of the state was found in the table.

Building on the command we used in the previous section, please refer to Fig 5.12 to see the output and note that the states are returned in a random order.

Most of the time, this is not what you are looking for. You will want to see the values in a specific order, such as alphabetical or based on a time value. `sort` will allow you to sort the output into any order you wish.

The following command will sort the output by the `State` column:

```
StormEvents
| distinct  State
| sort by State
```

A sample of the output is as follows:

State	≡
> WYOMING	
> WISCONSIN	
> WEST VIRGINIA	
> WASHINGTON	
> VIRGINIA	
> VIRGIN ISLANDS	
> VERMONT	
> UTAH	
> TEXAS	
> TENNESSEE	
> SOUTH DAKOTA	
> SOUTH CAROLINA	

Figure 5.13 – The sort command showing states listed in descending alphabetical order

Note that the output is in alphabetical order, but it is in the default descending order. While this may be what you want, if you wanted to see the states that start with *A* first, you will need to specify that you want the sort to be done in ascending order. The following command shows how to do that:

```
StormEvents
| distinct State
| sort by State asc
```

In the following output, you can see that those states that start with *A* are now shown first:

State	≡
> ALABAMA	
> ALASKA	
> AMERICAN SAMOA	
> ARIZONA	
> ARKANSAS	
> ATLANTIC NORTH	
> ATLANTIC SOUTH	
> CALIFORNIA	
> COLORADO	
> CONNECTICUT	
> DELAWARE	
> DISTRICT OF COLUMBIA	
> E PACIFIC	
> FLORIDA	
> GEORGIA	
> GUAM	

Figure 5.14 – The sort command showing states listed in ascending alphabetical order

Note that `order` can also be used in place of `sort`, so the following command will do exactly the same thing that we just saw:

```
StormEvents
| distinct  State
| order by State  asc
```

As you can see, the `sort` command is extremely useful when you need to see your output in a specific order, which will probably be most of the time.

The join command

The `join` operator will take the columns from two different tables and join them into one. In the following contrived example, all the rows from `StormEvents` where `State` equals `North Carolina` will be combined with the rows from `FLEvents` where they have a matching `EventType` column:

```
let FLEvents = StormEvents
| where State == "FLORIDA";
FLEvents
| join (StormEvents
| where State == "NORTH CAROLINA")
on EventType
```

You will use the `join` command quite a bit when writing your queries to get information from multiple tables or the same table using different parameters. Next, we will examine the `union` command and how it differs from the `join` command.

The union command

The `union` command combines two or more tables into one. While `join` will show all the columns of the matching rows in one row, `union` will have one row for each row in each of the tables. So, if table 1 has 10 rows and table 2 has 12 rows, the new table that's created from the union will have 22 rows.

If the tables do not have the same columns, all the columns from both tables will be shown, but for the table that does not have the column, the values will be empty. This is important to remember when performing tests against the columns. If table 1 has a column called KQLRocks and table 2 does not, then, when looking at the new table that's created by the union, there will be a value for KQLRocks for the rows in table 1, but it will be empty for the rows in table 2. See the following code:

```
let FLEvents = StormEvents
| where State == "FLORIDA";
let NCEvents = StormEvents
| where State == "NORTH CAROLINA"
| project State, duration = EndTime - StartTime;
NCEvents | union FLEvents
```

In the following example, when looking at the rows where the state is NORTH CAROLINA, all the columns other than State and duration will be empty since the NCEvents table only has the State and duration columns. When looking at the rows where State is FLORIDA, the duration column will be empty since the FLEvents table does not have that column in it, but all the other columns will be filled out. The let command will keep the FLEvents and NCEvents variables around for later use. See the *The let statement* section for more information.

If we run the preceding code and scroll down a bit, we will see the output shown in the following screenshot. As you can see, most of the fields where State equals North Carolina are empty since the table that we created with the let command only contains the State and duration fields:

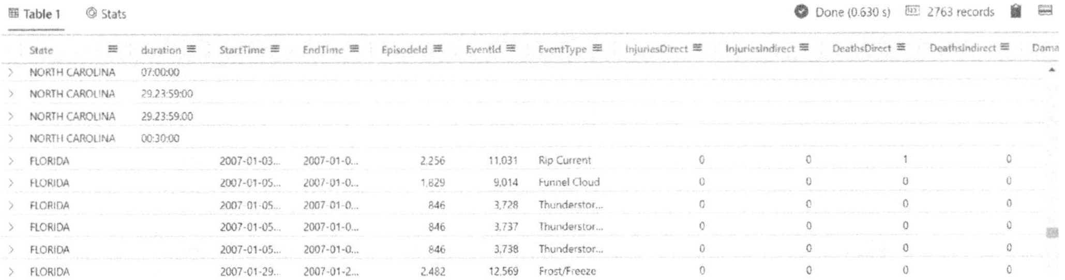

State	duration	StartTime	EndTime	EpisodeId	EventId	EventType	InjuriesDirect	InjuriesIndirect	DeathsDirect	DeathsIndirect	Dama
NORTH CAROLINA	07:00:00										
NORTH CAROLINA	29.23:59:00										
NORTH CAROLINA	29.23:59:00										
NORTH CAROLINA	00:30:00										
FLORIDA		2007-01-03...	2007-01-0...	2.256	11.031	Rip Current	0	0	1	0	
FLORIDA		2007-01-05...	2007-01-0...	1.829	9.014	Funnel Cloud	0	0	0	0	
FLORIDA		2007-01-05...	2007-01-0...	846	3.728	Thunderstor...	0	0	0	0	
FLORIDA		2007-01-05...	2007-01-0...	846	3.737	Thunderstor...	0	0	0	0	
FLORIDA		2007-01-05...	2007-01-0...	846	3.738	Thunderstor...	0	0	0	0	
FLORIDA		2007-01-29...	2007-01-2...	2.482	12.569	Frost/Freeze	0	0	0	0	

Table 1   Stats   Done (0.630 s)   2763 records

Figure 5.15 – Output of the union command

Use the union command when you need to see all the columns from the selected tables, even if some of those columns are empty in one of those tables.

The render command

The `render` operator is different from all the other commands and functions we have discussed in that it does not manipulate the data in any way, only how it is presented. The `render` command is used to show the output in a graphical, rather than tabular, format.

There are times when it is much easier to determine if something is being asked by looking at a time chart or a bar chart rather than looking at a list of strings and numbers. By using `render`, you can display your data in a graphical format to make it easier to view the results.

If we run the following command, we'll get a tabular view of the data. While this is useful, it doesn't show any outliers:

```
StormEvents
| project State, EndTime, DamageProperty
| where State =="CALIFORNIA"
```

The partial output is as follows:

State	EndTime	DamageProperty
CALIFORNIA	2007-01-01 04:35:00.0000	0
CALIFORNIA	2007-01-01 04:37:00.0000	0
CALIFORNIA	2007-01-01 11:35:00.0000	0
CALIFORNIA	2007-01-02 03:36:00.0000	0
CALIFORNIA	2007-01-02 06:30:00.0000	0
CALIFORNIA	2007-01-02 11:00:00.0000	0
CALIFORNIA	2007-01-02 11:00:00.0000	0
CALIFORNIA	2007-01-02 11:00:00.0000	0
CALIFORNIA	2007-01-02 11:00:00.0000	0
CALIFORNIA	2007-01-04 19:14:00.0000	0
CALIFORNIA	2007-01-05 03:36:00.0000	0
CALIFORNIA	2007-01-05 04:36:00.0000	0
CALIFORNIA	2007-01-05 04:57:00.0000	350,000

Figure 5.16 – Results shown in tabular format

While it does show there was an instance of a storm event on January 5, 2007, that caused a lot of damage, was it the one that caused the most damage? We could look through the rows and look at the **DamageProperty** column for each row to find this out, but there is an easier way to do this.

If we run the following command, a line chart will be generated that shows the same data but in a graphical view:

```
StormEvents
  | project State, EndTime, DamageProperty
  | where State =="CALIFORNIA"
  | render linechart
```

The output from this command is shown in the following screenshot. It is instantly recognizable that, while the storm we saw in January caused a lot of damage, it is nowhere near the damage caused by the storm on June 30:

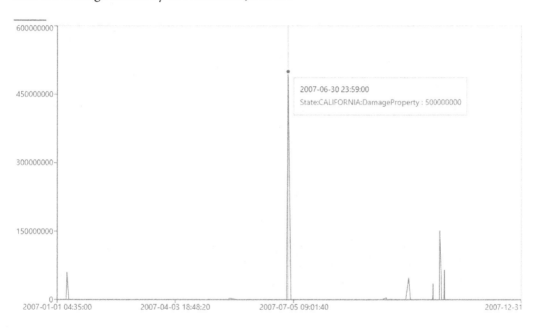

Figure 5.17 – Viewing storm damage as a graph

As shown in the preceding graph, there are times when a graphical representation of the data is more valuable than just looking at the textual output.

Information Box

The *x* axis is a bit misleading here with the labeling but, as you can see, when you hover your mouse over the data, the storm did occur on June 30.

Some of the other charts that can be rendered include a pie chart, an area chart, and a time chart, and each may require a different number of columns in order to present the data.

Query statement

Query statements in KQL produce tables that can be used in other parts of the query and must end with a semicolon (;). These commands, of which we will only discuss the let command here, will return entire tables that are all returned by the query. Keep in mind that a table can consist of a single row and a single column, in which case it acts as a constant in other languages.

The let statement

The let statement allows you to create a new variable that can be used in later computations. It is different than extend or project in that it can create more than just a column – it can create another table if desired.

So, if I want to create a table that contains all the StormEvents for only NORTH CAROLINA, I can use the following commands. Note the ; at the end of the let statement since it is indeed a separate statement:

```
let NCEvents = StormEvents
| where State == "NORTH CAROLINA";
NCEvents
```

The let statement can also be used to define constants. The following command will work exactly like the one earlier. Note that the second let actually references the first let variable:

```
let filterstate = "NORTH CAROLINA";
let NCEvents = StormEvents
| where State == filterstate;
NCEvents
```

The let statement is very powerful and one that you will use quite a bit when writing your queries.

Scalar functions

Scalar functions take a value and perform some sort of manipulation on it to return a different value. These are useful for performing conversions between data types, looking at only part of the variable, and performing mathematical computations.

The ago() function

ago is a function that is used to subtract a specific time space from the current UTC time. Remember that all times stored in the Log Analytics log is based on UTC time, unless it is a time in a custom log that is specifically designed not to be. Generally, it is safer to assume that the times stored are based on UTC time.

If I wanted to look for events in the StormEvents that ended less than an hour ago, I would use the following command. Note that this command doesn't return any values as the times stored are from 2007:

```
StormEvents
| where EndTime > ago(1h)
```

In addition to using h for hours, you can also use d for days, among others.

The bin() function

The bin function will take a value, round down as needed, and place it into a virtual bin of a specified size. So, the print bin(7.4,1) command will return 7. It takes 7.4 and rounds down to 7. Then, it looks at the bin size, which is 1 in this case, and returns the multiple of the size that fits, which is 7. If the command is changed to print bin(7.4,4), the answer is 4. 7.4 rounded down is 7, and that fits into the second bin, which is 4. Another way of looking at this is that the first bin for this command contains the numbers 0,1,2,3, which will return a 0, the second bin is 4,5,6,7, which returns a 4 (which is why print bin(7.4,4) returns a 4), the third bin contains 8,9,10,11, which returns an 8, and so on.

This command is typically used with summarize by to group values into more manageable sizes, for example, taking all the times an activity occurred during the day and grouping them into the 24 hours in a day.

For example, if you wanted to see how many storms started during each day, you could use the following code:

```
StormEvents
| summarize count() by bin(StartTime,1d)
```

The output would appear as follows:

⊞ Table 1   ◎ Stats

StartTime ≡	count_ ≡
> 2007-01-01 00:00:00.0000	200
> 2007-01-02 00:00:00.0000	66
> 2007-01-03 00:00:00.0000	45
> 2007-01-04 00:00:00.0000	85
> 2007-01-05 00:00:00.0000	152
> 2007-01-06 00:00:00.0000	51
> 2007-01-07 00:00:00.0000	69
> 2007-01-08 00:00:00.0000	66
> 2007-01-09 00:00:00.0000	62
> 2007-01-10 00:00:00.0000	52
> 2007-01-11 00:00:00.0000	58
> 2007-01-12 00:00:00.0000	358

Figure 5.18 – Sample bin output

There are many more entries other than what is shown here. As you can see, bin can be quite useful to group results by date and time.

String operators

String and numeric operators are used in the comparisons of a where clause. We have already seen ==, which is a string equals operator. As we stated earlier, this is a case-sensitive operator, meaning that ABC == ABC is true but ABC == abc is false.

> **Note**
>
> You may need to carry out a case-insensitive comparison using =~. In this case, ABC =~ abc returns true. While there are commands to change text to uppercase or lowercase, it is good practice to not do that just for a comparison but rather do a case-insensitive comparison.

Some other string operators that can be used are as follows:

Operator	Description	Case Sensitive	Example (returns True)	Example (returns False)
==	Equal	Yes	"One" == "One"	"One" == "ONE"
=~	Equals	No	"one" =~ "ONE"	"one" =~ "two"
contains_cs	Right-hand string is in left-hand string	Yes	"ONEtwo" contains_cs "ONE"	"ONEtwo" contains_cs "one"
contains	Right-hand string is in left-hand string	No	"ONEtwo" contains "one"	"ONEtwo" contains "three"
startswith_cs	Right-hand string is in the beginning of the left-hand string	Yes	"ONEtwo" startswith_cs "ONE"	"ONEtwo" startswith_cs "one"
startswith	Right-hand string is in the beginning of the left-hand string	No	"ONEtwo" startswith "one"	"ONEtwo" startswith "two"
endswith_cs	Right-hand string is in the ending of the left-hand string	Yes	"oneTWO" endswith_cs "TWO"	"oneTWO" endswith_cs "two"
endswith	Right-hand string is in the ending of the left-hand string	No	"oneTWO" endswith "two"	"oneTWO" endswith "one"
in	Left-hand string is in one of the right-hand list of strings	Yes	"one" in ("alpha","beta","one")	"ONE" in ("alpha","beta","one")
in~	Left-hand string is in one of the right-hand list of strings	No	"ONE" in ("alpha","beta","one")	"TWO" in ("alpha","beta","one")

In addition, by placing ! in front of any command, that command is negated. For example, !contains means does not contain and !in means not in.

For a complete list of operators, go to https://docs.microsoft.com/en-us/azure/kusto/query/datatypes-string-operators.

Summary

In this chapter, you were introduced to the Kusto Query Language, which you will use to query the tables in your logs. You learned about some of the tabular operators, query statements, scalar functions, and string operators. Finally, we will provide some quick questions to help you understand how to use these commands to perform your queries.

In the next chapter, you will learn how to take what you learned here and use it to query logs that are stored in Azure Sentinel using the Logs page.

Questions

1. How many storms occurred in California?

2. Provide a list that shows only one occurrence of each different state.

3. Provide a list of storms that caused at least $10,000 but less than $15,000 worth of damage.

4. Provide a list of storms that show the state, amount of property damage, amount of crop damage, and the total of the property and crop damage only.

Further reading

For more information on KQL, see the following links:

*   Performing queries across resources: `https://docs.microsoft.com/en-us/azure/azure-monitor/log-query/cross-workspace-query#performing-a-query-across-multiple-resources`

*   Complete KQL command documentation: `https://docs.microsoft.com/en-us/azure/kusto/query/index`

*   Running your KQL queries with sample data: `https://portal.azure.com/#blade/Microsoft_Azure_Monitoring_Logs/DemoLogsBlade`

*   Additional graphical formats for queries: `https://docs.microsoft.com/en-us/azure/azure-monitor/log-query/charts`

*   Date/time formats in KQL: `https://docs.microsoft.com/en-us/azure/azure-monitor/log-query/datetime-operations#date-time-basics`

6
Azure Sentinel Logs and Writing Queries

In the previous chapter, we looked at the **Kusto Query Language** (**KQL**) and gave a brief introduction on how to use it. In this chapter, we will learn about the Azure Sentinel **Logs** page. The Azure Sentinel **Logs** page is where you can see the various logs in your workspace, determine the type of data that makes up the logs, create the queries that will be used in the Analytics rules and threat hunting, as well as being able to save these queries for later use. This will help you in creating rules and investigating incidents and is an integral part of investigating incidents.

As part of this chapter, we will provide an overview of the page, learn about the various sections, and look at how to use KQL to write queries. We will review the Logs screen in Azure Sentinel and how to look at logs' columns using both the UI and using KQL. We will also look at the steps you can take to help develop your queries.

In a nutshell, the following topics will be covered:

- An introduction to the Azure Sentinel Logs page
- Navigating through the Logs page
- Writing a query

An introduction to the Azure Sentinel Logs page

The Log Analytics workspace follows a hierarchical pattern regarding how it organizes its information. At the top is the Log Analytics workspace. This is the container for all the individual logs for your instance of Azure Sentinel. This is equivalent to a database in SQL.

Within each workspace are individual logs, also known as **tables**. These are equivalent to a table in SQL. These are the entities that hold data. These have a set of columns, and zero or more rows of data.

Within each of those logs are the columns that hold the data. The columns can hold different data types including text, date/time, integers, and others.

> **Note**
>
> A lot of the documentation you will read will use the terms table and log interchangeably. We are choosing to use the term log, as that seems to be the default, with the understanding that Microsoft may change the wording of various parts of this page and in the documentation later.

Navigating through the Logs page

The **Logs** page is where you can see a listing of all the logs that belong to your instance, view some existing queries, write your own queries, view the results, and much more. Let's explore this page.

To get to the **Logs** page, select **Logs** from the Azure Sentinel navigation section. This will open the following page:

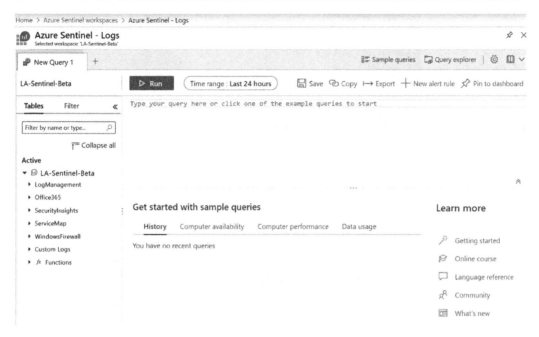

Figure 6.1 – Azure Sentinel Logs page

The page is broken down into different sections, such as the following:

- Page header

- Tables pane

- Filter pane

- KQL code window

- Sample queries/results window

These sections can be seen in the following screenshot:

Figure 6.2 – Azure Sentinel Logs page sections

Let's describe each of these sections in more detail.

The page header

The page header is located at the top of the page and contains useful links, including sample queries, the query explorer, settings, and help, as shown in the following screenshot:

Figure 6.3 – Logs page header

You will not need to use these links to create new queries although they can assist with some predefined code, as you will read about. We will look at each individual button, starting from the left side.

Sample queries

Azure Sentinel has a few sample queries that have been provided to help you get started looking at tables. Follow these steps to use them:

1. Click on the **Sample queries** button. This will change the sample queries results window and instead show some sample queries as follows:

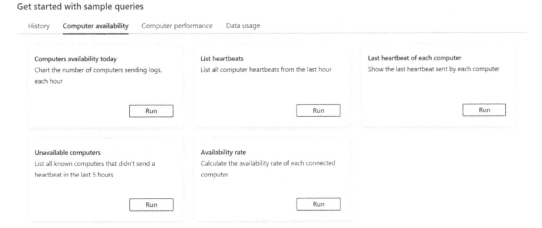

Figure 6.4 – Logs page sample queries

Each time you press the **Sample queries** button, a new KQL code window will open to avoid interfering with any queries you may have already been working on.

Also, the **Computer availability** tab will be shown by default. The queries are all related to showing the availability of the various computers that are logging data into your Log Analytics workspace.

2. Click the **Run** button on any of the entries to load the query and run it. In the following screenshot, the **Computers availability today** query was run. Your results will vary depending on how many computers are reporting. If you do not see any results, it may be that you do not have the proper data connector set up; in this case, you need to have at least one computer associated with this Log Analytics workspace. For a refresher, See *Chapter 3, Data Collection and Management*, on setting up data connectors, and *Chapter 2, Azure Monitor – Log Analytics*, on attaching computers to Log Analytics workspaces:

Figure 6.5 – Sample query results

The other tabs, **Computer performance** and **Data usage**, show other queries that are pertinent to their tab's title. You can click on the **Run** button on either of them to run that query.

Let's move on to the next button on the page header, which is the **Query explorer**.

Query explorer

The **Query explorer** button is similar to the **Sample queries** button except that you can add your own queries to this listing, which will be discussed later. If you have marked any queries as favorites or saved any queries yourself, these will show in this window:

1. Click on the **Query explorer** button. This will open the **Query explorer** blade as follows:

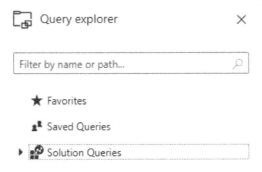

Figure 6.6 – Query explorer

2. Expand the **Solution Queries** tree; you will see that there are other groupings under it. Let's try this out. Expand the **Log Management** entry to see a listing of queries that are related to log management as shown in the following screenshot:

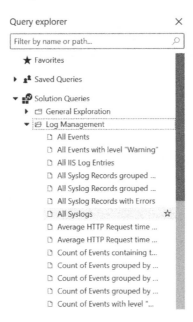

Figure 6.7 – Query explorer sample queries

3. As you can see in the preceding screenshot, the **All Syslogs** query has been selected. If the star on the right side of the name is selected, the query will be saved as a favorite. The entry will be listed under the **Favorites** section, and the star will turn black, as shown in the following screenshot:

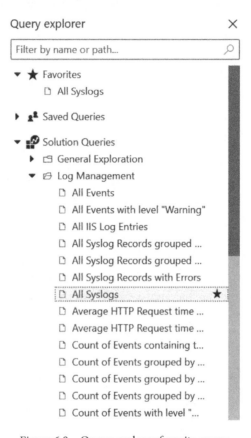

Figure 6.8 – Query explorer favorite query

4. Clicking on any entry will also load that query into the KQL window. In the following screenshot, the **All Syslogs** query was clicked on but not yet run. Notice that the title of the KQL code window has been changed to match the name of the selected query:

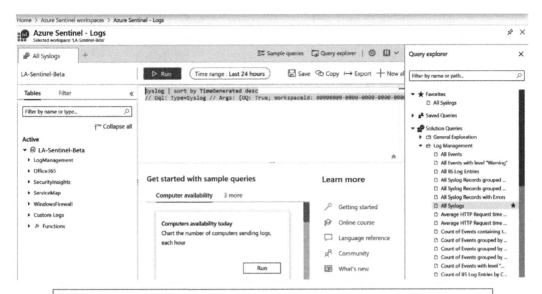

> **mportant note**
>
> It should be noted that when you click on the query, a new query tab will open. However, if you were to click the same query again, it would not open a new tab for that query again. It would actually switch back to the original tab that held the query.

Settings (the gear icon)

The Azure Sentinel **Logs** page has a few settings that can be modified. Follow these steps to change them.

Click on the **Settings** button. This will open the **Settings** blade as follows:

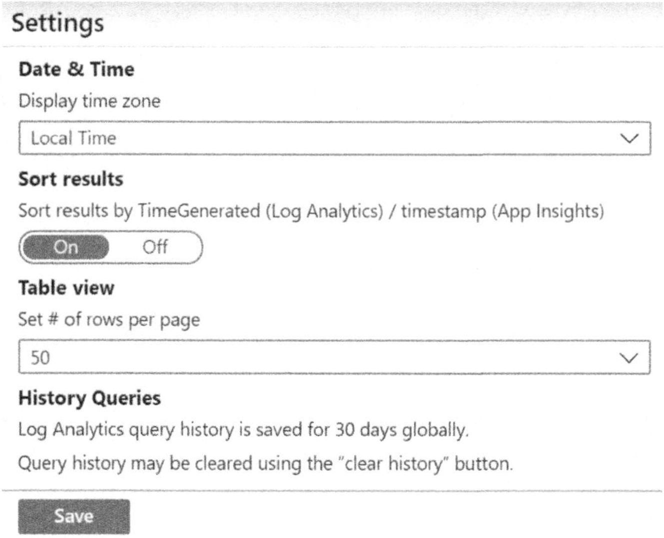

Figure 6.10 – Logs page Settings pane

Here you can choose from the following options:

- **Date & Time**: Select which time zone to use when displaying the date and time. This will change how any of the date and time fields, such as **TimeGenerated**, are displayed. By default, the fields will be displayed using **Universal Time Coordinated (UTC)**, which is also known as **Greenwich Mean Time (GMT)** or **Zulu (Z)**. Use the drop-down menu to change this to whichever time zone you desire. You can also use the **Local Time** entry to have the date and time displayed in whatever the local time zone is your computer is using.

> **Tip**
> Changing the date and time field here will change how the date and time are displayed whenever you show a time field in the results. You can also change the time zone used to display the time on a result-by-result basis in the header of the **Results** section. See the *Results window* section for more information.

- **Sort results**: Choose whether you want to automatically sort the results using the **TimeGenerated** field or not. If this is set to **On**, the default, then whenever the results are shown, they will be sorted using the **TimeGenerated** field. If this is set to **Off**, the results are shown in whatever order they were stored. Note that any sorting performed in the query will override this selection.

- **Table view**: How many rows to show on each page. The drop-down menu allows you to select **50**, which is the default, **100**, **150**, and **200**. Selecting higher values will allow more rows to be shown on a single page.

- **History Queries**: There is nothing to modify here, it is just to tell you how long the query history is stored and how to clear the query history.

Let's take a look at the book icon next.

Help (the book icon)

This icon has no name assigned to it, but it is the one on the far-right side of the header that looks like a book.

Click on it to find other options that can help you learn more about the **Logs** page and writing queries in general:

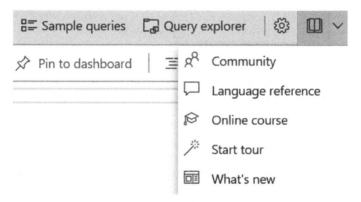

Figure 6.11 – Logs page help

Here you have the following options:

- **Community** will open a new tab and take you to the Azure Log Analytics Tech Community page.

- **Language reference** will open the KQL reference page in a new tab.

- **Online course** will open a new tab and will take you to Pluralsight's page, where you can view the free **Kusto Query Language (KQL) from Scratch** course.

- **Start tour** will restart the tour of the **Logs** page. This will be the same tour that started the first time you accessed the page. This can be quite useful if you forget how a certain feature works.

- **What's new** will open the Azure Log Analytics updates page in a new tab.

> **Tip**
>
> Notice that all of these entries are also duplicated on the right-hand side of the page under the **Learn more** heading.

That's it for the page header section of the **Logs** page. Next, we will look at the **Tables** pane, on the left side of the page.

The Tables pane

The **Tables** pane will list all the logs (AKA tables) that are part of your Log Analytics workspace, grouped together using predefined groups.

Click on **Tables** and, looking at figure 6.12, you will see that some of the logs are listed under a group called **LogManagement**. There can also be groups called **Office365**, **SecurityInsights**, **WindowsFirewall**, and others.

> **Tip**
>
> Do not be concerned if you have more or fewer groups than what is shown here. The group will only show if there are any logs in it and the logs will only show if they are either part of Azure Sentinel or a connector is being used to populate them. For instance, the Office365 group will only show if the underlying OfficeActivity log is present and that will only show if the Office365 connector has been enabled and has received data.

Expanding a group will show all the logs under that group. In the following screenshot, the **LogManagement** group was expanded showing all the logs under it:

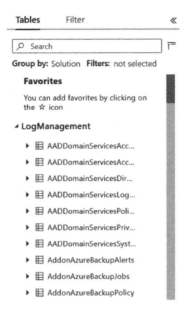

Figure 6.12 – The Tables pane

If you mouse-hover over any of the entries, you will see a star icon and an eye icon showing up on the right of the log's name.

Clicking on the star icon will save this entry as a favorite. It will show at the top of the list under the **Favorites** section. This will be an identical entry so that you can expand it to see its columns and mouse-hover it to see the eye icon, described next.

Clicking on the eye will open a new pop-up window and will show the first 50 rows of the log as shown in the following screenshot. If you want to see this query in the KQL query window, click on the **See in query editor** button at the bottom of the page. This will automatically generate the KQL code for the query and paste it in the window:

Resource Type: Virtual machines   Category: Virtual Machines   Solution: LogManagement

Preview Data

TenantId	SourceSystem	TimeGenerated [Local Time]	Source	EventLog
bfc2c181-b094-4120-bba1-748b98...	OpsManager	2/18/2020, 6:17:18.753 AM	Service Control Ma...	System
bfc2c181-b094-4120-bba1-748b98...	OpsManager	2/18/2020, 6:17:31.627 AM	Service Control Ma...	System
bfc2c181-b094-4120-bba1-748b98...	OpsManager	2/18/2020, 6:10:40.423 AM	Service Control Ma...	System
bfc2c181-b094-4120-bba1-748b98...	OpsManager	2/18/2020, 6:10:53.253 AM	Service Control Ma...	System
bfc2c181-b094-4120-bba1-748b98...	OpsManager	2/18/2020, 6:19:48.177 AM	Service Control Ma...	System

See in query editor

Figure 6.13 – Sample records from the log

If you look at the top of the pop-up window, just above the **Preview Data** heading, you will see there are three boxes that are labeled **Resource Type**, **Category**, and **Solution**. These are the categories that this entry will fall under when performing the grouping. If you look back at figure 6.12, you will see there is a **Group by** section right under the search box. This will allow you to search by the three different categories.

Sorting by **Resource Type** will sort all the entries based on the Azure type they belong to, including **Application Gateways**, **Logic Apps**, and **Virtual Networks**. Sorting by **Category** will sort the entries based on the Azure category they belong to, including **Audit**, **Containers**, and **Network**. Sorting by **Solution** will sort the entries based on the solution that populates the logs, including **LogManagement**, **SecurityInsights**, and **WindowsFirewall**.

So, looking at the preceding screenshot, the event log will belong to the **Virtual machines** group when sorted by **Resource Type**, the **Virtual Machines** group when sorted by **Category**, and the **LogManagement** group when sorted by **Solutions**.

To the right of the **Group by** section is the **Filters** section. This will allow you to filter the view of the tables by any of the same categories that the **Group By** section has.

You can also expand a single log to see all the columns that make up the log, as well as the data type of the column. In the following screenshot, the **Event** log was expanded. You can see the various columns that make up the log and to the left of the name is an icon that shows the data type: an italic **t** for text, and a pound sign, **#**, for number. There is also a clock for date/time, a **B** for Boolean and {} for the dynamic type:

Figure 6.14 – Event log columns

Next, let's us move on to the **Filter** pane.

The Filter pane

The **Filter** pane is useful after you run a query; before that, it will be empty. This pane will analyze the results of the query being run and generate useful filters for that query.

Clicking on any of the checkboxes in the **Filter** pane and then clicking **Apply & Run** at the bottom of the screen will modify the query to use those filters. Only the top 10 values for each filter will be shown so it may be possible that you will not see the value that you want to use to filter. In that case, you will need to apply the filter on the individual column. Let's try this out.

In the following screenshot, a query to show entries from the **Event** log was run and the **Filter** pane was selected to show useful filters. A listing of the columns that are part of the result set will be shown and up to 10 entries that represent the values for the column will be displayed:

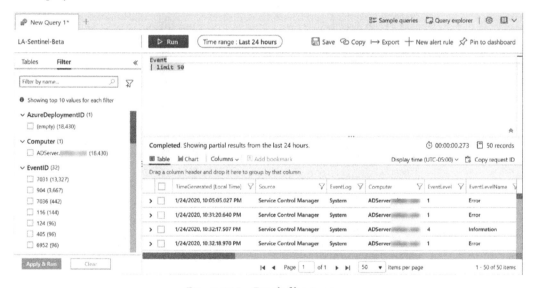

Figure 6.15 – Result filtering pane

If there are additional columns that you want to filter on that are not listed, click on the funnel icon to add them. This will open a new pop-up window that will show all the columns that are being returned by the query, as shown in the following screenshot. All the columns that are currently in use will be selected. Select any of the others that you wish to add and then click **Update**. The new columns will be shown as available filters now:

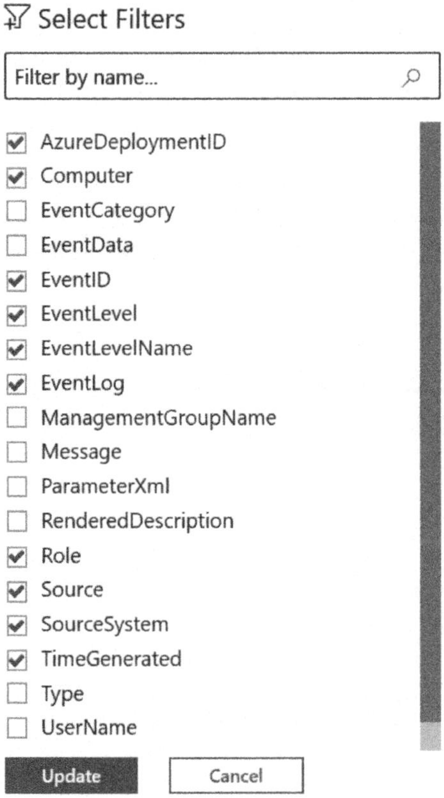

Figure 6.16 – Filter pop-up window

> **Tip**
> Be cautious selecting new columns to show in the **Filter** pane. There is usually a good reason they were not chosen, including having too many entries or just one entry.

To use a filter, select the checkbox next to the name. You can select any number of entries under any number of columns in order to perform a filter. Each entry you select will be treated as an `and` in the query so that if you select an entry called `Alpha` and one called `Beta` the row must have both `Alpha` and `Beta` in it for it to be shown in the result set.

When you have selected all the needed filters, click on the **Apply & Run** button to apply the new filters. You can also click the **Clear** button to remove all the selected filters.

In the following screenshot, the **EventID** of **7031** and the **EventLevel** of **1** were selected and the **Apply & Run** button was clicked. It shows the new query and the updated results. Note that the **Filter** values have changed due to the new results:

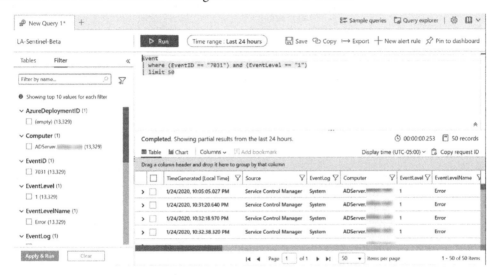

Figure 6.17 – Updated result-filtering pane

Next, let's explore the KQL code window.

The KQL code window

To the right of the **Schema** and **Filter** panes is the KQL code window. We have already worked with this window a bit previously, when we were looking at predefined queries.

The KQL code window is where you enter the KQL code you want to run. While you can create your code using any text editor, including programs such as Notepad or Notepad++, there are some advantages to using the code window, including the following:

- The code window knows about your logs so it can help you write your code. If you start typing in `Alert` in an empty code window, you will see suggestions of logs that contain that phrase, as shown in the following screenshot. This makes it much easier to start writing your queries:

Figure 6.18 – Log IntelliSense

- The code window knows KQL so it can help write your queries that way as well. If, in an empty code window, you type in `Alert` and press *Enter*, two things will happen: First, a new line is created with the | KQL delimiter already added. Second, a list of suggested KQL commands will be displayed, as shown in the following screenshot. You can start typing and the list will shorten to include only those entries that contain the text you have typed. If the command you want is highlighted, press the *Tab* key to have it automatically filled in.

This makes it much faster and easier to create your KQL query:

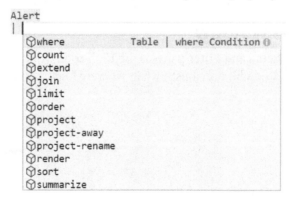

Figure 6.19 – Query IntelliSense

Just like the page header, the KQL code window also has its own header. Let's explore it.

The KQL code window header

The KQL code window has its own header comprised of buttons that allow you to perform actions against your queries, including running, saving, copying, and exporting them, as shown in the following screenshot:

Figure 6.20 – The KQL code window header

Each of the buttons will be discussed, working from the left to the right.

Run

Click on the **Run** button to execute whatever KQL code is in the window. Make sure that the query is selected before clicking this button to make sure your query is run.

Time range

This will determine how far back your query will look, unless there is a statement in your KQL code that specifically states how far back to look. This works the same as all the other **Time range** buttons and will not be discussed here in more detail.

Save

This will allow you to save your query for future use. Clicking on this button will open the **Save** pane as follows:

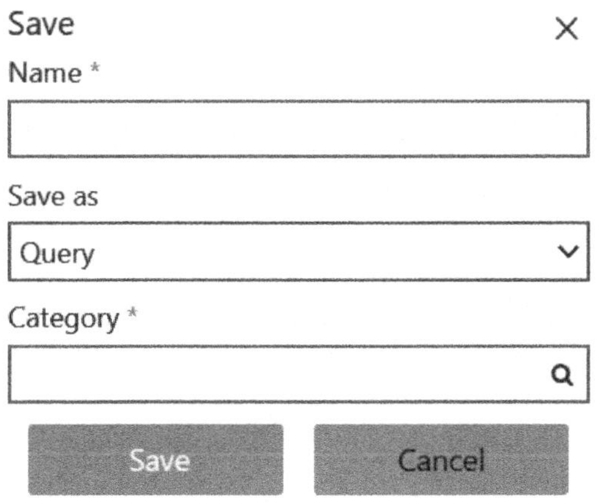

Save   ✕

Name *

[   ]

Save as

[Query   ∨]

Category *

[Q]

[Save]   [Cancel]

Figure 6.21 – The Save pane

Fill in the necessary fields:

- **Name**: Provide a useful name for this query so that it can easily be determined what this query does.

- **Save as**: Select either **Query** or **Function**. If **Function** is selected, you will be asked to provide a **Function Alias**, which is a short identifier so that they can easily be referenced in a query, as well as a checkbox asking whether this should be saved as a computer group. Refer back to *Chapter 2, Azure Monitor – Log Analytics* for a refresher on computer groups.

- **Category**: Enter the name of the category that will be used to group queries together. You can use the lookup icon to find ones that have already been used.

Click the **Save** button to save your query or function.

Copy link

This will allow you to copy either the link, the query, or the results to the clipboard. The options under this are as follows:

- **Copy link to query**: This will copy the URL for this specific query to the clipboard. This can be useful if you want to share a query with others.

- **Copy query text**: This will copy the query text to the clipboard. This is useful if you need to save your KQL query somewhere else, such as a DevOps file.

- **Copy result**: This will copy the URL for the results (which is the same as the URL for the query) to the clipboard.

Let's take a look at the **New alert rule** button.

New alert rule

This has an entry under it called **Create Azure Sentinel alert** and, once clicked, it will take you to the new Analytics rule page where you can create a new scheduled rule that has the query already filled in. Refer to *Chapter 7, Creating Analytics Rules,* for more information.

Export

This will provide you with three options:

- **Export to CSV – All Columns**: This will export all the columns, shown or not, into a CSV file. When this is clicked, a file called **query_data.csv** will be created and downloaded with the actual step determined by your browser settings.

- **Export to CSV – Displayed Columns**: This will work as in the first bullet point except that only those columns that are shown in the **Results** window will be saved. Refer to the *Results window* section to see how to hide/show columns.

- **Export to Power BI (M Query)**: This will create and download a file called `PowerBIQuery.txt` and will provide you with instructions on how to load this query into the Microsoft PowerBI application.

Let's look at the **Pin to dashboard** option.

Pin to dashboard

This will allow you to pin this query to an Azure portal dashboard so that you can easily see the results of the query. The creation and usage of dashboards is out of scope for this chapter; however, you can go to `https://docs.microsoft.com/en-us/azure/azure-portal/azure-portal-dashboards` for more information.

Prettify query

This will reformat the KQL code to make it more readable. It has internal rules that it uses to determine what is more readable so you may or may not agree with how it reformats the code.

Running a query

Once you are satisfied with your query, click on the **Run** button to see the results. As stated previously, make sure that all the code in your query that you want to run is selected before clicking on the **Run** button.

The results will be shown in the results window , which is described next.

The results window

Immediately below the query window is the results window. As the name implies, this is where you will view the results of your queries. You can also perform tasks such as hiding or showing columns, filtering the results, and changing how the results look:

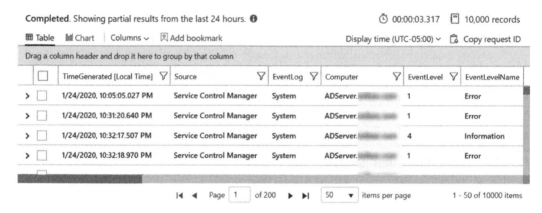

Figure 6.22 – Query results

> **Note**
> If you have not run any queries yet, this will display the **History** tab, which that will show queries that you have run previously, if you have any, as well as the tabs for the various categories of sample queries.

The Results window header

At the very top of this window is a header that provides information regarding the results. On the left side is a message telling you information regarding the query. In Figure 6.20, it is stating that the query is **Completed** and that it is showing a partial listing from the last 24 hours. The reason it is showing only partial results, in this case, is that there is a hard limit of 10,000 results that can be shown and there are more rows than the query can return. This message will change depending on the query results and it does provide valuable information regarding your query's results.

> **Important note**
> The maximum number of records that are returned when running a query in the **Logs** page is 10,000.

To the right of that is a stopwatch icon and the time it took your query to run, just over 3 seconds in the preceding screenshot. This is a valuable tool to help determine whether your query is running inefficiently. While your query is running, this value will be updated periodically so you can see it is still running.

On the far right is the total number of records returned. This can be any number from 0 to 10,000 and lets you know whether you need to refine your query further.

The Table tab

On the left side of the page are two tabs to help you define and filter your queries. On the far left is a tab that shows the default **Table** view, which shows the results in a column/row format. Next to that is the **Chart** tab, which will try to show the results in a chart if at all possible.

Depending on which of those tabs is selected, there will be different information shown to the right. The following screenshot shows what it will look like when the **Table** tab has been selected:

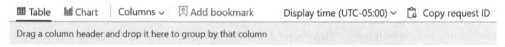

Figure 6.23 – Table results

The **Columns** drop-down menu will allow you to select which columns you want to show or hide. There is also the option to allow you to group your results based on a column. If this is enabled, then you will see a grey area under the **Table** tab where you can drag columns to group by that column. The following screenshot shows the results when they are grouped by **EventLevel**. Compare this to the results shown in Figure 6.17:

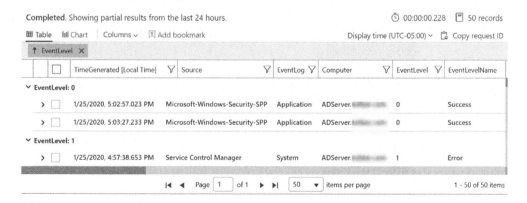

Figure 6.24 – Grouped query results

To the left of the **Columns** drop-down menu is the **Add bookmark** link. This allows you to create bookmarks from selected result items. Refer to *Chapter 10, Threat Hunting in Azure Sentinel,* for more information on bookmarks.

No matter whether you have selected the **Table** or the **Chart** tab, the next two items will always be shown:

- **Display time**: This will show you what time zone is being used to show the time in the results window. Use the drop-down menu to change the time zone. Refer to the **Settings** section to see how to change this for all the results windows.

- **Copy Request ID**: On the far right side is the **Copy request ID** button. Click this to have the GUID that represents the request copied into the clipboard. This is useful if you need to contact Microsoft for support. By providing the request ID, they can easily locate the query and assist you.

Underneath the grouping area, if it is enabled, is the listing of the result columns that have been selected to be shown. Click on the name of the column to sort the results using that column. The first time you click on the column, it will sort in ascending order; clicking it again will sort in descending order.

Each column name will have a funnel icon to the right of the name. Click on the funnel icon to perform a filter on the column as shown in the following screenshot:

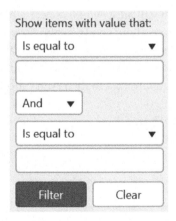

Figure 6.25 – Column filter

This is different than filtering using the **Filter** pane. If you were to select a value to filter a column using the **Filter** pane, the query itself would change and the query would need to be rerun to see the changes. If you just enter a value to filter a column in the results window, the query itself will not change; only the rows displayed will change to match the filter immediately. Note that will not be a list of possible values that you can filter on.

You can also change the comparison operator from **Is equal to** to other options, including **Not equal to, Contains, Has value, Has no value**, and others. This can give you a much more precise filtering experience than using the **Filter** pane although it takes a bit more work to set up the filter since you have to know the filtering values.

To the left of each row is a greater-than button (>). Click on that to expand the result row to see all the data in it displayed as rows rather than columns. If any of the columns contain compound data, such as JSON, it will have another greater-than button which, when clicked, will expand that row to see the data inside of it, as shown in the following screenshot. This is very useful to see all the data that a row contains, whether or not the column is set to be visible in the **Table** view:

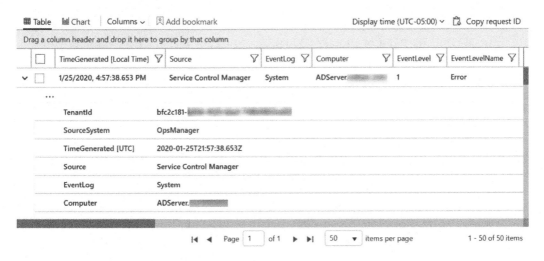

Figure 6.26 – Result row expanded

While being able to view your results in a table view is very useful, there are times when it is much easier to look at the results in some sort of graphical view, such as a line or pie chart. Let's see how to do this next.

The results footer

When you are looking at your results using the **Table** tab, at the bottom of the screen is the results footer, as shown here:

Figure 6.27 – Results footer

This footer will allow you to page forward and back through your results, show you which page number you are on, as well as changing how many items to show on the page for this specific result window. Each part is described in the following list:

- The go to the first page button will take you to the first page of results. This is only active if you have more than one page of results and you are not on the first page of results.

- The go to the previous page button will take you to the previous page of results. This is only active if you have more than one page of results and you are not on the first page of results.

- The page X of Y listing shows you the current page you are on, denoted by X here, as well as the total number of pages, denoted by Y here. In the preceding screenshot, we are on page 2 out of a total of 200 pages. You can enter the page number you wish to go to and press *Enter* to go directly to that page.

- The go to the next page button will take you to the next page of results. This is only active if you have more than one page of results and you are not on the last page of results.

- The go to the last page button will take you to the last page of results. This is only active if you have more than one page of results and you are not on the last page of results.

- The drop-down menu for **items per page** will allow you to change how many rows of results are shown on this specific page of results. You can select from **50, 100, 150**, or **200** items per page.

Next, let's move on to the **Chart** tab.

The Chart tab

To view the results graphically, select the **Chart** tab. Depending on the type of chart that is selected, the fields to the right will be different. There will always be a drop-down menu where you can change the type of chart being shown, which will be called the name of the currently selected graphical choice, but the fields will differ after that.

As you can see in the following screenshot, a **Pie** chart has been selected and the fields are specific to a pie chart. In this case, it is showing the fields that are being used to generate the chart's data. After those is a checkbox to show or hide the labels:

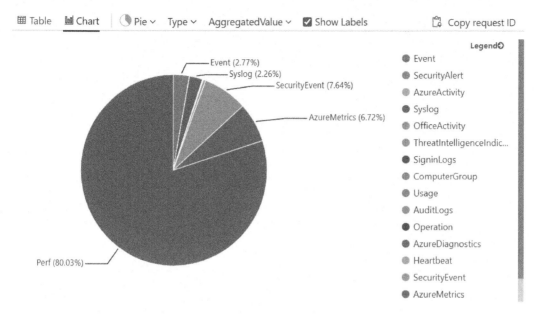

Figure 6.28 – Pie chart

This chart was generated by clicking on the **Sample queries** button in the page's header and then selecting the **Data Usage** tab. In this tab, select the **Run** button in the **Usage by data types** box. This will generate a pie chart showing the percentage of data added to each log during the time period. It will look similar to the preceding screenshot. Again, the logs shown may be different than what is shown in the screenshot, depending on what activity your tenant has had during the selected time period.

> **Note**
>
> This is an interactive chart so if you were to hover your mouse over one of the rows in the legend, that slice of the pie would be shown and the others would become dimmer to make it easier to see that one slice. Likewise, when you hover your mouse over a slice of the pie chart, it will highlight the selected row in the legend.

Click on the chart type drop-down menu; you will be presented with the graphical representations of the available charts, as shown in the following screenshot. Keep in mind that not all charts will make sense for the data you have selected. Also, remember that the button will represent the currently selected graphical choice, which is a pie chart in this case:

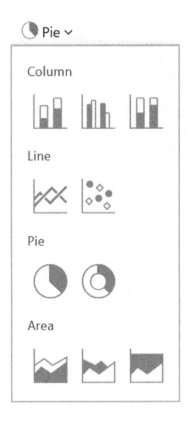

Figure 6.29 – Graphic view choices

You can use the chart type drop-down menu to change what type of chart is being shown or use the other drop-down menu(s) to change what column is being used to display the data, although in this query, no other columns are available.

> **Important note**
> While you are limited to just those chart types available in Azure Sentinel when running your queries, you can use Jupyter Notebooks or third-party charting tools such as Grafana to access the same data and use third-party charting tools to get different chart types. For more information, refer to *Chapter 10, Threat Hunting in Azure Sentinel.*

Now you have learned how to use a pre-built query, or use your own, to generate results. You can manipulate these results to perform actions including limiting what columns are shown or expanding a single result row to see all the columns that it contains. You have also learned how to change the view of the results from a straight text view into a graphical representation such as a pie chart.

Learn more

This section contains all the same links as the book icon in the page header. Refer back to the *Book icon* section for a refresher.

The information is duplicated here as an easy way to refer to the links when entering the **Logs** page for the first time. As soon as a query is run, the results window will expand to overwrite this area so you will need to use the book icon to get to these links.

You have learned quite a bit about the Azure Sentinel **Logs** page and how to select and run built-in queries to get the results. You have also learned how to manipulate those results further and how to change how they are displayed.

Now it is time to start learning how to write your own queries. You already have the basic knowledge of KQL from *Chapter 5, Using the Kusto Query Language (KQL),* so now let's go over the steps to consider when writing your own query.

Writing a query

Now that you have seen how to use the **Logs** page in Azure Sentinel, it's time to use your new skills to write your own queries. No matter what the query is, there are a few basic steps you will take to create your query.

1. Have an idea of what information you are looking for. Do you need to know which computers are currently active? What actions a user performed in SharePoint? What data has been ingested? This will give you an idea of what log(s) you will need to look at. Look at *Chapter 10, Threat Hunting in Azure Sentinel,* for information on one way to keep track of this data.

2. Once you have an idea which log you want to look at, the next step is to look at a small number of rows in that log to get a better understanding of the data that is stored in the log.

One of the easiest ways to do this is to find the log in the **Tables** pane and click on the eye icon to the right of the name. This will create a new KQL code window that will return up to 50 rows from the selected log. Take a look at some of the rows, expanding them to see all the information. Is this some, or possibly, all of the information that will be needed?

3. If it is, now you can create the query using the log and applying any filtering that may be needed.

4. Finally, determine what would be the best way for these results to be displayed. If you are using these in an analytics query, then they must be returned as a table view. However, if this is for threat hunting or for use in a workbook, then possibly a graphical view would be better.

Now that you have seen how to write your own queries, here are some that are not part of Azure Sentinel that you may find useful. As you are reading these, keep in the back of your head what steps would have been needed to develop these queries. What table would be needed? What information from the table? How would you filter it? How would you display it?

The billable data ingested

You have already seen the query to get a pie chart based on the amount of data being ingested. While this is useful, it only shows the percentage against the total; it does not show the size of the data actually being ingested.

If you want to see how much billable data has been ingested in the last 31 days, use the following query:

```
Usage
| where TimeGenerated > startofday(ago(31d))
| where IsBillable == true
| summarize TotalVolumeGB = sum(Quantity) / 1024. by
bin(TimeGenerated, 1d), Solution
| render barchart
```

This will look at the Usage log, which holds all the information regarding log ingestion, for the last 31 days, and check the IsBillable column to make sure the ingested data is billable. If you want to see all the data, billable or not, remove the following line:

```
| where IsBillable == true
```

It then summarizes the data by gigabytes (the `Quantity` field stores information in megabytes hence the division by `1024`), by the day that the data was ingested and by the solution, which is where the data came from. Finally, it will generate this data in a stacked column bar chart for easier viewing.

If you want to see the amount of data from a single solution, you can add the following line after the other lines that begin with `where`, substituting "`Security`" for whichever solution you wish to view:

```
| where Solution == "Security"
```

Map view of logins

Another one that is useful when used in conjunction with the map visualization in the workbooks (see *Chapter 8, Introducing Workbooks,* for more information) is one that looks at all the Azure sign-ins and gets the latitude and longitude so the location can be mapped:

```
SigninLogs
| extend latitude = toint(LocationDetails.geoCoordinates.
latitude), longitude = toint(LocationDetails.geoCoordinates.
longitude)
| extend country = strcat(tostring(LocationDetails.
countryOrRegion)," - ",tostring(LocationDetails.state))
| summarize count() by latitude, longitude, country
```

This query will look at all the entries in the **SigninLogs** log, which holds all the login information. Since there is no time limit applied in the code, it will use the default time limit based on the **Time range** drop-down menu.

Rather than having to pass in the long string to obtain the latitude and longitude, it creates new variables for the latitude and longitude. `toint()` is used to convert `LocationDetails.geoCoordinates.latitude` from a dynamic data type into an integer data type so they can be used in the `summarize` command at the end:

```
| extend latitude = tostring(LocationDetails.geoCoordinates.
latitude)
```

The same conversation will take place for the `longitude` variable.

There is a new feature of KQL exposed here: using a period to access information stored within a dynamic type. In the case of the `latitude` value, it is part of the `geoCoordinates` value, which is in turn part of the `LocationDetails` value, hence the need to traverse down the variable chain using the period to get to the value that is needed.

You could use a `where` command to make sure that both the `latitude` and the `longitude` variables have values; however, you may miss some logins as there are cases where the `latitude` and `longitude` values are not passed into the log. It is up to you whether you consider that important or not.

Another new variable is created that takes the country and adds the state to the end. This was done to provide some names for the locations on the map:

```
| extend country = strcat(tostring(LocationDetails.
countryOrRegion)," - ",tostring(LocationDetails.state))
```

Finally, it does a summary based on the variables so the total number of logins per `latitude`, `longitude`, and `country` will be returned:

```
| summarize count() by latitude, longitude, country
```

This is just an incredibly small sampling of some useful queries. There are many, many more in the **Query explorer** that was discussed earlier. Go ahead and play around with some to get a better idea of how to interact with the log tables to get the information you need.

Other useful logs

As you can see, the `Usage` log is quite useful to determine how your data is growing and `SigninLogs` is useful to determine when and where your users signed in. You can imagine using the first query shown to see how your data is growing daily, and we will do just that in *Chapter 8, Introducing Workbooks*.

There are other logs that are just as useful. The following table lists just a few of them:

Name	Description
AzureActivity	View the activity within Azure along with the category of the action performed
AzureDiagnostics	Look at the actions in Azure and whether they succeeded or not
Event	Windows Events
Heartbeat	The heartbeat of the computers that are attached to this Log Analytics workspace
Perf	Performance counters of the computers that are attached to this Log Analytics workspace
SigninLogs	Azure Active Directory Sign-in logs
W3CIISLog	IIS Web server logs from any computer running IIS if that data is being collected
SecurityAlert	The Alerts generated by Azure Sentinel including any other Azure security systems if the Analytic queries for those systems are being used
OfficeActivity	Office 365 logs. Requires that the Office 365 connector be enabled.

> **Tip**
>
> Ashwin Patil, one of our technical reviewers, maintains a wiki of data source schemas that is a good place to start when looking at the various logs:
> `https://github.com/Azure/Azure-Sentinel/wiki/`
> `DataSource-Schema-Reference.`

Summary

In this chapter, we explored the **Logs** page of Azure Sentinel. We saw how to use the various sections of the page, such as the page header, the **Tables** pane, the **Filter** pane, and the code and results pages to run built-in queries and determine the way results are displayed. Besides this, we also learned how to write our own queries using KQL.

With the help of the **Logs** page and by writing useful queries, you are now ready to carry out your own log analysis for investigation. You can use it to your advantage for trend analysis, visualizations, and troubleshooting.

In the next chapter, you will learn how to take the queries you build in the **Logs** page and use them in analytics queries.

Questions

1. What are two ways you can see pre-made queries?

2. If I am viewing the results from a query that shows me a listing of all the computers, how can I filter the results to only show specific computers without changing the query?

3. What is the easiest way to see a preview of the entries of a log?

4. What is the easiest way to show up to 200 results on a page when viewing all results pages?

5. How can I show up to 200 results on a page when viewing a single results page?

Further reading

-   Overview of log queries in Azure Monitor: https://docs.microsoft.com/en-us/azure/azure-monitor/log-query/log-query-overview

-   Getting started with log queries in Azure Monitor: https://docs.microsoft.com/en-us/azure/azure-monitor/log-query/get-started-queries

-   Logs in Azure Monitor:https://docs.microsoft.com/en-us/azure/azure-monitor/platform/data-platform-logs

Section 3: Security Threat Hunting

In this section, you will learn how to use various tools to create analytic rules, hunt for threats, and respond to security incidents.

The following chapters are included in this section:

- *Chapter 7, Creating Analytic Rules*
- *Chapter 8, Introducing Workbooks*
- *Chapter 9, Incident Management*
- *Chapter 10, Threat Hunting in Azure Sentinel*

7
Creating Analytic Rules

Now that you have connected your data to Azure Sentinel and know how to write your own KQL queries, you need to know how to use those queries to detect suspicious events. This is where Azure Sentinel Analytics comes into play.

Analytics is the heart of Azure Sentinel. This is where you will set up analytic rules and queries that can run automatically to detect issues that you may have. These rules can run queries, which you build on your own or they can come from the ever-growing list of templates that Microsoft provides. This is exactly what we will learn to do in this chapter.

This chapter will take you through the following topics:

- An introduction to analytic rules
- The various types of analytic rules
- Creating rules from templates
- Creating new rules and queries using the wizard
- Managing rules including editing and deleting

An introduction to Azure Sentinel Analytics

Azure Sentinel Analytics is where you set up rules to find issues with your environment. You can create various types of rules, each with its own configuration steps and niche for the types of abnormalities you are trying to detect.

Types of analytic rules

There are currently four types of rules: scheduled, Microsoft Security, machine learning, and fusion. Each type of rule fills a specific niche. Let's explore each of these in turn.

Scheduled

As the name suggests, these rules run on a set schedule to detect suspicious events. For instance, you can have a rule run every few minutes, every hour, every day, or at other time period. The queries for these rules will use KQL to define what they are trying to find. These rules will make up a large pro portion of your analytic rules and, if you have used other SIEM systems, are probably the ones you are most familiar with.

Microsoft Security

Microsoft Security rules are used to create Azure Sentinel incidents from alerts generated from other Microsoft Security solutions. At the time of writing, the following security solutions can have their alerts passed through:

- Microsoft Cloud App Security
- Azure Security Center
- Azure Advanced Threat Protection
- Azure Active Directory Identity Protection
- Microsoft Defender Advanced Threat Protection

These rules are very useful to set up to provide a single location to go to to see all of the alerts from Azure Security applications.

Machine learning behavioral analytics

Currently, these rules can only be created from templates that Microsoft provides. They use proprietary Microsoft machine learning algorithms to help to determine suspicious events. By harnessing the power of artificial intelligence and machine learning, these queries can help to detect abnormalities in how your users behave. For example, if a user normally only logs in to a server Monday – Friday and then starts logging in on the weekend, it could be an action worth investigating.

Fusion

Fusion is another Microsoft machine learning technology that will combine information from various alerts to generate alerts about things that may otherwise be very difficult to detect. This can be very powerful as some lower-severity alerts may not mean much looking at each one separately, but when combined they can indicate a much larger issue.

> **Note**
>
> For more information on the Fusion technology in Azure Sentinel, look at this page: `https://docs.microsoft.com/en-us/azure/sentinel/fusion.`

Those are the various types of analytic rules available. As you can see, they cover a wide variety of use cases from fully automated machine learning to scheduled rules that you create yourself. In the next section, we will look at the **Analytics** home page.

Navigating through the Analytics home page

The **Analytics** home page is where you can view, create, and manage various alerts. Let's navigate through this page.

To access the Analytics home page, select **Analytics** from the left-hand navigation bar. The following screen will open:

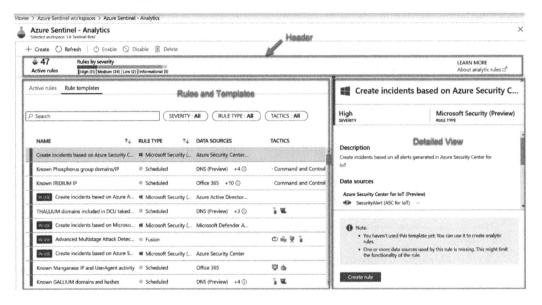

Figure 7.1 – Analytics home page

You will notice that the home page is broken into three main parts:

- The header bar
- The listing of rules and templates
- The detailed information section

Each of these parts will be described in further detail in the following sections.

The header bar

The following screenshot shows the header bar. Take a closer look at it. On the left is the number of **Active rules**; this is the number of rules that are currently in use. To the right of that is a listing of those rules broken down by the severity of the alert they will create. On the far right is a link that will open a new tab where you can learn more about analytic rules:

Figure 7.2 – Analytics header bar

Under the heading bar is a selector to select either **Active rules** or **Rule Templates**. Each of these tabs has different information. Let's take a look at them now.

Rule and template listings

Click on **Rule Templates**. It will show all of the rule templates that Microsoft has pre-loaded from Azure Sentinel's GitHub repository for you to use. Note that these are templates only; you must create a rule from them to use them, and there will be more on this later:

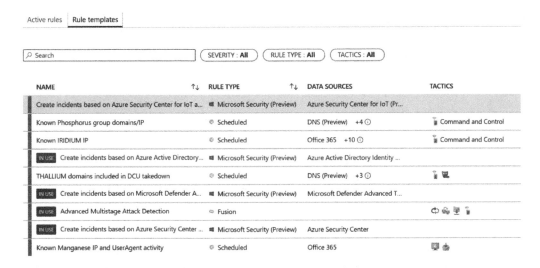

Figure 7.3 – Active rules/rule templates

If you notice in the preceding screenshot, the fourth rule template in the list states it is **IN USE**. This means that a rule has been created from this template already. Some of the rule templates, mainly any machine learning behavioral analytics or Fusion rules, will only allow you to create a single rule from the template, so if you see this message on those rules types, you know you cannot create another rule from the template. The other rule types have no such restrictions, so the message is more of a notification that there is at least one rule created from that template. See the *Creating a rule from a rule template* section for more information.

For each rule, the name, the rule type, the required data sources, and tactics (see the MITRE ATT&CK callout later) will be displayed. You can sort the name and rule type fields but not the required data sources or tactics fields since they can have multiple values. Now, click on **Active rules** and you will see those rules that you have either created yourself or have used a rule template to create. The following screenshot shows an example of what this looks like. We will go into more detail about this view later in this chapter:

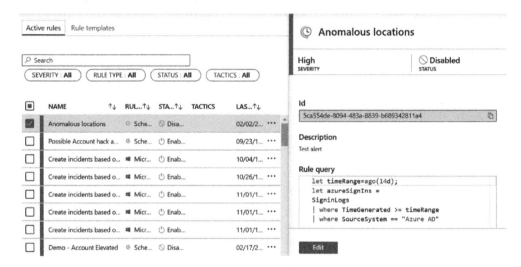

Figure 7.4 – Active rules

Immediately under those tabs is a search box and filters as shown in the following screenshot. The tab you are viewing will determine where the search and filters will look. If you are viewing the **Rule templates** tab, then the filter and search will only look for rule templates that match. Likewise, if you are viewing the **Active rules** tab, the search and filter will only look for active rules that match.

Use the search box to search for the **Rule templates** or **Active rules** for which you know at least part of the title. Filters allow you to filter your view based on **SEVERITY**, **RULE TYPE**, or **TACTICS**. If you are looking at the **Active rules** tab, you can also filter on **STATUS**. Click on the filter to see a drop-down list of all of the available options:

Figure 7.5 – Search box and filters

Under the filters is a listing of either the **Rule templates** or the **Active rules**, depending on which tab you are in. Let's explore these next.

Now draw your focus to the left of the **NAME** field in both the tabs (**Active rules** and **Rule templates**). There is a colored column. This matches the severity of the alert that will be created. Red is for high, orange for medium, yellow for low, and gray for informational. This field is used as the default for sorting the rows.

Details pane

Click on any row (in the following screenshot, we clicked on the **Known Phosphorus group domains/IP** template from the rule templates). This will show the details pane to the right of the listing as shown in the following screenshot. In that pane, you can see as much of the full name that fits, preceded by an icon to match the rule type. Under the name are the severity and the textual rule type:

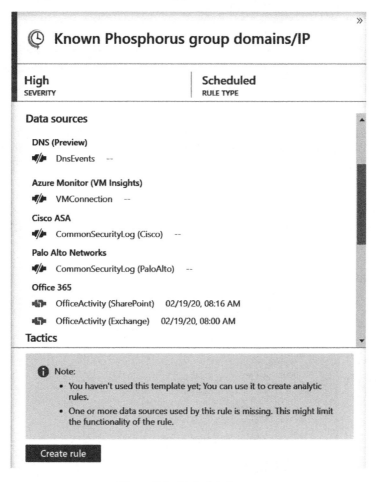

Figure 7.6 – Rule detail pane

There are currently four icons and they represent the rule types discussed in the *Types of Analytics rules* section from earlier. The icons are as follows:

Icon	Description
🕐	Scheduled
⊞	Microsoft Security
⚗	ML Behavior Analytics
⊘	Fusion

Figure 7.7 – Icons for each rule type

The description is below that line and gives you more information regarding what the rule will be doing and any other useful information.

Below that is a listing of any required data sources. If the icon to the left of the data source name is gray, that indicates that the data source is not available, and you will be unable to use this rule. If the icon is green, then the data source is present. All of the data sources must be green to use this rule template. This information will not be shown when looking at **Active rules**.

Now scroll the page down. You will see that under the required data sources is a listing of tactics that this rule uses, as shown in the following screenshot. This will show what types of tactics this rule is looking for:

Figure 7.8 – Rule detail pane continued

MITRE ATT&CK® Tactics

The MITRE organization describes the ATT&CK® tactics as follows:

"MITRE ATT&CK® is a globally-accessible knowledge base of adversary tactics and techniques based on real-world observations. The ATT&CK knowledge base is used as a foundation for the development of specific threat models and methodologies in the private sector, in government, and in the cybersecurity product and service community."

While the full discussion of tactics is beyond this book, understand that these are standard ways of designating how adversaries are trying to access your system and can be used to denote what your rules are attempting to detect. For more information, visit `https://attack.mitre.org/`.

The rest of the fields depend on the type of rule being looked at. Fusion and the ML behavior analytics rules will not have any further information.

If the rule is a scheduled rule, then the rule query will be shown under the tactics listing as shown in the following screenshot. This is the KQL query that will be run to determine whether an alert needs to be generated. Only scheduled rules will have this field as other rule types hide their queries:

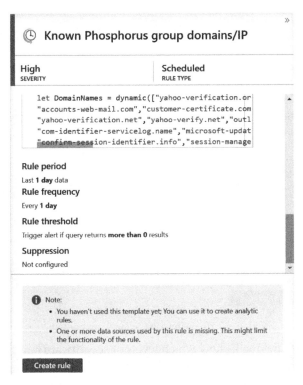

Figure 7.9 – Rule detail pane continued

Below the rule query are a few additional details:

- **Rule period**: This is how far in the past the query will look for its data. In this case, it will look through the data that was ingested in the last day.

- **Rule frequency**: This determines how often the query will be run.

- **Rule threshold**: This determines how many occurrences of the query finding a result there needs to be before an alert is generated.

- **Suppression field** (not shown): This will state whether the query has been suppressed and if so, for how long.

If the rule is a Microsoft Security rule, then instead of those fields discussed earlier, the **Filter by Microsoft security service** field will state which other Microsoft service is being used to generate the alerts, as shown in the following screenshot:

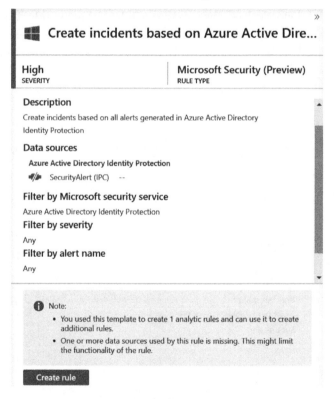

Figure 7.10 – Microsoft Security detail pane

The **Filter by severity** field will show which levels of severity are being used to filter the incoming alerts and **Filter by alert name** will do the same for the names of the alerts. These fields will be discussed in the *Microsoft incident creation rule* section later.

You have now learned about the Azure Sentinel Analytics home page including how to view the various rules that have been created, both in the summary and detail views. You have an understanding of what a rule template is and now it is time to learn how to use those rule templates to create a new rule and how to create a new rule from scratch using the built-in wizards.

Creating an analytic rule

As mentioned before, there are two ways to create rules. You can either use a rule template to create a rule or you can create a new one from scratch using the built-in wizards. Let's first try and do this using a rule template.

Creating a rule from a rule template

To use a rule template to create a rule, all you need to do is to select the rule in the list of rule templates. If you are able to create the rule, which can mean that you have all of the needed data sources and, in some cases, you have not already used this rule template to create a rule, then at the bottom of the rule details pane on the right side of the screen will be a **Create rule** button. Click it to create the rule.

> **Note**
>
> As stated previously, if this button is grayed out, then there will be some highlighted text above it explaining why. Referring back to figure 7.8 you will notice that we are unable to create a rule from the selected template due to missing data sources.

When you click on **Create rule**, you will be taken to the **Rule creation wizard** pages. Depending on the type of rule you are creating, there will be different questions on the pages that need to be answered and these pages will be discussed in the next section. Note that the name and description will be automatically filled in and cannot be changed.

For instance, the rule templates based on the Fusion and machine learning rule types only allow you to select whether or not the rule is enabled when creating a rule from the template. Both the schedule and Microsoft Security rule types allow you to modify all of the fields although a lot of default values have already been filled in for you. The following section covers what the fields are and how to fill them in.

Creating a new rule using the wizard

Azure Sentinel provides a wizard to help you to create new analytic rules. This wizard is comprised of either two or four pages depending on the type of rule being created. As shown in the following figure, there are two different types of rules that can be created using the wizard: Scheduled query and Microsoft incident creation. The creation of each is presented here:

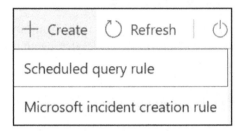

Figure 7.11 – Create a new analytics rule

We will create a new rule using the **Scheduled query rule** link first.

Creating a scheduled query rule

Remember, a scheduled rule is one that will run on a set schedule and uses KQL code to perform the query. It also has the added benefit of being able to associate an Azure Sentinel Playbook to perform actions when this rule generates an alert.

This allows you to create a rule where you enter your own KQL query. Let's see how to do it:

1. Click on the **+ Create** link at the top of the page. This will present you with a drop-down list where you can select **Scheduled query rule**.

2. Once you select the option from the drop-down list, you will be presented with the **General** screen, as follows:

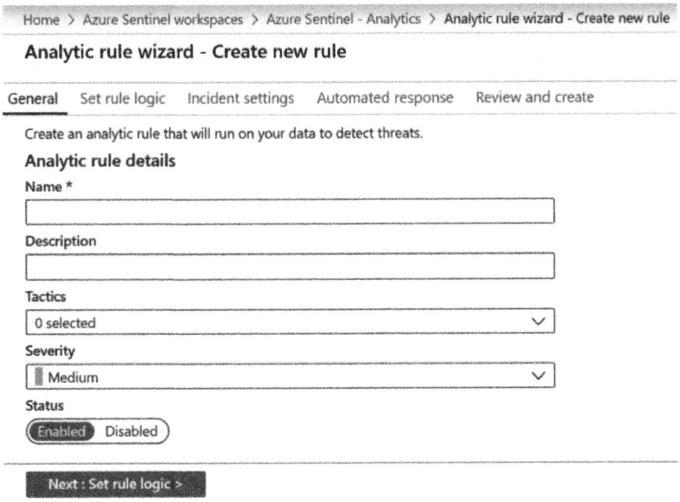

Figure 7.12 – Create new rule – General page

Fill in the details for each field. The following table provides further details to help you out:

Field name	Description
Name	This is the name of the rule. Make this as descriptive as possible. The user should be able to easily tell what type of activity the rule is trying to find. For example, `Security Event log cleared` clearly tells you it is checking to see whether the security event log has been cleared.
Description	This is the description of the rule. Add enough information so that whoever is reading the description knows what the rule does.
Tactics	These are the MITRE tactics that this rule uses. Go to `https://attack.mitre.org/tactics/` for more information.
Severity	What is the severity of the alert that gets created by this rule? There are no hard and fast rules for what severity to choose but make sure the severity matches what you are looking for. Having someone fail to log in to their account five times in ten minutes is probably not a hyphenate issue since it could be that the user just changed their password and is trying to remember it. However, having someone fail to log in five times in ten minutes and then log in to a server they have not logged in to before could indicate a brute force password attack and would merit a high severity.
Status	This is either **Enabled** or **Disabled**. You can disable a rule if you expect to perform actions that would result in many false positives being generated. Just remember to enable the rule when you are done testing.

3.   When you have all of the fields filled in, click on **Next: Set rule logic** > to continue. The **Set rule logic** page is where you add your KQL code and entities and set the schedule and alert threshold. The screen is shown here, followed by a description of the fields:

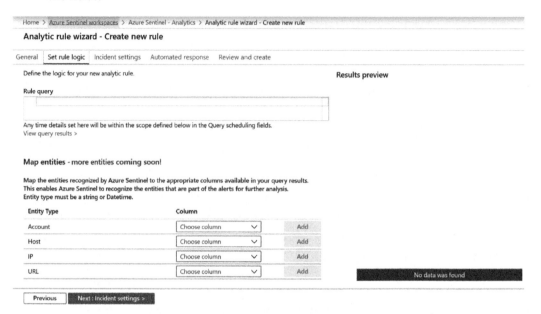

Figure 7.13 – Create rule – Set rule logic

Once again, fill in the details for each field. The following table provides further details to help you out:

Field Name	Description
Rule query	This is where you enter your KQL query string. Once it has been entered and you leave this field, the **Results** preview on the right will show the number of results in a graph.
Map Entities	These are the entities needed to be able to perform an in-depth analysis of the alerts via the **Investigation** graph. Fill these in where it makes sense. For each field, select the appropriate column and click on the **Add** button before adding the next one.
Account	This will typically be the username that performed the action if known.
Host	This will typically be the host that the action was performed on if known.
IP	This will typically be the IP address of the machine that performed the action if known.
URL	This will typically be the URL of the action that was performed if known. Using the URL detonation capability, Microsoft can determine whether this URL is malicious or not with high accuracy.

4. Now, scroll down the page and you will find some more fields related to the **Query scheduling** and **Alert threshold**, as shown here:

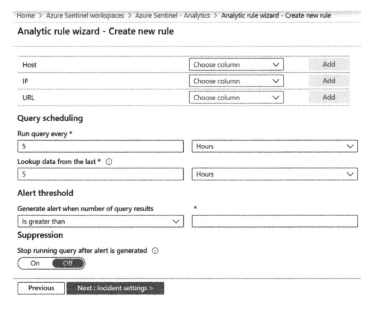

Figure 7.14 – Create rule – Set rule logic continued

The following table provides further details for each entry:

Field Name	Description
Run query every	Select the numeric value and the time span (minutes, hours, or days) to determine how often the query runs. While there are no additional charges for running a query often, consider how often the suspicious activity would occur and how quickly you need to know about it. It is tempting to run every query as quickly as possible but that can lead to alert overload. Do you need to be notified as quickly as possible about the hyphenate event of someone entering the wrong password five times in ten minutes? This is the **Rule frequency** when viewing the rule on the **Overview** page.
Lookup data from the last	Select the numeric value and the time span (minutes, hours, or days) to determine how far back in time to look for data. Usually, this will be the same as the **Rule frequency.** This is the **Rule period** when viewing the rule on the **Overview** page.
Stop running query after alert is generated	This determines whether the rule will be paused after an alert has been generated. This can either be on or off. If on, elect the numeric value and the time span (minutes or hours) to determine how long the rule will be paused before reactivating. This can be very useful when testing a new query. You want to be able to validate that it is working correctly and that the incident generated is accurate before continuing, so by setting this, you can get one new incident that you can investigate to make sure the query is accurate.
Alert threshold	This determines how many times the rule finds a positive result before an alert gets generated. This can be set to **Is greater than, Is less than, Is equal to,** or **Is not equal** to a numeric value. This is can be used to limit the number of incidents that get generated to avoid overload. For instance, you may set the number of times a failed login occurs before generating an incident much higher than you would set something like a new account being granted admin rights. This is the **Alert threshold** when viewing the rule on the **Overview** page.

5. When you have all of the fields filled in, click on **Next: Incident Settings** > to continue. If you need to change some values on the previous screen at any moment, click on the **Previous** button.

6. The **Incident settings** page allows you to determine whether you want this alert to create an incident and whether you want this alert to group incidents together, and it is shown here:

Home > Azure Sentinel workspaces > Azure Sentinel - Analytics > Analytic rule wizard - Create new rule

Analytic rule wizard - Create new rule

Incident settings

Azure Sentinel alerts can be grouped together into an Incident that should be looked into.
You can set whether the alerts that are triggered by this analytics rule should generate incidents.

Create incidents from alerts triggered by this analytics rule

(**Enabled**   Disabled)

Alert grouping

Set how the alerts that are triggered by this analytics rule, are grouped into incidents.
Grouping alerts into incidents provides the context you need to respond and reduces the noise from single alerts.

Group related alerts, triggered by this analytics rule, into incidents

(Enabled   **Disabled**)

Limit the group to alerts created within the selected time frame

| 5 | Hours |

Group alerts triggered by this analytics rule into a single incident by

(●) Grouping alerts into a single incident if all the entities match (recommended)

(○) Grouping all alerts triggered by this rule into a single incident

(○) Grouping alerts into a single incident if the selected entities match:

| Select entities | ∨ |

Re-open closed matching incidents

(Enabled   Disabled)

| Previous | | Next : Automated response > |

Figure 7.15 – Create rule – Incident settings page

The following table provides further details for each entry:

Field Name	Description
Create incidents from alerts triggered by this analytics rule	By default, each alert that gets triggered will create an incident. If this is not the desired functionality, select **Disabled**. One reason you may want to disable this is if you want to perform more computations on the alert in a playbook before creating the incident.
Group related alerts, triggered by this analytics rule, into incidents	Enable this if you want all of the incidents that this alert will create to be grouped into one incident. This can make it easier to perform the investigation if there are multiple occurrences of the alert that are identical.
Limit the group to alerts created within the selected time frame	Select how far back to look for matching alerts. Enter the number and then select either minutes, hours or days from the drop-down list.
Limit the group to alerts created within the selected time frame	This has three options that you can select to determine how the alerts are matched: Grouping alerts into a single incident if all the entities match (recommended): Selecting this will match the alerts if and only if all of the entities in the alerts match. Grouping all alerts triggered by this rule into a single incident: This will match all of the alerts created by this rule into the same incident regardless of whether or not the entities match. Grouping alerts into a single incident if the selected entities match: If this is selected, then the drop-down list under it will list all of the entities that have been associated with this rule. Select the one or more that you want to match.
Re-open closed matching incidents	Enable this if you want previously closed incidents to re-open when a new alert is matched. You may want to do this if you feel that having additional alerts that match previously closed ones would warrant further investigation into those that were previously closed.

7. When you have all of the fields filled in, click on **Next: Automated response** > to continue. If you need to change some values on the previous screen at any moment, click on the **Previous** button.

The **Automated response** page allows you to select a playbook that gets run automatically when an alert is generated, as shown here:

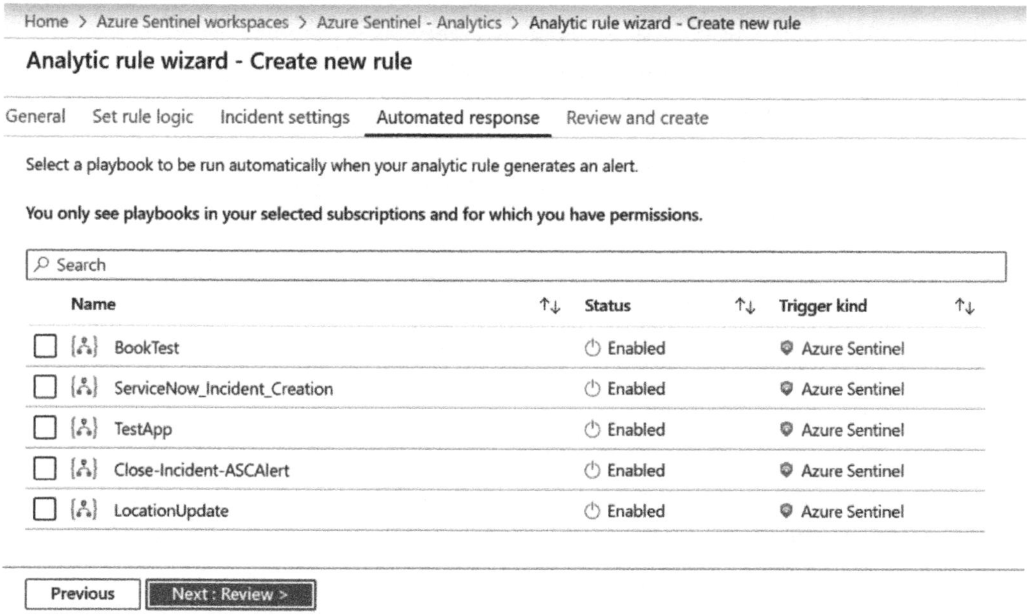

Home > Azure Sentinel workspaces > Azure Sentinel - Analytics > Analytic rule wizard - Create new rule

Analytic rule wizard - Create new rule

General   Set rule logic   Incident settings   Automated response   Review and create

Select a playbook to be run automatically when your analytic rule generates an alert.

You only see playbooks in your selected subscriptions and for which you have permissions.

Name		Status		Trigger kind	
☐ {⋏} BookTest	↑↓	⏻ Enabled	↑↓	⦿ Azure Sentinel	↑↓
☐ {⋏} ServiceNow_Incident_Creation		⏻ Enabled		⦿ Azure Sentinel	
☐ {⋏} TestApp		⏻ Enabled		⦿ Azure Sentinel	
☐ {⋏} Close-Incident-ASCAlert		⏻ Enabled		⦿ Azure Sentinel	
☐ {⋏} LocationUpdate		⏻ Enabled		⦿ Azure Sentinel	

Previous   Next : Review >

Figure 7.16 – Create rule – Automated response

In the preceding screenshot, there are multiple playbooks available to be selected. If there are no playbooks listed, then you have not created any that have **Azure Sentinel** set as the **Trigger kind**. See *Chapter 11, Creating Playbooks and Logic Apps*, for more information on creating Azure Sentinel playbooks.

8.   To choose the playbook that you want to run when this analytic rule generates an alert, click on the name of the playbook. The screen will then change to show the selected playbook, as shown here:

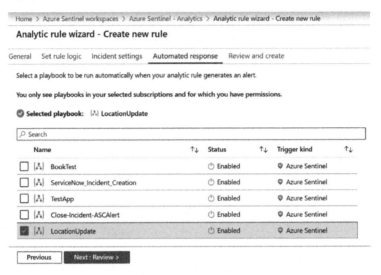

Figure 7.17 – Create rule – Automated response with the selected playbook

9.   When you have all of the fields filled in click, on **Next: Review** > to continue. If you need to change some values on the previous screen, click on the **Previous** button.

The **Review and Create** screen will show you a review of all of your choices and validate your entries to make sure they are valid. If there are issues, you will see a screen like the one shown here:

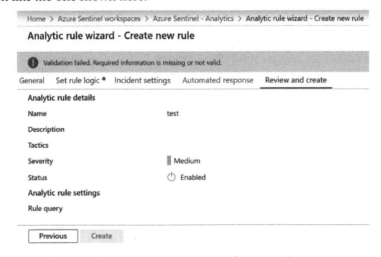

Figure 7.18 – Create rule – Review and create with an error

You can see there is an error message telling you there is a validation failure and a red dot next to the page name that has an error. In this case, it is the **Set rule logic** page, as indicated by the red dot to the right of the tab's name.

If there are no errors, you will see a page like the one shown here:

Home > Azure Sentinel workspaces > Azure Sentinel - Analytics > Analytic rule wizard - Create new rule

Analytic rule wizard - Create new rule

✓   Validation passed.

General   Set rule logic   Incident settings   Automated response   **Review and create**

Analytic rule details

Name   test

Description

Tactics

Severity   ▌ Medium

Status   ⏻ Enabled

Analytic rule settings

Rule query   Heartbeat

| Previous | Create |

Figure 7.19 – Create rule – Review and create with no errors

10. Finally, after filling in and verifying all of the details, you can then click on the **Create** button to create your rule.

Now you know how to create a scheduled rule. These are going to be the vast majority of the rules that you create and use. As you can see, they are quite flexible, not only in terms of the KQL query that gets run, but in terms of when it runs, whether it creates a new incident or adds new information to an existing one, and what happens automatically when this rule generates an alert. Next, we will look at creating a Microsoft incident rule.

Creating a Microsoft incident rule

When creating one of these rules, you are telling Azure Sentinel to take the alerts passed in by another Azure security system such as Microsoft Cloud App Security, apply any filters, and create the alert in Azure Sentinel. To create this type of rule, follow along with these steps:

1. Click on the **+ Create** link at the top of the page. This will present you with a drop-down list where you can select **Microsoft incident creation rule**.

2. Once you select the option from the drop-down list, you will be presented with the **General** screen, as follows:

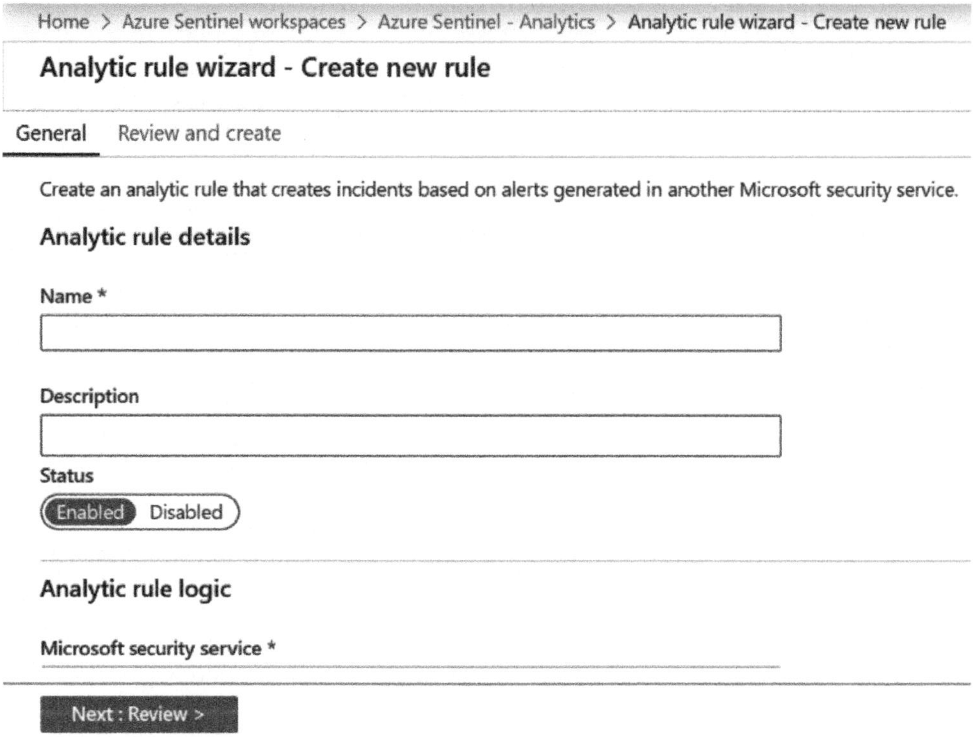

Figure 7.20 – Create Microsoft incident rule

The following table provides further details for each entry:

Name	Description
Name	This is the name of the rule. Make this as descriptive as possible.
Description	This is the description of the rule. Add enough information so that whoever is reading the description knows what the rule does.
Status	This is either enabled or disabled. You can disable a rule if you expect to perform actions that would result in many false positives to be generated. Just remember to enable the rule when you are done.

3.   Scroll down and you will see more fields to fill in, as shown here:

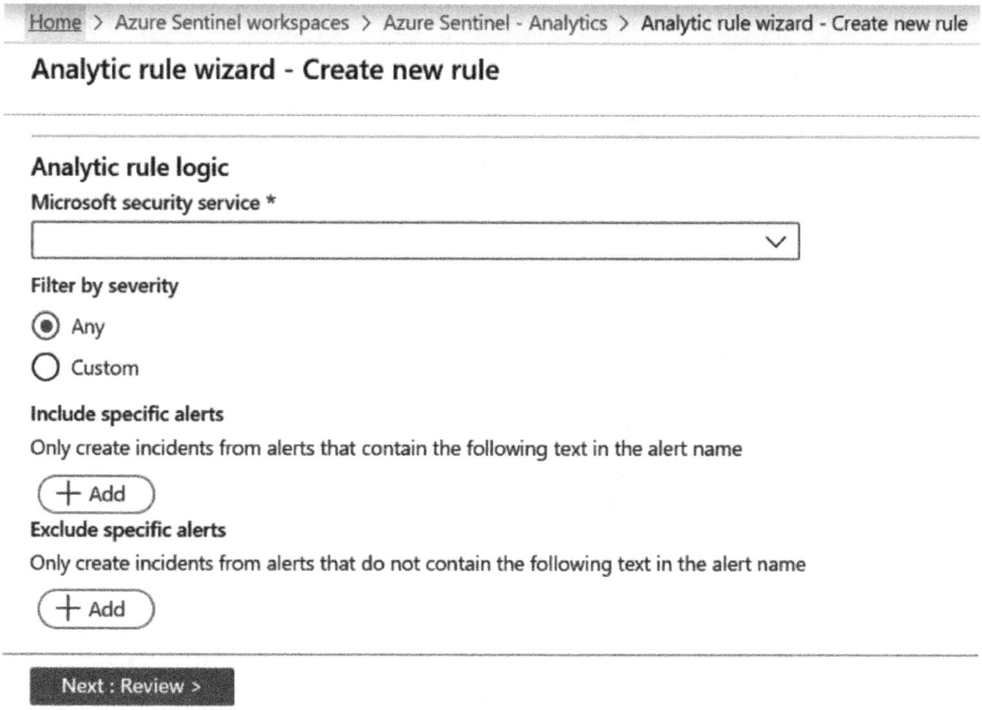

Figure 7.21 – Create Microsoft incident rule continued

The following table provides further details for each entry:

Name	Description
Microsoft security service	Use the drop-down list to select the Azure resource from which you want to ingest the alerts. This includes Microsoft Cloud App Security, Azure Security Center, Azure Advanced Threat Protection, and more.
Filter by severity	This can either be **Any** or if you select **Custom**, you can select one or more from **High**, **Medium**, **Low**, or **Informational**. This will filter those alerts to only allow the selected severity to pass through.
Filter by text contained in the alert name	This can either be **Any** or if you select **Custom**, you can enter one or more terms that will be used for filtering. This will filter only those alerts that contain any of the terms entered.

4. When you have all of the fields filled in, click on **Next: Review** > to continue. The **Review and Create** screen will open, which shows you a review of all of your choices and allows you to check your entries to make sure they are valid. If there are issues, you will see a screen like the one shown here:

Figure 7.22 – Create Microsoft incident rule – Review and create with an error

You can see there is an error message telling you there is a validation failure and a red dot next to the page name that has an error. In this case, it is the **General** page, as indicated by the red dot next to the tab's name.

If there are no errors, you will see a page similar to the one shown here:

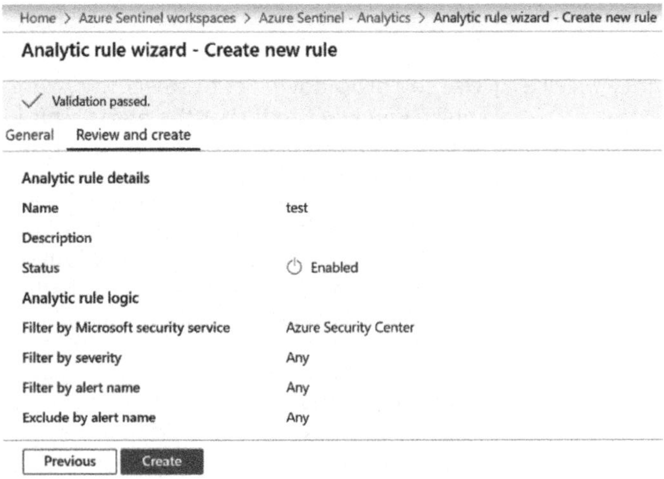

Figure 7.23 – Create Microsoft incident rule – Review and create with no errors

5. Finally, click on the **Create** button to create your rule.

We have looked at the three different ways to create a new analytic rule; using a template, creating a new scheduled rule from scratch, and creating a new Microsoft incident rule from scratch. All three ways have their uses and you will most likely use all three while setting up Azure in your environment. Next, we will look at how to manage existing analytic rules.

Managing analytic rules

Once your rules are created, you will need to manage them on an ongoing basis to ensure they remain useful. You may need to tweak a rule to give better results, change the playbooks assigned to a scheduled rule, disable a rule, or even delete ones that are no longer needed.

You can only manage those rules listed in the **Active rules** tab. So, follow along to complete these two simple steps:

1. Click on the **Active rules** link first.

2. In the listing of rules, to the right of the **Last Modified** column is the context menu, the three periods in a row, for each rule. Click on it and you will see a drop-down list, as shown in the following screenshot:

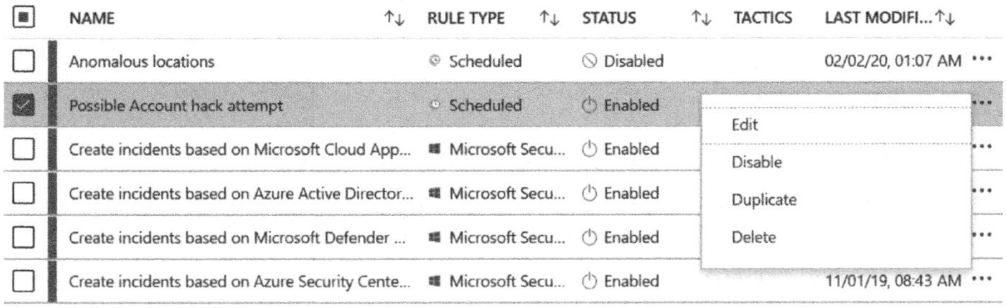

■	NAME	↑↓	RULE TYPE	↑↓	STATUS	↑↓	TACTICS	LAST MODIFI... ↑↓
☐	Anomalous locations		⊙ Scheduled		⊘ Disabled			02/02/20, 01:07 AM •••
☑	Possible Account hack attempt		⊙ Scheduled		⏻ Enabled		Edit	•••
☐	Create incidents based on Microsoft Cloud App...		▦ Microsoft Secu...		⏻ Enabled		Disable	•••
☐	Create incidents based on Azure Active Director...		▦ Microsoft Secu...		⏻ Enabled		Duplicate	•••
☐	Create incidents based on Microsoft Defender ...		▦ Microsoft Secu...		⏻ Enabled		Delete	•••
☐	Create incidents based on Azure Security Cente...		▦ Microsoft Secu...		⏻ Enabled			11/01/19, 08:43 AM •••

Figure 7.24 – Analytic rule context-sensitive menu

Let's see how to use these options:

- **Edit**: This entry will allow you to edit the rule so that you can modify any of the fields as needed. You can also edit the rule by clicking on the **Edit** button on the details blade. Editing a rule will take you through the same pages as creating the rule with all of the saved parameters filled in. Make the necessary changes and save them.

- **Disable**: This entry will allow you to disable the rule. If the rule is disabled, then this entry will be labeled **Enable** and it will allow you to enable the rule. You can disable a rule if you think it is no longer needed before deleting it or if you are going to perform operations that you know will trigger the rule unnecessarily. Just remember to re-enable it when you are done!

- **Duplicate**: This button will create an exact copy of the selected rule that you can then edit. The name will be that of the existing rule appended with `- Copy X` where X is the next number in the series starting with `1`. So, if there is a rule called **Test Rule** and the **Duplicate** entry is selected, the new rule will be named `Test Rule - Copy 1` and if **Duplicate** is selected again, the new rule will be called `Test Rule - Copy 2`, and so on.

- **Delete**: This entry will allow you to delete the rule. A pop-up box will ask for confirmation before the rule is deleted. For example, if you have a rule set up to check for abnormalities in equipment that is no longer running, you can delete the rule as it is no longer needed. A best practice is to disable the rule for a time period to make sure that the rule isn't needed anymore before deleting.

By effectively managing your rules, you are able to make sure your rules stay valid. You can modify the queries as needed and update any actions that get taken when a new alert is created from a scheduled rule. You can help to avoid alert overload by reclassifying an alert's severity if it is deemed to be too high (or too low). You can also delete any rules that are no longer needed.

Summary

This chapter introduced you to Azure Sentinel Analytics queries and the Analytics page. You not only learned about the different rule types but also how to create your own rules using the analytic rules templates that Microsoft has provided to make it easier. In addition, you learned how to create both a scheduled and a Microsoft incident creation rule. Finally, you learned how to manage your existing analytic rules.

You are now ready to start creating the rules needed to monitor your environment. Take a look at the extensive list of rule templates that Microsoft provides and see which of those will be useful. Then, create your own rules to fill in the blanks.

The next chapter will introduce Azure workbooks, which allow you to create very useful tables, charts, and graphs to get a better understanding of your data.

Questions

1. What are the four different rule types?

2. If I want a rule to run on a set interval, which rule type should I use?

3. Can you have alerts from other Azure security systems create incidents in Azure Sentinel?

4. What would you need to do to have a playbook automatically run when a scheduled alert fires?

5. What two ways can I use to delete a rule I no longer need?

Further reading

You can refer to the following link for more details:

- *Create custom analytic rules to detect suspicious threats*: `https://docs. microsoft.com/en-us/azure/sentinel/tutorial-detect-threats-custom`

- *Azure Sentinel correlation rules: Active List out; make_list() in, the AAD/AWS correlation example*: `https://techcommunity.microsoft.com/t5/ azure-sentinel/azure-sentinel-correlation-rules-active-lists-out-make-list-in/ba-p/1029225`

8
Introducing Workbooks

Azure Sentinel workbooks are a way to create and show customizable and interactive reports that can display graphs, charts, and tables. Information can be presented from Log Analytics workspaces using the same **Kusto Query Language** (**KQL**) queries that you already know how to use. These workbooks are based on the workbook technology that has been in use with other Azure resources, including Azure Monitor and Log Analytics workspaces.

Azure Sentinel provides a number of templates that are ready for use. You can use these templates to create your own workbook that can then be modified as needed. Most of the data connectors that are used to ingest data come with their own workbooks, to allow you better insight into the data that is being ingested through the use of tables and visualizations, including bar and pie charts. You can also make your own workbooks from scratch, if required.

In this chapter, you will learn the following topics:

- An overview of the Workbooks page
- Walking through an existing workbook
- Creating workbooks
- Editing a workbook

- Managing workbooks
- Workbook step types

> **Note**
>
> You may come across old documentation and websites that discuss Azure Sentinel dashboards. Dashboards were replaced with workbooks to provide a more interactive user experience.

An overview of the Workbooks page

To go to the **Workbooks** page, select **Workbooks** from the Azure Sentinel navigation blade. A new screen will appear that will look similar to the one shown in the following screenshot:

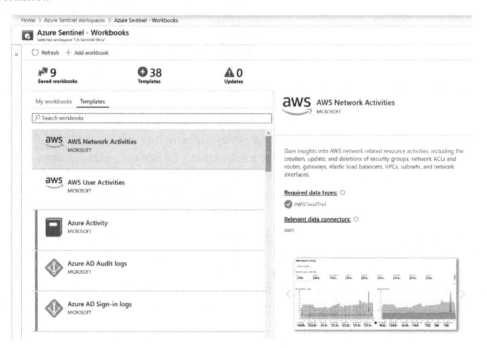

Figure 8.1 – Azure Sentinel Workbooks page

The header at the top of the page in the preceding screenshot shows the **Refresh** and **Add workbook** buttons. Adding a new workbook will be discussed in the *Adding a new workbook from scratch* section.

Let's discuss the different components of the **Workbooks** page in detail in the following sections.

The workbook header

Under the **Refresh** and **Add workbook** buttons is the total number of workbooks that have been saved. The number **9** in the following screenshot will include all the workbooks that have been saved, whether they are saved as a personal or as a shared workbook. So, this number can be different, depending on who is accessing the page:

Saved workbooks   Templates   Updates

Figure 8.2 – Workbook header

To the right of that is the total number of templates available to use. This number may change as new workbook templates are added.

On the far-right side is the total number of templates that can be updated. As new versions of the templates are added, this number will increment to inform you of this fact. The actual template that can be updated will have an icon to let you know it has an update.

> **Note**
> Note that this will update the template only. It will not update any saved versions of the workbook based on the template.

Let's take a look at the **Templates** view.

The Templates view

Below the workbook header are two tabs, **My workbooks** and **Templates**, as shown in the following screenshot. The **My workbooks** tab will show all the workbooks to which the user has access, including those that are shared and personal. The **Templates** tab shows all the templates that are available to be used:

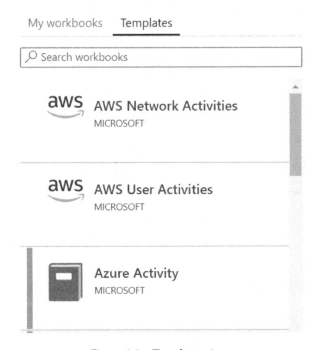

Figure 8.3 – Templates view

No matter which tab you select, each template or report will be shown on a single row. On the far left will be a green bar, indicating that this template has been saved previously and can be viewed under **My workbooks**. If you are looking at the **My workbooks** tab, then every report will have a green bar since every report is available to view. After that is an icon representing the company that created the template, followed by the template name, and the name of the company under this.

Looking at the first template listed in the preceding screenshot, you can see the icon for **Amazon Web Services (AWS)**. This is followed by the template name, **AWS Network Activities**, with the company that created it, **MICROSOFT**, under the template name.

Workbook detail view

Selecting a workbook will show its information in the details window on the far-right side of the **Workbooks** page, as shown in the following screenshot:

Figure 8.4 – Workbook detail view

This window will again show the icon, name, and company name at the top of the screen. Under that is a detailed description of the workbook.

Missing required data types

Below the workbook detail view is the list of required data types. This will list one or more data types that are needed for this workbook to function correctly. If your environment has the required data source, a green checkbox icon will show, but if it does not, then a cross check icon will show in its place, as shown in the following screenshot:

Figure 8.5 – Missing required data types

Unlike the Analytics query templates discussed in *Chapter 7*, *Creating Analytic Rules*, you can create a workbook from a template, even if you do not have the required data types. The only thing that will happen is that no information will be shown in the workbook, and there may be an error.

Workbook detail view (continued)

Below the **Required data types** field is the relevant data connectors that show which data connector(s) are used to ingest the needed data.

Scrolling down in the details pane will show one or more reports that represent how the report will look. This can be very useful to see what the workbook would look like, especially if you do not have the requisite data source populated yet, and an example of this can be seen in the following screenshot:

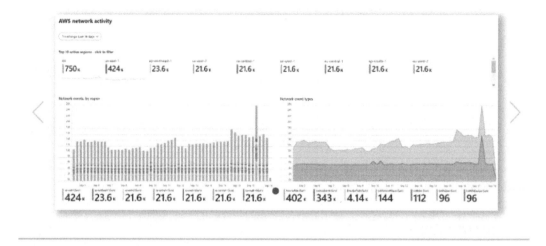

Figure 8.6 – Workbook detail view (continued)

Clicking on the left and right arrows will switch the displayed report if there is more than one available.

Saved template buttons

At the bottom of the screen are a series of buttons that change depending on whether you have saved the template or not. Figure 8.6 in the preceding section shows the buttons for a template that has not been used to create a workbook, and the following screenshot shows the buttons for a template that has been saved:

Figure 8.7 – Saved template buttons

Let's discuss each of these buttons in detail:

- If you have saved the template as a workbook, the first button that will be shown is **View saved workbook**. This will allow you to look at the workbook you have created from the template, including any changes that you have made to it. This activity will be discussed in the *Creating workbooks* section later. If you have not saved the template as a workbook, then the **Save** button will be displayed, as shown in figure 8.6. Clicking this will allow you to create a new workbook from a template. Refer to the *Creating a workbook using a template* section for more information.

- The next button is **View template**. This will show whether or not you have saved the template as a workbook already, as you can see in both figures 8.6 and 8.7. This will allow you to view the template. This is a fully interactive view of the template, although the only action you can perform is to refresh the template. You will not be able to save or modify the template from this view.

- The next button will depend on whether or not you have saved the template as a workbook. If you have saved the template, the **Delete** button will be displayed, as shown in figure 8.7. Clicking this will cause a validation popup to appear. If you confirm the deletion, the saved workbook, including any changes you have made, will be deleted.

The **My workbooks** tab will show the same information as the **Templates** tab, except that it will only show those workbooks that have been saved from a template or created from scratch. Also, at the bottom of the detailed description window, the buttons have changed.

If you have created a workbook from scratch, without creating it from an existing template, then the buttons will be shown as in the following screenshot. Since there is no template to view, the **View template** button will not be shown:

Figure 8.8 – Buttons for creating a workbook from scratch

You now have a good understanding of the workbook's overview page. You know how to look at a workbook template, determine whether you have the needed data sources, and create a new workbook using a template. Next, we will look at an existing workbook to give you an idea of what you can do with workbooks.

Walking through an existing workbook

We are going to take a look at an existing template that has most of the features available to workbooks. This may give you an idea of what you can do with your workbooks, or at least show you how to set up a workbook to do what you want.

The Azure Active Directory (Azure AD) **Sign-in logs** template has a wide variety of charts and graphs in it. In addition, it shows how to allow users to change parameters, and it shows how you can make columns in a table and display information in a more graphical way.

If you do not have the `SigninLogs` data type available, which the **Azure AD Sign-in logs** workbook uses to get its information, it is recommended that the Azure AD connector be enabled for your Azure Sentinel instance. Refer back to *Chapter 3, Data Collection and Management,* for guidance on how to do this. If you cannot get this connector activated, for whatever reason, you can follow along in the book. However, you will have a better experience if you can look at the workbook yourself.

Select the **Azure AD Sign-in logs** template and click the **View template** button. If you have created a workbook from this template, you can click the **View saved workbook** button. It will make no difference in this case. You will see a screen similar to the following. It is expected that the values are different, and some of the columns may not display the same graphics, as in the following screenshot:

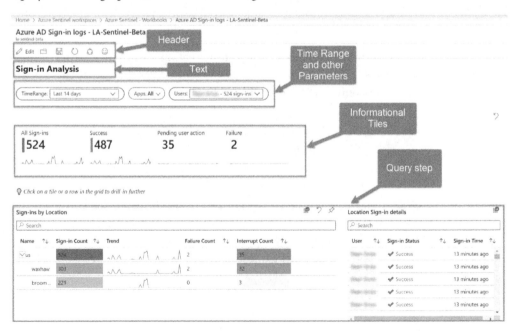

Figure 8.9 – Azure AD Sign-in logs workbook

A workbook is made up of small sections called **steps**. Each step has a unique name that can be pretty much anything, and this name can be referenced in other steps. Each step can run on its own, although some may require parameters either from a parameter step, as with the one discussed later, or from other steps.

The header at the top of the page does not concern us at this point. It will be explained in the Editing a workbook section later in this chapter. Notice that the page has a title called **Sign-in Analysis**. This is an example of straight text being shown.

Beneath that are some parameters that allow you to change what the workbook is looking at—in this case, **TimeRange**, **Apps**, and **Users** can be changed. In this way, the user can either select to look at the entire report, or narrow it down to a specific date, app, and user, or anything in between.

Under that is the first example of a query section. This is using a KQL query to obtain the data, and then displaying it in different ways. In this case, the information is being displayed as tiles; one tile per column is returned.

Below that is another example of a query section. In this case, the information is being displayed as a table, but individual columns have been modified to show graphical information, which others show as straight text. If you look at the second column from the left, it is showing a heatmap along with the textual value. The third column, called **Trend**, is showing a sparkle line instead of the text values.

Another interesting thing to note about these query sections is that they are shown side by side. Normally, when a new query is added to a workbook page, it is set to take up the entire width of the page. This can be modified so that the individual queries take up as much or as little width as desired. If another query can fit beside the first one, it will do so.

Remember that workbooks are interactive, meaning that they can be defined in such a way so that if you click on one value, others can change. In this workbook, if you select a row from the **Sign-ins by Location** query shown in the preceding screenshot, the **Location Sign-in details** will be filtered to show only those users who belong to the selected location.

The rest of the workbook's sections are pretty much the same as the ones already discussed. This should give you an idea of what you can do with your workbooks to display relevant information.

Go ahead and look at some of the other workbook templates available to see what else you can do. Remember: you can just click on the template and look at the provided report to get an idea of what the workbook will look like. You will see that you can show bar charts, pie charts, area charts, and more.

Creating workbooks

Now that you have an idea of what you can do with workbooks, it is time to see how to create your own. There are two ways of doing this:

- Using a workbook template
- Creating one from scratch

Either way, we will get a working workbook; however, you may find it easier to create workbooks from templates to begin with, to get a better understanding of how workbooks function and what you can do with them. There is no reason why you cannot create your own workbook, using the queries from a workbook created from a template as the starting point.

In order to be able to create a new workbook, you will need to have the proper rights. Refer to `https://docs.microsoft.com/en-us/azure/sentinel/roles#roles-and-allowed-actions` to see the rights that are required to create and edit workbooks.

Creating a workbook using a template

The following steps show how to create a workbook using a template. This makes it easier to create a new workbook, as you have a basis to start from:

1. While looking at a template's details page, click on the **Save** button.

2. A pop-up window, as shown in the following screenshot, will ask you which location to use to save the new workbook. Select the appropriate location. This should be the same location as the location where your Log Analytics workspace resides, so as to avoid egress charges:

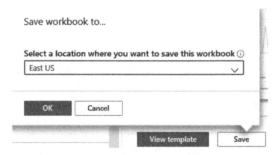

Figure 8.10 – Choosing your workbook location

3. Click **OK**. This will cause a new workbook to be created under **My workbooks**, with the same name as the template.

You now know how to create a workbook using a template as the baseline. This is a very easy method to get a workbook created that you can then modify as needed. Next, we will discuss creating a workbook from scratch, without using a template as the baseline.

Creating a new workbook from scratch

Creating a workbook from scratch is a bit more complicated. It involves creating the workbook, and then you need to edit it, since the workbook created is already saved with a default query assigned to it. To create a workbook from scratch, perform the following steps:

1. Click the **Add workbook** button in the header.

2. This will create a workbook like the one shown in the following screenshot. Note that the actual values will most likely be different:

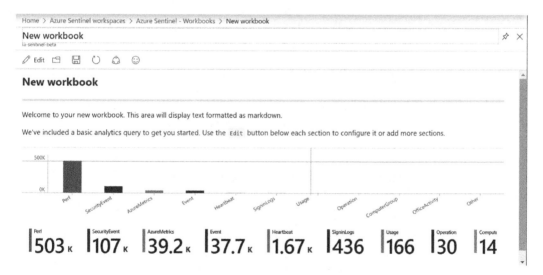

Figure 8.11 – A new workbook created from scratch

3. Notice that it comes already populated with text and with a query step already included, to get you started.

4. Click the **Save** icon in the header to save this workbook. Clicking it will open the **Save** dialog box, as follows:

Figure 8.12 – Save workbook screen

The relevant field options are discussed in the following table:

Name	Description
Title	The name of the workbook. This should be descriptive enough so that users can easily tell what kind of information will be shown.
Save To	This will determine whether this is a private workbook or a public one. Selecting My reports means that only you can see the workbook, while selecting Shared reports means that everyone can see it. Usually, you will save the workbook to My reports first while you are working on it, and then move it to Shared reports once it is completed. Refer to the Managing workbooks section later on in this chapter for information about how to move it.
Subscription	Select the subscription where this workbook will reside. It should be the same subscription as your Log Analytics workspace.
Resource group	Select the resource group where this workbook will reside. It does not matter if it resides in the same resource group as your Log Analytics workspace. For instance, you could have one resource group for all resources related to your Azure Sentinel instance, or one resource group just for your workbooks and anything in between. Follow your corporate standards on where to place items, if you have any.
Location	Select the location where your workbook will reside. You will want this to be the same location as your Log Analytics workspace to avoid egress charges.

5. Click **Save** to save the workbook.

> **Note**
>
> It is not actually necessary for you to save the new workbook before you edit it. It is generally recommended that you do so to make sure you have a saved copy of it that you can revert to, should your edits not work correctly.

That is all there is to it. Now, you will need to edit the workbook so that you can edit or remove the existing steps or add your own steps. Refer to the next section, where we will cover more details on what can be done to modify your workbook.

Editing a workbook

There will be times when you need to edit a workbook. As you saw in the previous section, you need to edit a workbook created from scratch in order to add what you need to it. You can also edit workbooks created from templates to modify them to suit your needs.

If you are not already viewing your workbook, you will need to view it first. If you are already viewing your workbook, you can skip this next step and move directly to the editing portion.

To edit a workbook, perform the following steps:

1. Go to either of the tabs.
2. Select the workbook in question.
3. Then, select the **View saved workbook** button in the workbook's detail pane.

> **Note**
> You cannot edit a workbook template directly. It must be saved first, and then the saved workbook can be edited. If you have created a workbook from scratch, you must go to the **My workbooks** tab since these workbooks have not been created from a template and only show up there.

At the top of the page will be a header of buttons, shown as follows. The one we care about in this section is the first one on the left, called **Edit**:

Figure 8.13 – Saved workbook header bar

When you click the **Edit** button, the workbook view will change to edit mode, which will look like the following screenshot:

Figure 8.14 – Workbook in edit mode

Each step in the workbook will have its own **Edit** button so that you can make changes to that individual step. More information on the various types of steps can be found in the *Workbook step types* section. Note that all the steps will be displayed, even those that have been set to be hidden when viewing the workbook.

The list of buttons in the edit mode header changes is as follows:

Figure 8.15 – Edit mode header buttons

The following table briefly describes each button:

Icon	Name	Description
Done Editing	Done Editing	This button will change from edit mode to view mode. All the individual edit buttons will disappear.
	Open	Open another dashboard. Refer to the Managing workbooks section for more information.
	Save	Save all the changes made to this workbook.
	Save as	Save this workbook with another name.
	Settings	Allows you to change some of the advanced settings for this workbook, including resources, styles, tags, and trusted hosts. The discussion of these topics is outside the scope of this chapter.
✕	Revert changes	Discard any changes made and revert back to the last saved version.
○	Refresh	Refresh the page. Will recalculate any queries on the page.
	Share	Allows you to share this workbook directly with others. Will open a pane with the URL, which you can copy and send to others. Note that a workbook must belong to the Shared Workbook group before you can share it. If the workbook is not shared, you will be prompted to move it to Shared Workbooks before you can share it.
	Show pin options	This will open the pin options, where you can pin the entire workbook to a dashboard or pin each section that can be pinned to a dashboard.
</>	Advanced editor	Switches the screen to show the JSON or Azure Resource Manager (ARM) code that gets generated automatically. Refer to the Advanced editing section for more information.
☺	Feedback	This allows you to provide feedback to Microsoft about workbooks and works like it does throughout the rest of the Azure portal.
? Help	Help	Opens the Microsoft workbook documentation page in another tab.

If you look at the bottom of the workbook you are editing, you will see a list of links matching the following screenshot. This is how you will add new steps, and each step will be described individually in the *Workbook step types* section:

Add text | Add query | Add metric | Add parameters | Add links/tabs

Figure 8.16 – Edit mode add links

Once you have finished making all your changes, click on the **Done Editing** button in the header bar to revert to the view mode. All the individual edit buttons will disappear, as will any steps, parameters, or columns that have been set to be hidden.

Take a look at your workbook to make sure the edits you just made are working as desired. Once you are satisfied with your changes, click on the **Save** button to save your changes.

Advanced editing

While the workbook's editing **graphical user interface (GUI)** allows to you completely create and edit an Azure Sentinel workbook, there may be times when you need to tweak a setting directly in the code. You may also wish to get the ARM template, which will allow you to easily reproduce this workbook elsewhere or store it as part of your DevOps process.

In either case, clicking on the **Advanced Editor** button will allow you to do that. When you click on the button, you will be taken to the **Gallery Template** view of the advanced editor, as shown in the following screenshot. This view will allow you to directly modify the JSON code. When you are done making the changes, click the **Apply** button to apply your changes, or the **Cancel** button to return to the GUI without saving your changes:

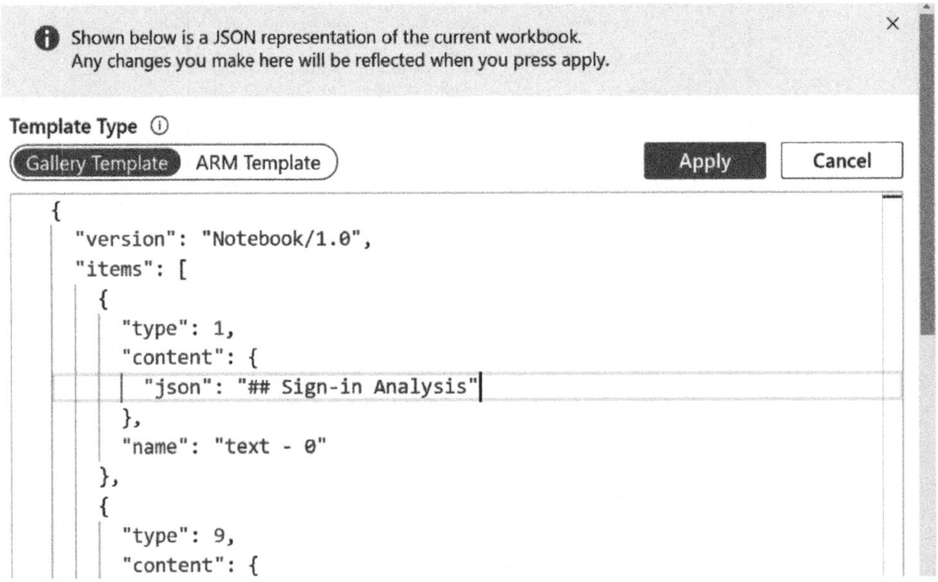

Figure 8.17 – Advanced Editor – Gallery Template view

> **Note**
> Do not modify the JSON code directly unless you are familiar with JSON and what needs to be changed. Any changes made here will apply to the GUI view as well, and if a mistake is made, you could render the workbook unusable.

If you want to see the ARM template that gets generated, click on the **ARM Template** button. This will switch the view to show you the ARM template that can be used to reproduce this. Copy the code and paste it into another file to use it, to recreate your workbook as needed. The **ARM Template** view can be seen in the following screenshot:

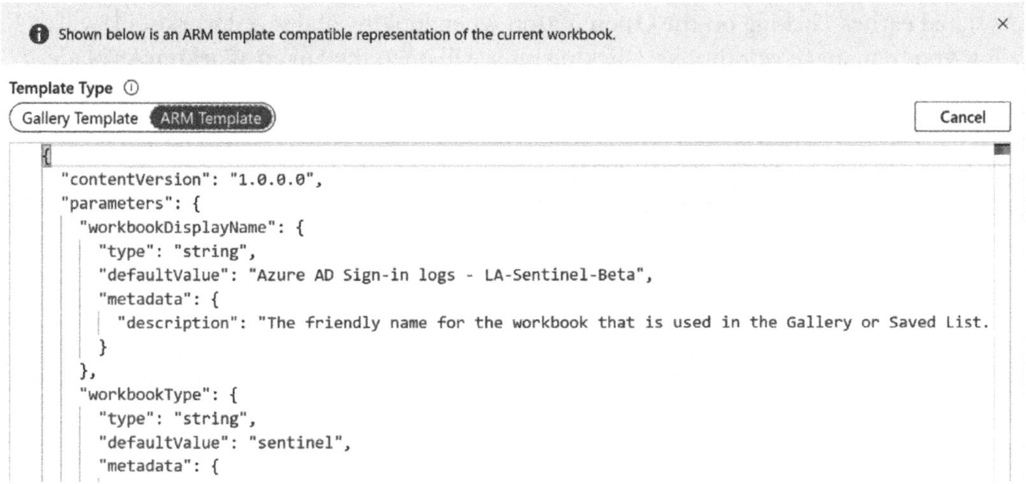

Figure 8.18 – Advanced Editor – ARM Template view

> **Tip**
>
> The discussion of ARM templates and how to use them is beyond the scope of this book. Go to `https://docs.microsoft.com/en-us/azure/templates/` and `https://docs.microsoft.com/en-us/azure/azure-monitor/platform/workbooks-automate` to learn more about them.

When you are done, click the **Cancel** button to return to the GUI view.

You have now seen how to edit a workbook using both the GUI and the advanced view, where you can edit the underlying code directly. You have also learned how to copy the JSON code that can be used in an ARM template to recreate this workbook as needed. Next, we will look at managing your existing workbooks.

Managing workbooks

You have seen how to add a new workbook, and now, you will learn how to manage the ones you have. This will include deleting, moving, and sharing workbooks. As a reminder, go to `https://docs.microsoft.com/en-us/azure/sentinel/roles#roles-and-allowed-actions` to make sure you have the proper rights needed to manage workbooks.

As stated earlier, clicking on the **Open** button when looking at a saved workbook will allow you to manage workbooks. Clicking on it will open the **Saved Workbooks** blade, which will look similar to the following screenshot:

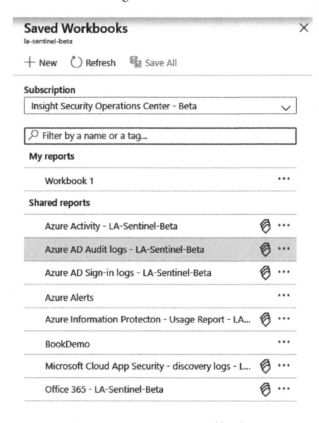

Figure 8.19 – Managing workbooks

At the top of the screen is the **New** button, which will allow you to create a new workbook; the **Refresh** button, which will refresh this view; and the **Save All** button, which will save all the changes made. Under that is the **Subscription** dropdown that will allow you to change the subscription you are looking at, followed by a search box where you can search for specific workbooks.

Below that is a listing of all the workbooks, separated into **My reports**, which only I can see, and **Shared reports**, which everyone can see. Clicking on any of the workbooks will change the workbook that you are viewing.

Each workbook will be shown in a separate row. It will display the name, and then an icon that will show whether the workbook has been created from a template, and then a context-sensitive menu. Clicking on the context-sensitive menu icon will show this menu.

This menu will allow you to delete this workbook, rename it, move it to **Shared reports** (if this workbook is already shared, it will allow you to move it to **My reports**), share it with others (if it is not a **Shared report**, you will be asked to make it a **Shared report** before you can share it), or pin it to a dashboard, which can provide a shortcut to get directly to this workbook. All of this can be seen in the following screenshot:

Figure 8.20 – Managing the workbook context menu

We have finished looking at how to manage your existing workbooks. You have learned about the **Saved Workbooks** pane, as well as the context-sensitive menu that will allow you to perform various management tasks on a workbook. Now, it is time to look at the various parts that make up a workbook, and how to use them.

Workbook step types

Each workbook is comprised of one or more steps. As stated earlier, a workbook is made up of small sections called steps. Each step has a unique name, which can be pretty much anything, and this name can be referenced in other steps. Each step can run on its own, although some may require parameters, either from a parameter step or from other steps.

There are five different types of steps: **text**, **query**, **metric**, **parameters**, and **links/tabs**. Each type of step will be discussed in more detail in the following sections. There will also be a section to discuss the **Advanced Settings** button, as the various step types have the same advanced settings.

To add a new step when editing a workbook, at the bottom of the screen is a list of links matching those shown in the following screenshot. Click on the appropriate link for the type of step you wish to add:

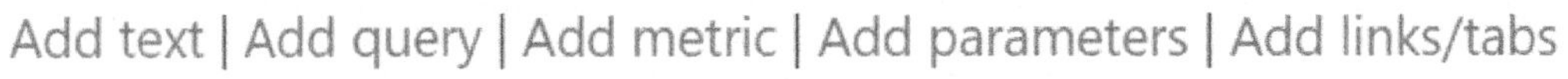

Add text | Add query | Add metric | Add parameters | Add links/tabs

Figure 8.21 – Edit mode add links

No matter which link you click, the list will change to look like the following screenshot:

Figure 8.22 – Edit mode add links after adding a step

Clicking the **Done Editing** button will change the selected step to view mode so that you can see how your changes look.

The **Go to advanced settings** button will take you to the **Advanced Settings** page. This is discussed more in the *Advanced settings* section.

The **Clone this item** button will create a duplicate of the step you are editing. This can be useful if you need to have two steps that are very similar, with only a few changes between them. Rather than having to create the two steps individually, you can create one, click the **Clone this item** button, and then make the necessary changes on the second one.

The **Move Up** button will move this step up one in the listing of steps so that it is displayed higher in the page. If there is a step below the one that you are editing, the **Move Down** button will display to the left of the **Move Up** button. If this step is at the top of the page, the **Move Up** button will no longer show.

The **Delete** button will remove this step. Note that there is *no* verification that you want to perform this step. Clicking on it will automatically remove this step. It pays to save often, just in case you accidently delete a step you didn't intend to, so that you can revert to a saved version.

Now that you know how to add a step, let's discuss each type in detail.

Text

As you may have guessed from the name, clicking the **Add text** link will add a step that displays text using the Markdown language. Clicking the link will add a new step with an empty textbox where you can enter your text, as shown in the following screenshot:

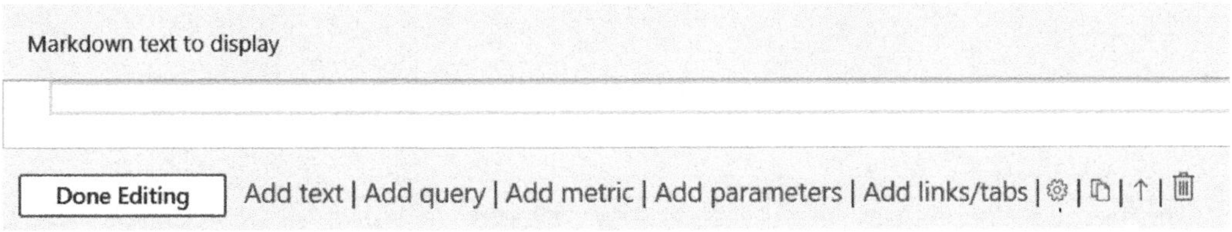

Markdown text to display

Done Editing   Add text | Add query | Add metric | Add parameters | Add links/tabs | ⚙ | ⎘ | ↑ | 🗑

Figure 8.23 –New text step

Enter the text you want, along with any of the Markdown formatting commands, and then click the **Done Editing** button to see your changes with the formatting applied.

The Markdown language is a text-based language that is used in many different systems, most notably GitHub. It was developed to allow people to write plaintext documents that contain the same formatting you would see in HTML documents. To see the various formatting commands, go to `https://www.markdownguide.org/`. Note that not all the Markdown formatting has been tried, so there is no guarantee that all formatting commands will work.

Query

The query step is the mainstay of the workbook. By using KQL queries, you can display data from the logs in various formats, including grids (or tables), area charts, various types of bar charts, line charts, pie charts, scatter charts, time charts, and tiles.

Currently, most of the visualization types are supported, with two of them—graph and map—in preview. Microsoft may make changes from time to time, so please refer to the official workbook docs for up-to-date information. The graph format allows you to show information in a graph view, much like what you see when investigating an incident. Refer to the *Investigating an incident* section in *Chapter 9, Incident Management,* to see what this looks like. The map format will show information in a non-interactive map. This means that you cannot adjust the scale to zoom in or out.

After you click on the **Add query** link, you will see that a new step has been added, which looks as follows:

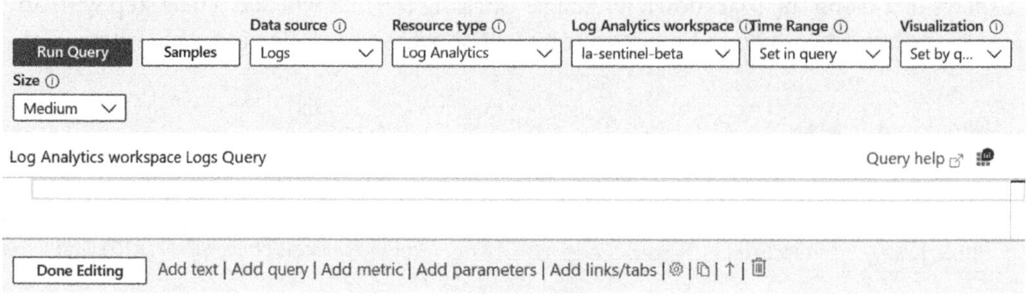

Figure 8.24 – New query step

Let's have a look at the different fields of the header bar:

- The **Run Query** button will run the query that has been added to the query window. In the preceding screenshot, there is no query, so clicking on the button will return an error.

- The **Samples** button will open a new pane and show some sample code. The code for the default query step that is added to a new workbook created from scratch is one of the samples available.

- The **Data source** dropdown will show a list of all the data sources that are available to query. Because of the other Azure technologies that use workbooks, there are more choices than just **Logs** available. However, for this chapter, that is the only data source we are concerned with.

- The **Resource type** dropdown will list what kind of resources can be used in the queries. Much like the **Data source** dropdown, this is used in other Azure resources, although we will only be concerned with using the **Log Analytics** entry.

- The **Log Analytics workspace** dropdown shows a listing of all the available workspaces that are available to use. The majority of the time, you should be using the one that your Azure Sentinel instance is using.

- The **Time Range** dropdown will show the various time ranges you can select, as shown next. If a value is selected here, it will tell your query to only look as far back as the value that has been set, with a few exceptions.

  Most of the entries should be familiar to you already. However, the top one, **Set in query**, and the bottom one, **TimeRange**, need some explanation. You may not see the **TimeRange** value listed, and the reason is explained here.

The **Set in query** value will read the time span directly from the query itself. If you have a query such as Heartbeat| where TimeGenerated < ago(1d), then because the time is set in the code, any value in the dropdown will be ignored. A best practice in cases such as this is to set the dropdown to the **Set in query** value so that anyone needing to edit this step can easily tell that the time span is set in the code.

The **TimeRange** value is added because there is a parameter called **TimeRange** that is set to be a time-range picker. This is explained more in the **Parameters** section. If you do not see this value, then you do not have a time-range picker set up as a parameter.

Remember that **TimeRange** is just the name given to the parameter. It could be called something else in your case. If there is anything listed under the **Time Range Pa...** header (which is a shortened version of **Time Range Parameter**), then that can be used too as the time-range value.

> Tip
> It is a best practice to use a time-range picker parameter in your workbooks as much as possible so that the workbooks can be as flexible as possible.

The **Time Range** dropdown is shown as follows:

Figure 8.25 – Time Range dropdown

- The **Visualization** dropdown determines how the output will be displayed. The values have already been discussed, but another entry that is available is **Set by query**. If this value is selected, then it means that the code itself has determined how to visualize the data using the `render` command.

- The **Size** dropdown is used to determine how much vertical space the step will take up, with the values shown in the following screenshot. Select the value that makes the most sense to you, and notice that the actual amount of space may vary, depending on the type of visualization selected:

Figure 8.26 –Available sizes

There is one more button that can show on the header and that is based on the type of visualization selected, and it is used to change the settings of the visualization. The grid, pie chart, tiles, graph, and map each have their own button that is shown to change the settings for that specific visualization.

The book would be far larger if we were to discuss every individual setting for each of these visualizations, so you will need to play around to see what the different settings do. One we will discuss, since it is very useful and is used to create some of the visual representations discussed in the overview of the **Azure AD Sign-in logs** workbook, is the grid's column renderer.

To see this in action, perform the following steps:

1. Enter `Heartbeat` into the **Log Analytics workspace Logs Query** area.

2. Change the **Time Range** to **Last 24 hours**.

3. The query should run automatically, but if it does not, click on the **Run Query** button to start the query.

4. When the query has finished, select **Grid** from the **Visualization** dropdown.

5. You will see a new button called **Column Settings** shown up in the header. Click it to open the **Settings** pane.

6. Select any column, and then the **Column renderer** dropdown will activate.

7. Click on it to see the listing of choices, including **Automatic**, **Text**, **Right Aligned**, **Date/Time**, and many others.

Most of the available entries will not make sense for an Azure Sentinel workbook, but others are useful. Some of the more useful ones are **Heatmap** and **Spark line**, which were used in the **Azure AD Sign-in logs** workbook, as well as **Text, Date/Time, Thresholds, Timeline, Icon**, and **Link** (which works like the **Link/Tab** step type described in the *Links/tabs* section).

> **Note**
> Depending on which one you select, other choices for settings can show up or disappear.

One other useful entry is **Hidden**. Selecting this will cause the column to not display in the grid. There may be times when you will need to have the column around, but do not want to show it. Set the column's renderer to **Hidden** for this to happen. It's outside the scope of the book to go into more detail on how to use these different renderers, but take a look at the **Azure AD Sign-in logs** workbook to get an idea of how to use the **Heatmap** and **Spark line**.

Beneath the header bar is the **Log Analytics workspace Logs Query** area. This is where you enter your KQL query to be run. On the right side of this screen are three icons, as shown here:

Figure 8.27 – Query step results buttons

The preceding list of buttons is explained as follows:

- The **Query help** icon will open a new tab and will take you to a page discussing how to write KQL queries.

- The icon next to it will open up the **Logs** page, in the same tab, and load the query you have in the **Log Analytics workspace Logs Query** area. This can be useful if you are having issues with your query and need to figure out what the problem is.

- The last icon will only show up once you have run a query. It will allow you to export your results into Excel for further processing.

The area directly under the **Log Analytics workspace Logs Query** area is where your results will show up. They will be displayed according to the value selected in the **Visualization** dropdown. Using the `Heartbeat` query we used earlier, run it, and then change the values in the **Visualization** dropdown to see how this area changes.

Metric

The metric step allows you to view metrics on different Azure resources. This step type is not that useful in regard to Azure Sentinel, so we will not discuss it in this chapter. To get more information on how to use the metric step, refer to `https://docs.microsoft.com/en-us/azure/azure-monitor/app/usage-workbooks#adding-metrics-sections`.

Parameters

As much as the query step is the mainstay of Azure Sentinel workbooks, they would not be as useful without parameters. A workbook that cannot change any of its inputs may just as well be an image rather than an interactive workbook that you can manipulate to query the results in different ways.

There are two types of parameters: those that get set in a parameter step, which we will discuss here, and those that are populated when an item in a query step is selected, which will be discussed in the *Advanced settings* section later in this chapter.

When you click the **Add parameters** link, you will see the following screen:

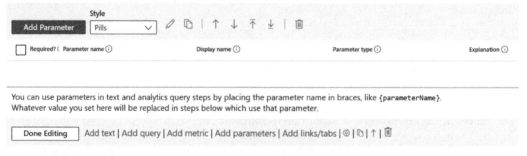

Figure 8.28 – New parameter step

Once you have parameters entered, they will be displayed in a table, one per row, as shown in the following screenshot. You can select a single checkbox to edit all the settings of an individual parameter. You can also change the **Required?**, **Parameter name**, and **Display name** fields directly from this screen. It will show the **Parameter type** and **Explanation** fields, although you cannot edit those fields from this screen. Refer to the *Adding a new parameter* section for an explanation of these fields:

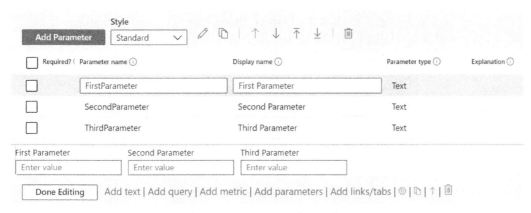

Figure 8.29 – Parameter step with sample parameters

Click on the **Add Parameter** button to add a new parameter. When you do, a new pane will open. This is where you will set up your new parameter. Refer to the *Adding a new parameter* section for more information.

The **Style** dropdown allows you to change how the parameters are displayed. By default, they are displayed as pills, as shown in the following screenshot.

When you click the **Add parameters** link, you will see the following. The parameters are displayed in a single line as much as possible. If they cannot fit on one line, then multiple lines will be used:

Figure 8.30 – Parameter inputs using the pill style

The other option is **Standard**, which will display the parameters as follows, with no border around them:

First Parameter   Second Parameter   Third Parameter

| Enter value | Enter value | Enter value |

Figure 8.31 – Parameter inputs using Standard style

Notice that you do not need to click the **Done Editing** button to see the changes. The parameters will show right above the button. This will be true even if you change the **Parameter name** or **Display name** as well. The header buttons are shown as follows:

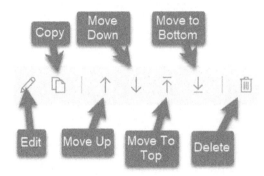

Figure 8.32 – Parameter header buttons

The header buttons are further discussed as follows, from left to right:

- The **Edit** button will allow all the entries to be edited in a single selected row.

- The **Copy** button will create a new copy of the parameter. This will open the same pane as adding a new parameter where the other fields are filled in from the original parameter except for the parameter's name. Fill in those details and click the **Save** button to create the copy.

- The **Move Up** and **Move Down** buttons will allow a parameter to be moved up and down in the list, respectively.

- The **Move to Top** and **Move to Bottom** buttons will move the parameter to the top of the list or the bottom of the list, respectively.

- The **Delete** button will delete the parameter.

Now that you have seen how the parameter step works, let's see how to add new parameters. These parameters will allow your users to have a more interactive experience with your workbooks.

Adding a new parameter

In order to add a new parameter, click the **Add Parameter** button. This will open the **New Parameter** screen with a description of fields, as shown in the following screenshot:

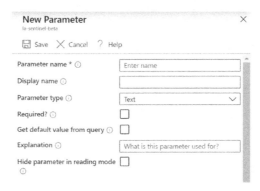

Figure 8.33 – New Parameter screen

The different fields of the **New Parameter** window are described in the following table:

Name	Description
Parameter name	This is the name of the parameter that you will use when you need to reference the parameter. No whitespace is allowed in the name, although underscores are allowed. Make the name descriptive enough to allow other users to know what it is used for.
Display name	This is the name of the parameter that will show on the screen when in reading mode. If this is left empty, the **Parameter name** will be used as the display name.
Parameter type	This will determine how the parameters are populated and what type of input is displayed. These types will be discussed in more detail later.
Required?	Select the checkbox if this is a required parameter.
Get default value from query	If this is selected, then there will be a new section of the screen that will open so that a KQL query can be entered. This works similar to entering a query for a query step, except there are no Visualization or Size dropdowns. The query should return a single row and a single value.
Explanation	Provide a brief explanation of the purpose for this parameter. It will show up as a tooltip when the parameter is selected.
Hide parameter in reading mode	If this is selected, then this variable will not be visible when in reading mode, but can still be used in other queries. This is a way of tricking the workbook itself into accepting parameters. Set up the parameter so it is not visible, and set it to have a default value. Set your KQL query to return the value you would want as the parameter.
Previews	These fields are read-only and will give you an idea of how the parameter will look when in edit and reading modes. It will also show you how to use the variable in your other steps, and what the value will be when the parameter is used.

Let's take a look at the different parameter types.

Parameter types

There are seven different parameter types:

- **Text**
- **Drop down**
- **Time-range picker**
- **Resource picker**
- **Subscription picker**
- **Resource-type picker**
- **Location picker**

Each works differently and can have additional fields show up in the **New Parameter** pane when selected. For instance, the **Text** type is very basic and will show a textbox for input, while the **Drop down** type will show the KQL window so that its values can be populated from a query; there will be a new field asking whether multiple selections can be made.

- **Text**: This is the basic parameter type. It will allow you to enter text—for instance, an email address—that can then be used to filter other queries.

- **Drop down**: The **Drop down** type allows you to enter a KQL query, or a JSON string, to provide the choices for the dropdown. This type will also have five additional fields:

Name	Description
Allow multiple selections	If selected, the user can select more than one entry from the dropdown.
Limit multiple selections	If selected, this will set the upper limit to how many items a user can select from the dropdown. Another field will show where the upper limit number can be entered.
Delimiter	If multiple entries are allowed to be selected, this is the delimiter that will be used to distinguish one entry from another.
Quote with	If multiple entries are allowed to be selected, this is the character that will wrap each entry at the beginning and end of that entry.
Include in the drop down	If the Any one checkbox is selected, then this parameter will not be used to filter.

- **Time Range**: This is probably the most widely used parameter type, and one that you will see on most—if not all—workbooks. It allows you to select how far back in time to look for your information. This type will also show a number of time-range entries—ranging from 5 minutes to 90 days—that can be selected to show as available choices, as well as one that allows users to enter a custom range.

- **Resource Picker**: This type will allow you to choose what types of Azure resources to show, and then the user will be able to choose one or more of them. For instance, it could be set up to allow users to choose from **virtual machines (VMs)**. This type will also have the same five additional fields as the **Drop down** type.

- **Subscription Picker**: This type will allow you to select one or more subscriptions from a list. This list can either be default subscriptions, all subscriptions, a KQL query, or a JSON string. This type will also have the same five additional fields as the **Drop down** type.

- **Resource Type**: This type will allow you choose a resource type from a list. This list can either be Known Resource Types, a KQL query, or a JSON string. This differs from the **Resource Picker** in that this one allows you to pick the type of the resource (that is, VMs, Virtual Networks, Logic Apps, and so on), while the **Resource Picker** selects individual resources from a given type. This type will also have the same five additional fields as the **Drop down** type.

- **Location Picker**: This type will allow you to pick Azure locations such as East US, East US 2, and West US, among many others. This type will also have the same five additional fields as the **Drop down** type.

> **Note**
>
> For those parameter types that have the **Include in the drop down** field, care must be taken in the KQL query that uses that parameter to account for the case where **All** is selected. The following code comes from the **Azure AD Sign-in logs** workbook and uses the `Apps` parameter. It can filter based on the selection, or can look for all apps:
>
> ```
> |where AppDisplayName in ({Apps}) or '*' in
> ({Apps})
> ```
>
> It is the second part, after the `or`, that allows the code to use the **All** entry.

That is all the various parameter types that can be selected. Notice that when you change the parameter type, the **Previews** section will change to show how each type of parameter will look, and this is described next.

Previews section

The second part of the **New Parameter** blade, at the bottom of the screen, shows a preview of how the variable will be displayed and how to use the variable in code. The following screenshot shows a parameter with no values filled in:

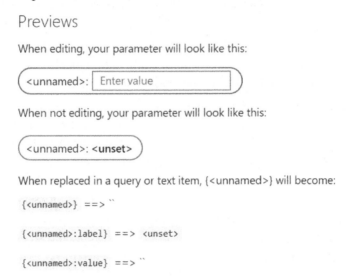

Figure 8.34 – New Parameter screen Previews section

The last part is very important as it shows how to use the variable in code. This is the **Parameter name**, not the **Display name**, surrounded by brackets, { }.

Links/tabs

The links/tabs step will allow you to either display links in different formats or tabs. This allows you to open a new website to show more information, show details about a selected cell, or display different tabs.

When you click on the **Add links/tabs** button, a new step will be added, as follows:

Figure 8.35 – New links/tabs step

This screen will allow you to add, edit, delete, or change the order of the links that you have added. Keep in mind that as far as workbooks are concerned, tabs are links that are displayed differently.

The **Update Links** button will update the links with any modifications that have been made during the edit process. The **Style** dropdown will change how the links will be displayed in a list. The following table shows how the various styles will affect how the links are shown:

Display Name	Sample
Bullet List	• First Link • Second Link • Third Link
List	First Link Second Link Third Link
Paragraph	First Link Second Link Third Link
Navigation	First Link | Second Link | Third Link
Tabs	First Link Second Link Third Link

The rest of the header buttons are as follows:

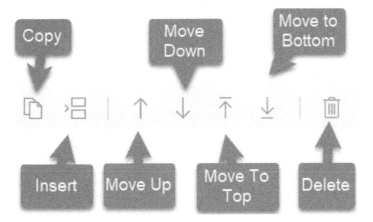

Figure 8.36 – Links/tabs step header buttons

The header buttons are discussed as follows, from left to right:

- The **Copy** button will create a duplicate of the selected link.

- The **Insert** button will insert a blank row above the selected row to allow for a new link to be created.

- The **Move Up** and **Move Down** buttons will allow a link to be moved up and down in the list, respectively.

- The **Move to Top** and **Move to Bottom** buttons will move the link to the top of the list or to the bottom of the list, respectively.

- The **Delete** button will delete the link.

Let's take a look at how to add a new link.

Adding a new link

To add a new link, start entering information in the blank row being shown in the listing. The different fields are described as follows:

- **Text before link**: Information entered into the **Text before link** textbox will be shown before the actual link. This field will not show if the selected **Style** is **Tabs**.

- **Link text**: The **Link text** is the actual text of the URL that will be shown.

- **Text after link**: Information entered into the **Text after link** textbox will be shown after the actual link. This field will not show if the selected **Style** is **Tabs**.

- **Action**: This is the action that will be performed when the link is selected. There are many different entries to choose from, but for this chapter, we will only look at **Url**, **Set a parameter value**, and **Scroll to a step**. Depending on which value you select, there may be a button or textbox showing up on the **Settings** field to provide more information, but a brief description of these fields is given in the following table:

Name	Description
Url	This will allow you to create a URL that you are used to seeing in internet browsers such as Edge and Chrome. You will need to set the URL in the Value field.
Set a parameter value	This allows you to set a parameter's value and is useful when working with Tabs. You will need to set the parameter's name in the Value field and the value for the parameter in the Settings field.
Scroll to a step	This will allow you to scroll directly to a step without the need to scroll manually. This is useful if you want the user to go to a specific step in a workbook without having to hunt for it. You will need to select the step from a dropdown that shows up in the Value field.

- **Value**: As discussed previously, this field changes dynamically depending on which **Action** was selected.

- **Settings**: As discussed previously, this field changes dynamically depending on which **Action** was selected.

- **Context Blade**: This field is only available when certain values in the **Action** field are selected. If enabled, any action that would cause a new blade to show—that is, **Cell Details** and **Generic Details**—will show in a pop-up window rather than a new blade appearing up the left-hand side of the screen.

- **Style**: The style that is in the header of the step deals with how the links are shown in a list. This style determines how an individual link is presented. Only certain values selected in the **Action** field will allow for all the entries in the **Style** field to be selected. For instance, if the **Url** is selected in the **Action** field, then the only available style will be **Link**. However, if **Set a parameter value** is selected, then both the **Button (primary)** and **Button (secondary)** will be shown. The following screenshot shows how the selected value will change how the link is displayed:

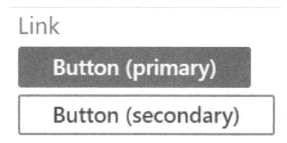

Figure 8.37 – Link formats

Now, let's take a look at how to add a new tab in the following section.

Adding a new tab

When adding a new tab, the **Style** field in the header needs to be set to **Tabs**. The only fields that will be shown are **Tab Name**, **Action**, **Value**, **Settings**, and **Context Blade**. You cannot set any text to show before or after the tab.

> **Note**
>
> There is no reason why you cannot use any of the other styles to do the same thing as the **Tabs** entry. The **Tabs** style is set up to minimize the amount of work needed to create a tab interface, including hiding unneeded fields and changing how the links are displayed to look like a traditional tabbed interface.

The value for the **Action** field for the tab will be **Set a parameter value**, as you will be using this value to either show or hide steps to make the tabs work. Enter the name of the parameter in the **Value** field and the value in the **Settings** field. It is recommended that you use the same parameter for all the tab entries, just changing the value to designate different tabs to show. This will be used along with the **Make this item conditionally visible** option in the advanced settings discussed in the following section.

Advanced settings

All steps have an **Advanced Settings** button in the step's footer that shows when the step is being edited. This will allow you to set items, including the step's name and visibility; if it exports parameters; what information to show when in view mode; as well as the step's width and other style settings. Not all step types will show the same fields, although all fields will be discussed here.

When you click the **Go to Advanced Settings** button, a new window will open up. The screen is broken into two tabs: **Settings** and **Style**. **Settings** is where you set the values that affect how the step will function, and **Style** is where you set the values that affect how the step will look. Let's have a look at them in the following sections.

Settings

This tab is where you set the values that affect how the step will function, including if the step is visible (and when); if the query shows; and if the step can be pinned to a dashboard. The following screenshot was taken from a query step window so it will show all the available fields, with the exception of the metrics step, which has two other fields discussed at the end of this section. Other steps will not have all the same entries:

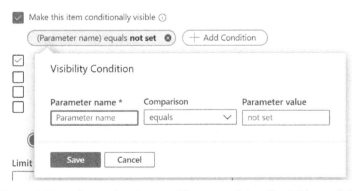

Figure 8.38 – Advanced Settings – Settings tab

The different fields from the **Settings** tab are explained as follows:

- **Step name**: This is where the name of the step is set. It can be any text, and should be descriptive enough so that users can easily tell what the step does. This is especially useful when used in dropdowns in links.

- **Make this item conditionally visible**: This will determine whether the step is always showing or just shows when certain conditions are met. If this is selected, a new button will show under it, called **Add Condition**. Clicking on that will open a new window where you can set the condition, as shown in the following screenshot:

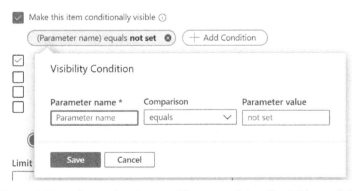

Figure 8.39 – Advanced settings – adding a conditionally visible condition

This is where you set the condition. You need to enter the **Parameter name**, the **Comparison** (equals to or not equals to), and then the **Parameter value**.

This is the field you will use when working with tabs. Each tab will have the **Parameter name** set to a different value, so when that tab is selected, the parameter will have a specific value, and that value will determine which step(s) to show.

You can have multiple conditions, and ALL of them must be met for the step to show.

- **Always show the pin icon on this step**: This will determine whether the pin icon will always show or whether it will follow the workbook's setting on showing the pin. Clicking on the pin icon will allow a user to pin this step to a dashboard so that a shortcut is created to this step.

- **When items are selected, export parameters**: If this is selected, when an item in this step is selected, a parameter will be set to the corresponding value. This allows for functionality such as filtering a listing of users based on status. If this is selected, a new button will show under it, called **Add Parameter**. Clicking on that button will open a new window, where you can set the parameter, as shown in the following screenshot:

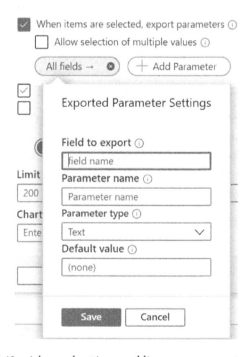

Figure 8.40 – Advanced settings – adding a new parameter to export

The **Field to export** is the name of the field from the query that will be used to populate the parameter's value. The **Parameter name** is the name of the parameter, and the **Parameter type** is the type of the parameter. For this book, we will always use text that includes integer, date/time, and Boolean values.

You can have multiple parameters exported at the same time. Remember to use the parameter in a query, surrounding the **Parameter name** with brackets { }.

- **Show query when not editing**: If this is selected, the KQL query will always show. This is not usually a good idea as it may confuse the casual user.

- **Show open external query button when not editing**: If this is selected, then the open external query button in the header will always show.

- **Show Export to Excel button when not editing**: If this is selected, the **Export to Excel** button will always show. This allows for the results to be exported into Excel for further analysis.

- **Columns to Export**: This will allow you to export only the columns that are shown in reader mode or all the columns, whether they are visible in reader mode or not.

- **Chart title**: This is the text that will appear at the top of a chart as its title.

- **No data message**: This is the text that will display if the query returns no results.

- **Show filter field above grid or tiles**: If this is selected, a search bar will appear above the results if the visualization type is a grid or tiles. Enter text into this field to filter based on that text.

- **Limit grid rows to**: This is how many rows will be displayed in a grid. You want this set to a high enough value that the user can get useful information, but not so high that it takes too long for the grid to display.

- **Show open in Metrics Explorer button when not editing**: This setting is only available when looking at a metric step and will determine whether the **Metrics Explorer** button will always show.

- **Limit resources to**: This setting is only available when looking at a metric step and will limit the number of resources that will be shown at one time. You want this set to a high enough value that the user can get useful information, but not so high that it takes too long for the grid to display.

That is everything you can do using the **Settings** tab. As you can see, each step in a workbook can be customized considerably. Next, we will look at the style changes you can make.

Style

The **Style** tab will allow you to change how the step will look when displayed. Unlike the **Settings** tab, all the fields are present in all the step types, as shown in the following screenshot:

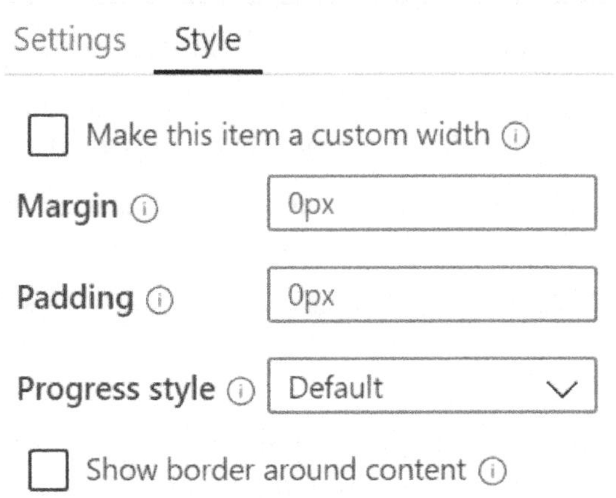

Figure 8.41 – Advanced settings – Style tab

The different fields from the preceding screenshot are explained as follows:

- **Make this item a custom width**: If this item is selected, two new fields show up under it: **Percent width** and **Maximum width**. The **Percent width** is how much of the overall width this step takes. If it is less than 100 and the previous or next step's width is also less than 100, the two steps will show side by side, assuming the sum of the widths is less than or equal to 100. Look at the **Azure AD Sign-in logs** workbook for examples of steps showing side by side. The **Maximum width** determines how wide a step can possibly be. It can either use a specific value, such as 150px, or a percentage.

- **Margin**: This specifies the margin that will show outside of the border of the step. Enter a value followed by a unit, such as px for pixels.

- **Padding**: This specifies the padding that will show inside the border of the step. Enter a value followed by a unit, such as px for pixels.

- **Progress style**: This determines which animated **Graphics Interchange Format (GIF)** file will show when the step is loading. While it is not possible to show the animation in a book, the following screenshot should give you an idea of what the various values will look like:

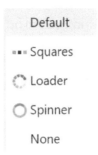

Figure 8.42 – Advanced settings – progress style choices

- **Show border around content**: This determines whether there will be a border shown around this step. Select it to show a border.

That ends our discussion of the step's advanced settings. As you have seen, these settings allow you to perform many actions, including stating when the step is visible, being able to export variables that other steps in the workbook can use, determining how much of the width of the page the step will take up, and more.

Summary

In this chapter, you learned about Azure Sentinel workbooks and how their interactive display is used to show information to users. Workbooks can be used to help determine if there is something in your environment that needs investigation.

You learned how to create and edit a new workbook, using the various step types provided. You learned how to define parameters using a new step, as well as coming from a query, and how to use those parameters to further filter your queries.

They can display a combination of texts, various graphs, metrics, and links including tabs. Using parameters, the workbooks can be made to change what information is presented, to help determine whether there is an incident that needs to be investigated.

Finally, you learned how to change the advanced settings on a step to change how it operates and how it looks. You learned how to get multiple steps to show up on the same row in a graph, and how one graph can communicate with another through parameters.

In the next chapter, you will learn about Azure Sentinel Incidents, which are generated from alerts and other queries, how to manage them, and how to investigate them.

Questions

1. What are the two ways to create a new workbook?

2. If I wanted to show the user instructions on how to use the workbook, what would be the best step type to use?

3. If I want to allow a user of the workbook to be able to change how far back in time every query in the workbook looks, which two actions would I need to take? Hint: The second action would need to be performed on every query step.

4. Is it possible to have a workbook step only show up when certain conditions are met?

5. How can I have two steps in the same workbook show side by side?

Further reading

For more information, you can refer to the following links:

- Azure Monitor Workbooks: https://docs.microsoft.com/en-us/azure/azure-monitor/platform/workbooks-overview

- Create interactive reports with Azure Monitor workbooks: https://docs.microsoft.com/en-us/azure/azure-monitor/app/usage-workbooks

- Azure Monitor workbook visualizations: https://docs.microsoft.com/en-us/azure/azure-monitor/platform/workbooks-visualizations

- Application Insights workbooks (GitHub repository of sample workbooks): https://github.com/Microsoft/Application-Insights-Workbooks

- Adding text and Markdown sections: https://docs.microsoft.com/en-us/azure/azure-monitor/app/usage-workbooks#adding-text-and-markdown-sections

9
Incident Management

In *Chapter 7, Creating Analytic Rules*, you learned that the rules in analytics create incidents. These incidents can represent potential issues with your environment and need to be looked at to determine whether they are indeed an issue. Are they false positives, irrelevant to your environment, or actual issues? The way to determine this is through incident management.

There are no hard-and-fast rules for incident management other than to look at the incidents and determine whether they are actual issues. There are various ways to do this and this chapter will look at the options Azure Sentinel provides to perform these investigations, including a graphical representation of the incident, viewing the full details of the incident, and running other queries to obtain more information.

In this chapter, we will cover the following topics:

- Using the Azure Sentinel Incidents page
- Exploring the full details page
- Investigating an incident

Using the Azure Sentinel Incidents page

To look at the Azure Sentinel Incidents page, click on the **Incidents** link in the left-hand navigation panel. This will take you to the Incidents page, which will look similar to what is shown in the following screenshot. The actual numbers and incidents listed may be different, of course:

Figure 9.1 – Azure Sentinel Incidents page

The page has been broken up into the header bar, the summary bar, the search and filtering section, the incidents listing, and the incident details pane. Each of these sections is described in more detail next.

The header bar

The header bar, shown in the following screenshot, at the top of the page has the usual **Refresh** button and timespan drop-down option. However, there is also another button called **Actions**:

Figure 9.2 – Incidents page's header bar

The **Actions** button will allow you to perform actions against multiple incidents at once, including changing the severity, assigning an owner, changing the status, and adding tags. See the *Using the Actions button* section for more information.

The summary bar

Under the header bar is the summary bar, shown in the following screenshot. This shows the total number of open incidents, the number of new incidents, and the number of incidents that are in progress:

Figure 9.3 – Incident page's summary bar

On the right side of the summary bar is a listing of the open incidents broken down by severity. By looking at the two different summaries of the incidents, you can get an idea of how your incidents are broken down.

The search and filtering section

Below the summary bar is the search and filtering section. This is where you can filter what results you see in the listing of all the incidents:

Figure 9.4 – Incident page's filtering section

Let's take a look at all the parameters under the search and filtering section:

- **Search by id or title**: This filter allows you to enter a search term to find specific incidents. This can either be text found in the title of the incident(s) or the incident ID number.

> **Note**
> If you search by ID number, the value entered must be an exact match to an incident's ID number.

You can also filter by the various fields that make up the incident display discussed next. As you can see, you can filter by **SEVERITY**, **STATUS**, **PRODUCT NAME** (which product generated the incident), and/or the **OWNER** (which is the person that is assigned to the incident).

- **SEVERITY**: This filter allows you to select one or more of **Select All**, **Informational**, **Low**, **Medium**, **High**, and/or **Critical**. By default, **Select All** is selected, which appears as just **All** in the summary bar, as shown in the preceding screenshot.

- **STATUS**: This filter allows you to select one or more of **Select All**, **New**, **In-Progress**, or **Closed**. By default, only the **New** and **In Progress** values are selected.

- **PRODUCT NAME**: This filter allows you to select one or more of **Select All**, **Microsoft Cloud App Security**, **Azure Security Center**, **Azure Advanced Threat Protection**, **Azure Active Directory Identity Protection**, **Azure Information Protection**, **Microsoft Defender Advanced Threat Protection**, and/or **Azure Sentinel**. By default, **Select All** is selected, which appears as just **All** in the summary bar, as shown in the preceding screenshot.

> **Additional products**
>
> As Microsoft adds more security-related products to Azure and the ability to create alert rules based on those products are added to Azure Sentinel, it is expected that this list will expand to include them.

- **OWNER**: This filter allows you to select one or more people to filter. Since anyone could be an owner of an incident, the actual list is too long and the values will not be listed here. Note that there are some special entries, including **All Users** and **Assigned to me**. **All Users** will show the incidents assigned to anyone, including those that are unassigned. **Assigned to me** will just show those incidents that are assigned to the user currently logged in.

> **Select All / All Users**
>
> The **Select All / All Users** entry in the filters section is a shortcut that allows you to select all the entries in the listing rather than having to select each one individually. By deselecting it, all the individual entries will be deselected as well, and each one can then be selected individually.

The search and filtering section is very useful for finding a specific incident. You can make use of these features to help you quickly locate incidents when there is a long list, especially if you just need to view those incidents to which you are assigned. Next, we will discuss what you do when you've found the incident you want.

Incident listing

Below the search and filtering section is the list of each incident, one per row, shown in the following screenshot. Here you can see a summary of the incident, including the incident ID, title, the number of alerts that make up the incident, the product names that created the incident, the date and time of creation, the owner, and the status:

	Incident id		Title		Alerts	Product names	Created time		Last update time	Owner
☐	1554		Account Deleted		1	Azure Sentinel	02/21/20, 10:37 AM		02/21/20, 10:37 AM	Unassigned
☐	1553		Mass Download		1	Azure Sentinel	02/21/20, 10:37 AM		02/21/20, 10:37 AM	Unassigned
☐	1552		Account Elevated		1	Azure Sentinel	02/21/20, 10:36 AM		02/21/20, 10:36 AM	Unassigned

☐ Select All   Showing 7 items

Figure 9.5 – Incident listing

On the far left is a checkbox. This checkbox is used to state that you want to perform an action on this incident. Refer to the *Using the Actions button* section for more information. You can also check the **Select All** checkbox at the top of this section to select all the incidents at once.

After that is a colored strip. The colored strip indicates the incident's severity: red for high, orange for medium, yellow for low, and gray for informational.

The remaining fields are described in the following table:

Name	Description
Incident id	This is the ID number of the incident that is publicly shown.
Title	The title of the incident. This will match the name of the alert rule that generated it.
Alerts	The number of alerts that created this incident.
Product names	The name of the product that generated this incident.
Created time	The time this incident was created.
Last update time	The time this incident was last updated.
Owner	The name of the person that owns the incident.
Status	The status of the incident.

You can sort by the **Incident id**, **Title**, **Created time**, **Last update time**, and **Status** fields. Clicking on any of these fields will sort the listings in ascending order. Clicking again will change the sort to descending order.

Each incident has its own row in the listing with its own properties, as we have just seen. You can use most of these properties to sort the rows to help you find the incident you want. Next, we will look at the incident details pane, which will provide even more information about the selected incident.

Incident details pane

When you select any incident from the list, the incident details pane will open, which shows more information about the selected incident. Of course, the information will be different depending on which incident you select:

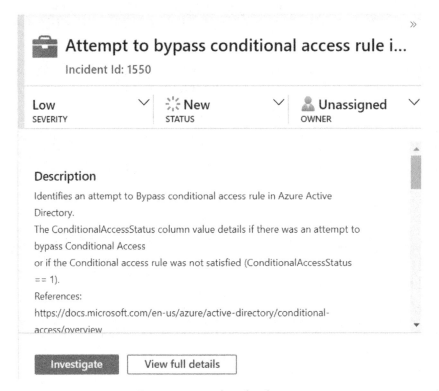

Figure 9.6 – Incident details page

At the top of the page is the title and the incident number appears directly beneath it. To the left of the title is a colored strip indicating the severity of the incident: red for high, orange for medium, yellow for low, and gray for informational.

Under that is the **SEVERITY** of the incident. This indicates how big of an issue this incident is and is defaulted from the analytic rule used to create this incident. You can change this value by using the drop-down list to select the new **SEVERITY** and then clicking on the **Apply** button to change the value, as shown in the following screenshot:

Figure 9.7 – Severity options

To the right of **SEVERITY** is **STATUS**. This indicates whether the incident is new, is being worked on, or is closed. Again, you can change the value by using the drop-down list to select the new status and then click the **Apply** button to change the value. Note that if you select **Closed** status, a new pop-up window will appear asking you to select the reason, either **True Positive** or **False Positive**, and add a comment. You will then have to click **Apply** again for the new status to take effect:

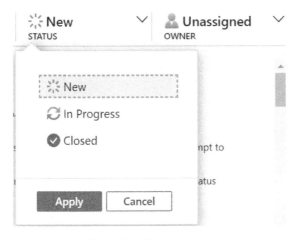

Figure 9.8 – Status options

On the far right is the owner of the incident. This is the person assigned to handle the investigation of the incident. Click the drop-down option to be presented with a list of possible owners, including an entry called **Assign to me**, which will assign the incident to the currently logged-in user, and **Unassign Incident**, which will remove the current owner of the incident. Click **Apply** once the owner has been selected to assign the incident to that user. Note that there can only be one owner for an incident, but it does not stop others from working on the incident:

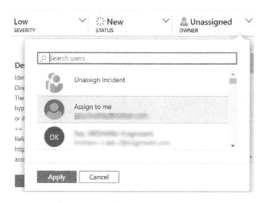

Figure 9.9 – Owner options

Under those dropdowns are descriptions of the incidents. This provides more details about an incident and can include items such as what the incident is looking for, how it was determined, and even external links to get more information.

Scrolling down on the details pane, we find **Incident link**, **Tags**, and **Last update time**, as shown in the following screenshot:

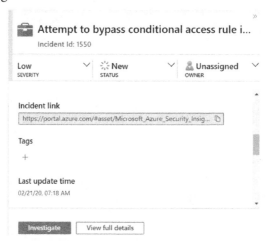

Figure 9.10 – Incident details page continued

The fields from the preceding screenshot are as follows:

- The **Incident link** provides a URL that you can provide to others that will take them directly to the incident's full details page, described in the *Full details page* section. This makes it easier to get to an incident as the person will not need to traverse the Azure portal's menus and then search for this incident.

- Under that are any tags that have been assigned to the incident. Tags are name/value pairs that enable you to categorize resources. Assigning a tag does not change the incident in any way; it just provides a way to filter incidents. Click the + button to add a new tag.

- Under **Tags** is **Last update time,** which tells you the last time the incident had any changes, including adding or removing a tag.

Scrolling down again, we find **Creation time**, **Close reason**, and **Evidence**, as shown in the following screenshot:

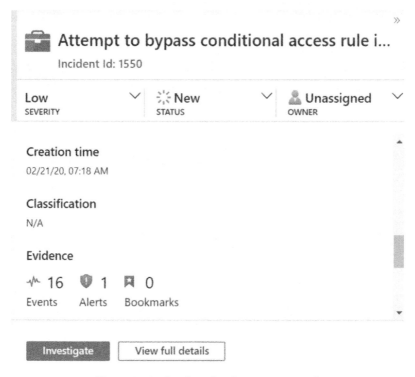

Figure 9.11 – Incident details page continued

The fields from the preceding screenshot are as follows:

- **Creation time** shows when the incident was created.

- **Close reason** will show the reason, either **True Positive** or **False Positive**, that was added if the incident was closed.

- **Evidence** shows the number of events that were found in the analytic rule that generated the alert. It is the total number of events from all the alerts that generated this incident, which is the number in the middle, and the number of bookmarks associated with the incident. Bookmarks will be described in the *The Bookmarks tab* section.

Scrolling to the bottom of the details pane, we find the **Entities** and **Last comment** fields as follows:

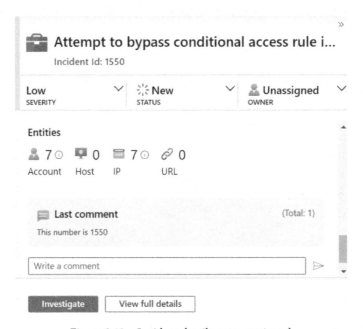

Figure 9.12 – Incident details page continued

The preceding fields are as follows:

- **Entities** are used by Azure Sentinel when investigating an incident. At the time of writing, there are four different entities that may have a value, as listed in the following table. Depending on how the incident was created, each of the entities can have zero, one, or more associated values. There needs to be at least one of these entities with a value for the **Investigate** button to be active. Investigation will be discussed in the *Investigating an incident* section. The entities are as follows:

Name	Description
Account	This is the user's account associated with the incident.
Host	This is the host that was found by the query.
IP	The IP address of the machine that performed the action that caused the incident to be created.
URL	The URL of the action that caused the incident to be created.

- At the bottom of the page will be the last comment that been added to the incident. To the right of **Last comment** is the total number of comments associated with this incident. Clicking on this number will take you to the **Comments** tab in the **View Full Details** page, described in more detail in *The Comments tab* section. To add a new comment, enter the text in the **Write a comment** text box and click on the submit button on the right. It will look like an arrow pointing to the right.

The **Investigate** button will open the investigation page, which will be discussed in the *Investigating an incident* section. The **View full details** button will open the full details page, which will be discussed in the *Exploring the full details page* section.

Now that you have seen how to look at and update a single incident, let's take a look at how you can update multiple incidents at once. This is done by using the **Actions** button in the page's header.

Using the Actions button

You have just learned how to change a single incident. What if you need to change more than one at a time? The **Actions** button from the header bar will allow you to do that.

The **Actions** button will allow you to make changes to multiple incidents at once. Looking back at the header in figure 9.2, you will see the **Actions** button. This button will allow you to perform the same action on multiple selected incidents.

First, in the listing of all the incidents, select the checkbox to the left of the incidents on which you want to perform the action. You can also select the checkbox called **Select All** to select all the incidents shown in the list.

After selecting the incidents that you want to handle, click on the **Actions** button and the **Actions** pane will open on the right, as the following screenshot shows:

Figure 9.13 – Incident actions

Make any changes to **Severity, Owner, Status,** or **Tags** that you wish and then click **Apply**. Refer to the *Incident details pane* section for a refresher on any of the fields.

Now you know how to change some of the settings, not only for a single incident but also for multiple incidents. This will help you keep your incidents up to date. Next, we will look at the full details page, which will show us even more information regarding an incident.

Exploring the full details page

The full details page shows you a lot more information about the incident than you would see in just the incident listings and the incident details pane. Some additional information includes details on the alert(s) that make up the incident, any bookmarks associated with this incident, details on any entities that are part of this entity, and any comments added to this incident.

Clicking on the **View full details** button in the incident details pane will take you to the incident's full details page, as shown in the following screenshot:

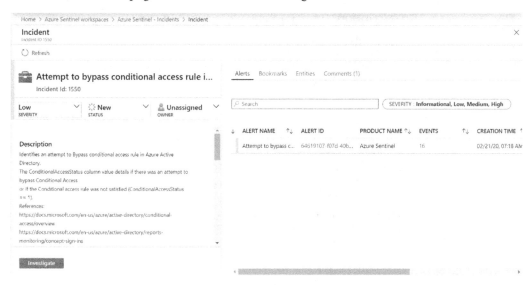

Figure 9.14 – Incident full details page

The left side of the page will show the same information as we saw in the *Incident details pane* section. As a matter of fact, the left side of the page is the same as the incident details pane. The right side of the page is broken up into tabs that show information about the alert itself, any bookmarks for this incident, the entities for this incident, and a list of all the comments. Each tab is described in further detail in the following sections.

The Alerts tab

This tab will show the one or more alert(s) that make up this incident. The following screenshot shows what it looks like, with a description of the fields following:

Figure 9.15 – Incident alert tab

First is a colored strip. The colored strip indicates the alert's severity: red for high, orange for medium, yellow for low, and gray for informational.

The rest of the fields are described in the following table:

Name	Description
ALERT NAME	The name of the alert that generated this incident.
ALERT ID	The internal ID of the alert. Clicking on it will take you to the Logs page, where a query will automatically be generated and run and show you more information regarding this alert.
PRODUCT NAME	The name of the product that was used in the alert rules to generate this incident.
EVENTS	The number of events that the analytic rule found when generating this alert. Clicking on the number will take you to the Logs page where a query will automatically be generated and run and show you more information on the events.
CREATION TIME	The creation time of the alert that generated this incident.
TIME FRAME	This will show the beginning and end dates that the alert looked at when generating this incident.
NUMBER OF ENTITIES	The number of entities from this alert. Look at the The Entities tab section for more information on entities.

At the far right of this screen is the **View playbooks** link. Clicking on it will open a new pane showing all the playbooks:

Figure 9.16 – Incident alert playbooks

You can click the **Run** button in each playbook's row to run the playbook against the alert's information, even if this was not the playbook associated with the analytic rule. Refer to *Chapter 11, Creating Playbooks and Logic Apps*, for more information on playbooks.

The Bookmarks tab

Clicking on the **Bookmarks** tab will show you all the bookmarks associated with this incident, as shown in the following screenshot. For more information on creating bookmarks, look at *Chapter 10, Threat Hunting in Azure Sentinel:*

Alerts	Bookmarks	Entities	Comments (1)

☐ Search

☐	Create Time ↕	Name	Created By ↑↓	Tags	↑↓
☐	02/14/20, 02:29 PM	Rare Audit activity initiated by ...	gary.bushey@nsitsec...		•••
☐	02/05/20, 03:17 PM	Rare Audit activity initiated by ...	gary.bushey@nsitsec...		•••
☐	01/27/20, 08:55 AM	Rare Audit activity initiated by ...	gary.bushey@nsitsec...		•••

Figure 9.17 – Incident Bookmarks tab

You can use the **Search** textbox to search for a specific bookmark.

For each bookmark, the **Create Time**, **Name**, **Created By**, and **Tags** fields will be displayed. At the far-right side of each listing is a context-sensitive menu where the only option is **Remove from incident**.

Clicking on the context-sensitive menu will automatically select the bookmark, and clicking on the **Remove from incident** entry will prompt you to confirm that you meant to remove the bookmark. Selecting **Yes** will remove the bookmark from this incident. Note that if you have selected multiple bookmarks, the entry will change to say **Remove X bookmarks from incident**, where **X** is the number of selected incidents.

The Entities tab

This tab will show all the entities associated with this incident as shown in the following screenshot. There will be one row for each of the entities associated with the incident:

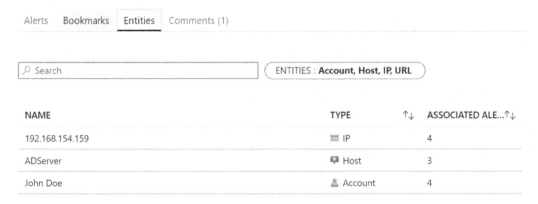

Figure 9.18 – Incident Entities tab

You can use the **Search** textbox to search for specific entities.

The **ENTITIES** filter allows you to select one or more of **Select All**, **Account**, **Host**, **IP**, and/or **URL**. By default, **Select All** is selected.

Each entity will be listed on a separate row. The name of the entity (which is also its value), the type, and the associated alerts will be shown. **ASSOCIATED ALERTS** tells you the number of other alerts that have been raised that contain the same entity. This information will be used in the *Investigating an incident* section.

The Comments tab

This tab will show all the comments associated with the incident. Note that the link will also show the total number of comments—in this case, **1**. You can also use this page to add new comments if desired:

Figure 9.19 – Incident Comments tab

Adding comments while performing your investigation will help you remember what you were doing. They will also help others that may need to come in later and either look at the same incident or investigate one that is similar. Next, we will look at how to go about investigating an incident.

Investigating an incident

Remember in *Chapter 7, Creating Analytic Rules*, you learned that the rules in analytics create incidents. Incidents are not worth anything if they just sit there without being investigated; after all, that is the reason they were created. An investigation is used to determine whether the incident is actually an issue. For example, an incident describing failed logons could be as simple as someone forgetting their password, or it could be someone trying to crack a password. You will not know which until an investigation is performed.

Now that you know how to look at an incident and retrieve all the information regarding it, it is time to see how to investigate an incident. The main way this is done in Azure Sentinel is via the graphical investigation page. This is a graphical interface that not only shows you the incident in question but can also be used to find related information.

When you are looking at an incident's details, at the bottom of the screen is the **Investigate** button. You click this to start the graphical investigation. If this button is grayed out, that means there are no entities associated with this incident. There needs to be at least one entity for the graphical investigation to work.

Clicking on the button will take you to a page that looks something like the following. Depending on the entities associated with your incident, the actual information presented will likely look different, but the functionality will be the same:

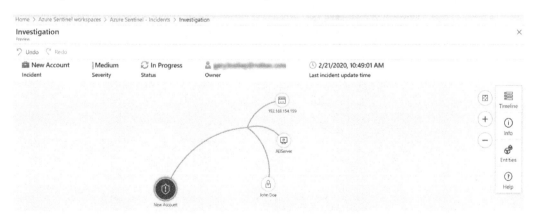

Figure 9.20 – Incident investigation screen

The header bar gives you general information regarding the incident including title, severity, status, owner, and last update time.

On the right side of the screen are two columns of buttons. The column on the left contains the screen control buttons. The top button will fit your diagram to the screen. This is useful if you zoom in or out too far. Under that is the zoom-in button, and at the bottom is the zoom-out button. You can also use your mouse's middle button to perform zooming if you have one. On the far right of the page are the buttons related to the incident itself, and each is described in more detail in the following sections.

This is an interactive user interface, so you can move the various objects shown on the screen around as needed, as well as the entire image. This can make it easier to see the part you are interested in when you zoom in.

While being able to see the incident graphically is nice, the real benefit comes when you look at the related alerts to get a bigger picture of the incident.

Showing related alerts

If you hover your mouse over an entity, this will show a pop-up window with more options, as shown in the following screenshot. This will vary a bit depending on the type of entity you have selected, but they will all show the **Related alerts** action:

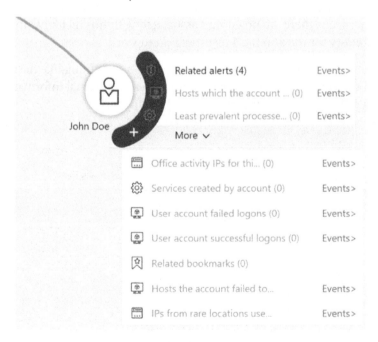

Figure 9.21 – Related alerts

Selecting this will bring up all the alerts related to that entity. In the following screenshot, the related alerts for the user entity are shown:

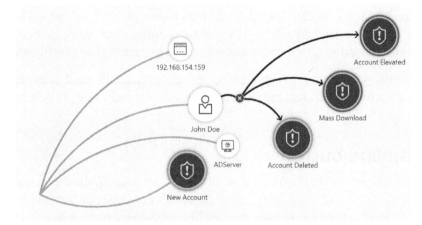

Figure 9.22 – Alerts related to the selected user entity

This will help you determine what else has occurred that is related to this entity. By seeing what other alerts are related to this user, in this example, you can see what else they have done. We can see that the user entity is also an entity in an **Account Elevated**, a **Mass Download**, and an **Account Deleted** incident.

Although it is called **Related entities,** since you are looking at an alert rather than an entity, you can perform the action that we just discussed. In the following screenshot, **Mass Download** was expanded. This has brought in a new host entity, **HRServer**, and the connections made:

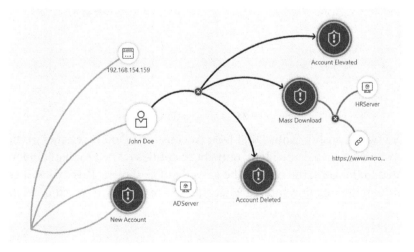

Figure 9.23 – Investigating user activities

The other actions available when you mouse over an entity, called **exploration queries**, will work similarly to how the related alerts action works. Looking back at Figure 9.21, you can see that there are entries called **Services created by this account**, user account failed logons, and more. In this case, all the entries have a **(0)** after the name, indicating that the query did not find any results. If any of these entries had one or more results, it would be worth selecting it to see what the results are as part of your investigation.

Now that we know how to look at an incident, its related incidents, and its exploration queries, let's discuss the incident buttons located on the far-right side of the screen in detail.

The Timeline button

The **Timeline** button shows the timeline of all the incidents being shown on the screen. If this incident was just opened, then there will probably only be one incident shown, but if you show a lot of related alerts, then the timeline will show a history of when the alerts occurred, as shown in the following screenshot:

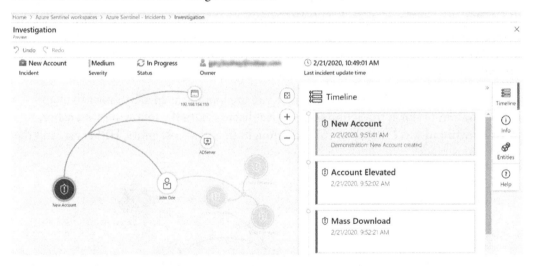

Figure 9.24 – Investigation timeline

In the preceding screenshot, notice that **New Account** incident is selected in the **Timeline** list. When you select a single incident, only those entities related to that incident will be highlighted in the view; the rest will be grayed out as shown. This makes it easy to progress through the timeline and see what entities are related to which incidents.

The Info button

The **Info** button will show information on whichever entity you have selected. For the IP, host, and account, this will show either **ADDRESS**, **HOSTNAME**, or **ACCOUNTNAME** depending on which type you have selected, and, no matter which type you selected, the **FRIENDLYNAME** of the selected entity as follows:

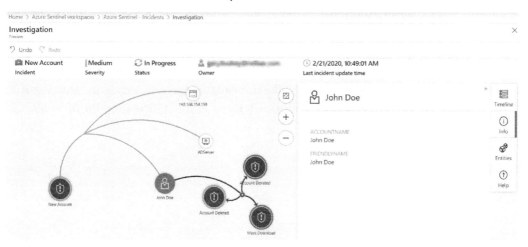

Figure 9.25 – Entity information

However, when you select a URL, what is shown in the pane will look very different from when you select any other entity. Azure Sentinel will perform URL detonation on all URL entity types. This means it will check the URL against a list of known bad addresses and will go out and grab a screenshot of the website at the time the alert fired.

The following screenshot shows what this may look like:

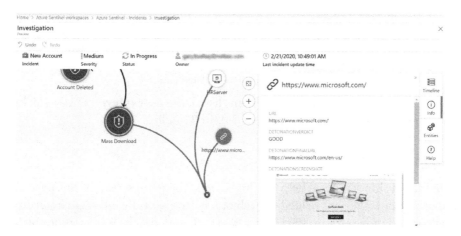

Figure 9.26 – URL investigation

URL is the URL entity from the incident. **DETONATIONVERDICT** is either **BAD** if the URL is deemed to be a bad site (for instance, one known to push malware), or otherwise **GOOD**. **DETONATIONFINALURL** is the final destination after all the URL redirects occur. **DETONATIONSCREENSHOT** is a screenshot of the site at the time the alert was fired. You can click on that image to see a larger view.

The Entities button

The **Entities** button will show a list of all the **Entities**, **Alerts**, and **Bookmarks** related to all the information being shown on the screen. If you are just starting to investigate this incident, then this will most likely just be the information for your incident. However, if you are looking at a lot of related alerts, this will show all the information for those alerts as well:

Figure 9.27 – List of related entities

If you hover your mouse over any of the items listed, the **user interface** (**UI**) will highlight the entities related to the item, much like it did for **Timeline**.

The Help button

The **Help** button shows general help for this screen. The main screen of this page shows the entities and how they are related to each other. This is a fully interactive screen, meaning you can move around the objects to get a better view as well as zooming in and out.

That was an introduction to how to start performing an investigation into an incident in Azure Sentinel. There is much more to performing investigations and the links in the *Further reading* section should help.

Summary

In this chapter, you learned about the Azure Sentinel Incidents page and its various components. You learned how to view an incident and change its values, including who owns that incident, its severity, and how to close an incident.

You also learned how to view more details about the incident along with the alert(s) that generated it, any bookmarks associated with it, the entities that incident contains, and all the comments added to it.

Finally, you learned about Azure Sentinel's graphical incident investigation feature. This allows you to not only view the incident in question but also the related alerts, the timeline of those alerts, and more information about the entities.

In the next chapter, you will learn about hunting for issues that alerts and incidents may not have found.

Questions

1. If I only want to see a listing of incidents that are in progress, what should I do?

2. Looking at an incident in the details pane, in what two ways can I tell what the incident's severity is?

3. I am looking at an incident in the incident details pane and the **Investigate** button is grayed out. What does that indicate?

4. If I want to get the full details of the first alert that generated an incident, what should I do?

5. How can I tell whether the URL in my URL entity is malicious?

Further reading

You can refer to the following links for more information on topics covered in this chapter:

- Use tags to organize your Azure resources: https://docs.microsoft. com/en-us/azure/azure-resource-manager/management/ tag-resources

- Keep track of data during hunting with Azure Sentinel: https://docs. microsoft.com/en-us/azure/sentinel/bookmarks

- Five steps of Incident Response: https://digitalguardian.com/blog/ five-steps-incident-response

- SANS Incident Response Policy template: https://www.sans.org/ security-resources/policies/general/doc/security-response- plan-policy

- SANS Sample Incident Handling Forms: https://www.sans.org/score/ incident-forms

- NIST Incident Response Guide: https://nvlpubs.nist.gov/nistpubs/ SpecialPublications/NIST.SP.800-61r2.pdf

10
Threat Hunting in Azure Sentinel

Threat hunting is part science, part art, and part intuition. Usually, you are looking for something that may have happened in your environment. It may be that you think something has happened due to external events, such as something odd showing up in the workbooks, a notice from a threat intelligence feed, or even something you just read about on the internet, and you want to investigate. No matter why you are performing your hunt, the tools in Azure Sentinel, including queries and Jupyter Notebooks, remain the same.

Threat hunting is a series of activities that you will perform during your investigation. While there is no set guidance on how to perform threat hunting, this chapter will introduce you to the tools that are available in Azure Sentinel to help you perform your investigations.

A brief introduction on how to perform threat-hunting activities will also be discussed, which will include aspects such as how to determine where to look for information. The cyclic process of threat hunting will be introduced as well.

In this chapter, we will cover the following topics:

- Introducing the Azure Sentinel Hunting page
- Working with Azure Sentinel Hunting queries
- Working with Livestream
- Working with bookmarks
- Using Azure Sentinel Notebooks
- Performing a hunt

Introducing the Azure Sentinel Hunting page

To access the **Azure Sentinel - Hunting** page, select the **Hunting** link in the Azure Sentinel navigation menu. This will show the **Azure Sentinel - Hunting** page, which will look like the following screenshot:

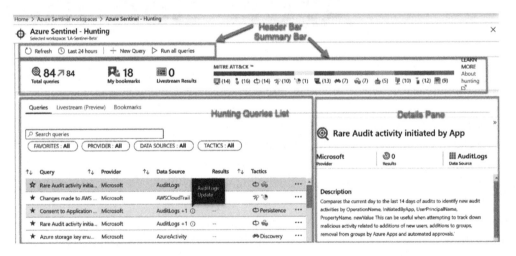

Figure 10.1 – Hunting page overview

Each of these sections will be described in more detail in the following sections.

The header bar

The header bar, at the top of the page, has the usual **Refresh** and timespan dropdown. There is also a **New Query** button that will allow you to create a new query (refer to the *Adding a new query* section for more information). The header bar can be seen in the following screenshot:

○ Refresh   ○ Last 24 hours | + New Query   ▷ Run all queries

Figure 10.2 – Hunting page's header bar

Finally, we have the **Run all queries** button. This button will run all the hunting queries in the background and will then update the hunting query list section with the number of results found. This is easier than running each query one after another, and should usually be one of the first actions you perform when accessing this page.

The summary bar

The summary bar shows the total number of queries that are available to run, the total number of bookmarks that you have (refer to the *Working with bookmarks* section for more information), the number of results from running Livestream queries (refer to the *Working with Livestream* section for more information), and then, how the queries are broken down based on their MITRE ATT&CK™ tactics, as shown in the following screenshot:

Figure 10.3 – Hunting page's summary bar

> **Note**
>
> You can visit `https://attack.mitre.org/tactics/enterprise/` to learn more about MITRE ATT&CK® tactics.

Clicking on any of the icons in the MITRE ATT&CK® breakdown will show you only those queries that have that specific attack type associated with it. So, if you click on the **Initial Access** icon (the first icon that looks like a monitor), it will only show those hunting queries that have **Initial Access** as one of their entries in the **Tactics** field.

The summary bar gives you a good overview of how your hunting queries are broken down. This can make it easier to find those queries that you need in your investigations.

The hunting queries list

Below the header is a listing of all the hunting queries. At the top of the listing is the search and filtering section. This works like other pages' search and filtering sections, so it will not be described in detail here. Refer to the *Search and filtering* section in *Chapter 9, Incident Management,* for a refresher on how this works.

Each row will show a star icon that shows whether it is a favorite. If it is a favorite query, the star will be selected; otherwise, it is not. Another benefit of making a query a favorite is that each time you go the **Hunting** page, the favorite queries will automatically run.

Each row will also list the name of the query, where it came from, the first data source that is required (note that in the following screenshot, the more information icon was shown with the mouse placed on it to display what the tooltip would look like if there are multiple data sources required), the number of results found for the query, and then, any of the MITRE ATT&CK® tactics selected for this query, as follows:

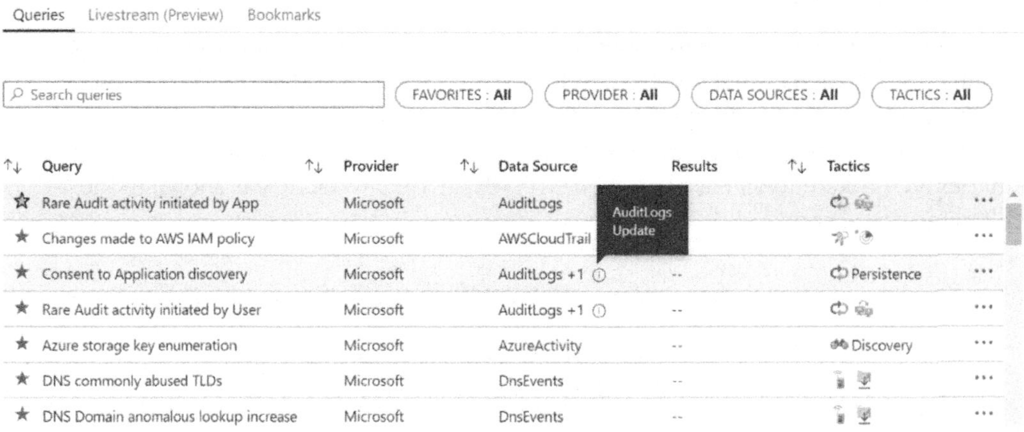

Figure 10.4 – Hunting queries list

At the very end, on the right-hand side, is the context-sensitive menu where you can run the query, add/remove the query to your **FAVORITES** list, edit the query (if you created it), clone the query (so that you can edit it), and delete the query (again, if you created it). Refer to the *Working with Azure Sentinel Hunting queries* section for more information.

This covers all the fields of the **Azure Sentinel - Hunting** page. As you saw, you can learn a lot about each hunting query from here. However, there is more information pertaining to the query, and you will read about that in the next section.

Hunting query details pane

When you select any query from the list, the hunting query details pane will open the query and will show more information about it. Naturally, the information shown will depend on which query was selected. An example can be seen in the following screenshot:

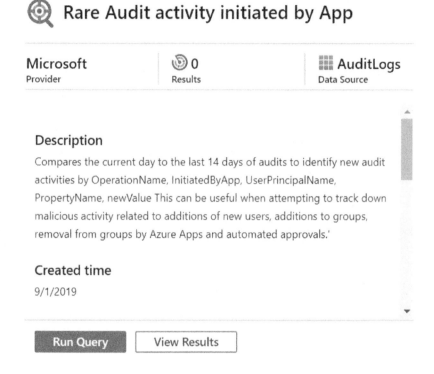

Figure 10.5 – Hunting query detail pane

At the very top of the page is the title of the page. Immediately under that is the name of the who that wrote the query. In this case, it is **Microsoft**, but if it is a query that you created, it will say **Custom Queries**. Next to that is the number of results for this query. On the right of that is the first data source that this query is using. If there is more than one data source for this query, you will need to hover your mouse over the more information icon to see them, as shown in Figure 10.4.

Under that is the description of the query. This will provide you with information as to how the query works and what it is looking for.

Under the **Description** field is the **Created time** field, which will tell you when this query was created. For any of the queries that came with Azure Sentinel, this will be when this Azure Sentinel instance was created.

Scrolling down, there are more fields, as shown in the following screenshot. The **Query** field will show the **Keyword Query Language (KQL)** query that this query will run. Under this is a link called **View query results**, which will take you to the **Logs** page and run this query. Refer back to *Chapter 6, Azure Sentinel Logs and Writing Queries*, for more information on the **Logs** page:

Figure 10.6 – Hunting query detail pane (continued)

Under that is a listing of **Entities** that will be filled in when this query is run.

> **Note**
> If there are no entities, this section will not show at all.

Under that is the **Tactics** section, which will provide more details about each tactic that is associated with this query, as well as a link to get more information on the tactics. If there are none, this section will not show at all.

At the bottom of the details page are the **Run Query** and the **View Results** buttons. The **Run Query** button will run the query in the background and will show the number of the results in the **Hunting Queries listing** section. The **View Results** button will work just like the **View query results** link described earlier.

Now that you have seen the various parts of the **Hunting** page, let's take a look at the hunting queries that you can run to start your investigation.

Working with Azure Sentinel Hunting queries

While there are a lot of pre-existing queries, with more being added all the time, there may be times when you need to add your own or modify an existing query to better suit your needs.

Adding a new query

To add a new query, click on the **New Query** button at the top of the **Hunting** page. This will open the **Create custom query** page, as shown in the following screenshot. This is very similar to creating a new scheduled query, as discussed in *Chapter 7, Creating Analytic Rules*, so you can read the *Creating a new rule using the wizard* section as a refresher:

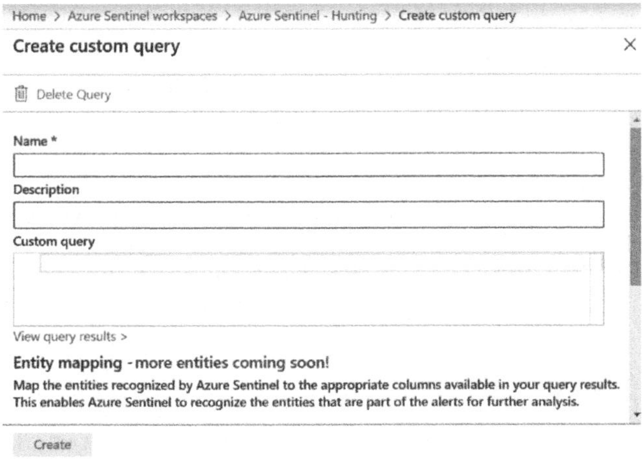

Figure 10.7 – Adding a new query

Fill in the **Name**, **Description**, and **Custom query** fields. If your query has any entities, use the **Entity mapping** section to add the entity mapping to the query. Remember to add them one at a time. Finally, select one or more tactics (not shown in the screenshot) that this query is using.

Once all the information has been filled in, click on the **Create** button to create the new query.

Now that you have added a new query, what happens if you need to make a change to it? The next section talks about editing a query and will answer that very question.

Editing a query

If a query is not working quite like you expect, or you want to update information about the query, you can edit it to make the needed changes.

To edit a query, click on the context-sensitive menu (denoted by the three periods at the far right of the line) to the right of the query's name in the **Query** list, and select **Edit Query**, as shown in the following screenshot:

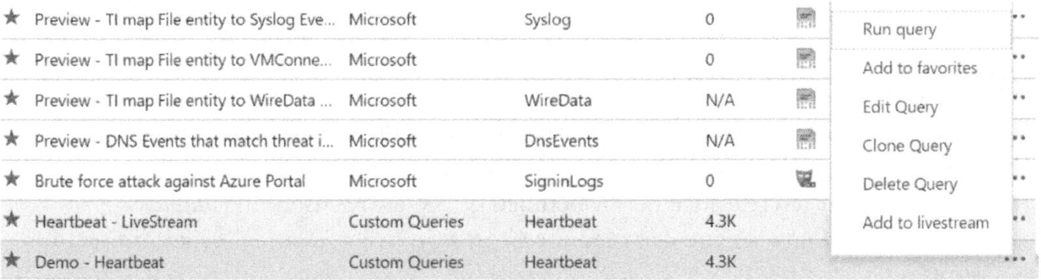

Figure 10.8 – Context-sensitive menu

This will bring up the same page that was shown in figure 10.7, when adding a query was discussed earlier. Make the necessary changes, and click on **Save** to save your changes.

You can always click on the **X** in the upper right-hand corner of the window to close the window without saving any changes. If you have made any changes, you will be prompted for verification that you want to close the window without saving your changes.

Now, you know how you can change a query as needed. What if you want to make a new one and change the new one? You can clone the query, as described in the next section.

Cloning a query

You may have noticed that you cannot edit a pre-existing query. If you need to modify a pre-existing query, you will need to clone it first to make a custom query, and then change the new custom query.

To clone a query, click on the context-sensitive menu, as shown in the previous section, and click **Clone Query**. This will open the same window that is shown when adding a new query, and all the fields will be filled in with the same information that the original query has, except for the **Name** field.

The **Name** field will be filled in with the name of the original query, but will have `Copy of` prepended to the name. This is done so that there are not two queries with the same name, which can lead to confusion, although there is nothing preventing you from having multiple queries with the same name.

When you have made all the necessary changes, click the **Create** button to create the new query.

At this point, you can add a new query, edit a query, and create clones of the queries. You may find that some of the queries are no longer needed, and so you may want to get rid of them. The next section will tell you how to delete queries that are no longer needed.

Deleting a query

If you need to delete a query, click on the context-sensitive menu and select **Delete**. This will show a pop-up window, asking to verify that you want to delete the query. Click on **Yes** to delete it.

Now, you know how to work with the individual hunting queries. Running these queries can be the first step of your investigation. Usually, you will need to perform more queries than just those, though, and being able to retrieve the results later can be quite useful.

The next section will discuss working with Livestream, a new feature that allows you to watch the results of a query in real time.

Working with Livestream

Livestream is a new feature for Azure Sentinel that will allow you to watch one or more hunting queries in real time, to see new results as they occur. This can be useful when performing an investigation, to watch whether a query has any new results without having to constantly rerun the query.

> **Note**
> At the time of writing this book, the Livestream feature was still in preview and, as such, the features and functionality may have changed.

Looking back to Figure 10.8, the last entry in the context menu is called **Add to livestream**. Selecting this will add the query to the **Livestream** window, as follows:

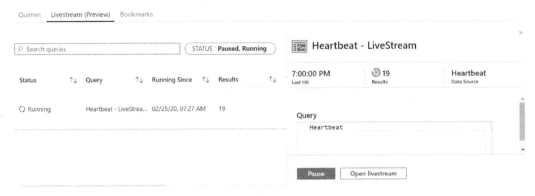

Figure 10.9 – Adding a query to Livestream

While this query is added to Livestream, it is not yet running. Click on the **Open livestream** button on the bottom of the query's detail page. If there is more than one query listed on the page, make sure to select the query you want to watch before clicking this button.

This will open the **Livestream** window. Here, you can start or stop the query, promote it to an alert rule, modify the query, and see the results, as shown in the following screenshot:

Figure 10.10 – Livestream page

At the bottom of the screen are all the results that have been added since the query started running. The columns that are displayed will depend on the query that is being run.

Adding a query to the **Livestream** and enabling it causes that query to be run every minute. If the query runs and the display increments, it means that a potential threat is active. Additionally, you can move away from the **Livestream** tab, and it will continue running. You will be notified through the Azure console notification system as new artifacts are incrementing during the **Livestream** session. You can also select the individual rows of the results and add them as bookmarks, which will be described in the next section.

Adding queries to **Livestream** can be a very useful tool to watch what is happening in your environment in almost real time. By watching one or more queries, you will get to see the results show up when they happen.

In the next section, we will discuss bookmarks, which will allow you to save the results from queries and associate them with an incident, to assist you further with your investigations.

Working with bookmarks

While carrying out investigations, there may be times when you need to keep track of the results from previously run queries. It could be that you need to work on another project and will come back to this investigation later, or another user will be taking over the investigation. You may also need to keep certain results as evidence of an incident. In any case, using a bookmark will allow you to save this information for later.

Creating a bookmark

In order to create a new bookmark, you must run a query from the **Logs** page—refer to *Chapter 6*, *Azure Sentinel Logs and Writing Queries*, for a refresher. While on the **Hunting** page, clicking the **Viewing Results** button in the query's details pane will open the **Logs** page showing your results, as follows:

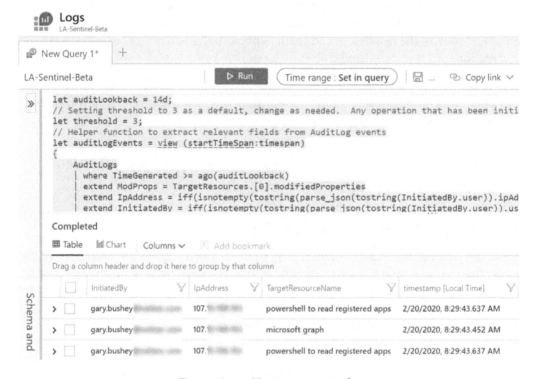

Figure 10.11 – Viewing query results

You may have noticed that there are checkboxes to the left of each result. To create a new bookmark, select one or more checkboxes. When at least one checkbox has been selected, the **Add bookmark** link will be enabled in the result's header bar.

When you click on **Add bookmark**, a new blade will open, as shown in the following screenshot (the actual title of the blade will be different if you select one checkbox from what it will be if you select multiple checkboxes):

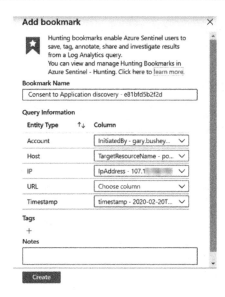

Figure 10.12 – Add bookmark blade

The **Bookmark Name** will be filled in with the name of the query followed by a random 12-digit hexadecimal number, so that if you create multiple bookmarks from the same query, they will each have a unique name. Below that is a list of all the available entities. If the query has any entities associated with it, those will be filled in.

Add any **Tags** and **Notes** that are needed. When adding **Notes,** make sure they provide enough information so that when you or someone else comes back to this bookmark, it will be easy to understand what is going on. Enter any **Tags** that will be useful to filter, to find the various bookmarks when needed.

Click **Create** to create the bookmark when all the fields have been filled in.

> **Note**
> If you select multiple checkboxes when creating a bookmark, the first bookmark created will follow the naming convention stated earlier. For the rest, a new bookmark will be created for each selected result, and the **Name** will have (x) appended to it, where x is the copy number of the bookmark. For example, if there are four checkboxes selected and the bookmark name was set to Test Bookmark - 123456789012, then the first bookmark will have that name; the second will be named Test Bookmark - 123456789012 (1); the third will be named Test Bookmark - 123456789012 (2); and the fourth will be named Test Bookmark - 123456789012 (3). This way, you can easily tell which bookmarks were created together.

It is very easy to add bookmarks when you are performing your queries. In the next section, we will discuss how to use them.

Viewing bookmarks

If you go back to the **Hunting** main page, you will see that there is a **Bookmarks** tab above the listing of all the queries. Clicking it will change the page to show the **Bookmarks** tab, as illustrated in the following screenshot:

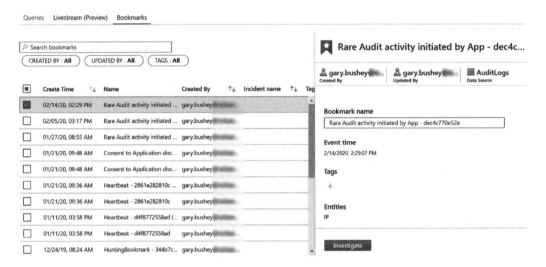

Figure 10.13 – Bookmarks tab

When a bookmark is selected, the details pane is opened on the right, showing more information about the bookmark, as illustrated in the following screenshot:

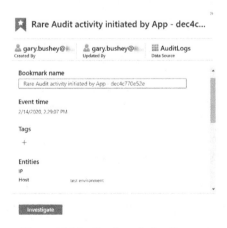

Figure 10.14 – Bookmark details pane

At the top of the page is the bookmark's name, and under that is who created it, who last updated it, and the data source used by the query that created the bookmark, or the first data source if there were multiple data sources.

Below that is another field that contains the bookmark name. This field is editable, so if you want to change the bookmark's name, you can make the changes here. Once you leave the field, the new change will be automatically applied.

Under that is the time the result was created, any tags associated with the bookmark, and also the entities that are associated with this bookmark.

Under that is the **Query result row**, which contains the values for all the columns displayed for the query result. You will need to scroll down to see all the fields. Directly under that is a link called **View source query**, which will allow you to view the source query itself. The text for this link is in a very small font, so it is easy to miss.

There is also the **Notes** section, where you can add any notes that you need to. This is an editable field, and any changes you make in this field will automatically be updated when you leave the field.

After that is the bookmark's internal ID, with a link to view the bookmark log for this query so that you can view the history of the bookmark. This will include items such as the creation of the bookmark, any changes to the bookmark's name, and when notes were added. Since there is nothing on the screen that tells you when notes were added or updated, this is a useful feature for determining when actions were performed against the bookmark.

> **Note**
>
> You may see a message stating *"Investigation cannot be used to investigate this bookmark because some of the data related to this bookmark is no longer stored."* This can occur if the results that were stored in a bookmark have been deleted due to your data retention policy. Refer back to *Chapter 2, Azure Monitor – Log Analytics,* for information on setting your data retention policy.

At the bottom of the screen is the **Investigate** button, which will only be enabled if there is at least one entity with a value. Clicking the button will open the investigation screen, which was described in detail in *Chapter 9, Incident Management*.

There is one change to the **Investigate** screen; since you are working with bookmarks rather than incidents, the main icon will look as follows:

Figure 10.15 – Bookmark investigation

You now know how to view the bookmarks that you have created. You can get more details about them and see how to view the information using the **Investigate** button. Next, we will learn how to associate the bookmark with an incident.

Associating a bookmark with an incident

Bookmarks, by themselves, are not that useful. In order to be useful, they need to be associated with an incident, either a new incident or an existing one. This section will discuss the various ways to associate the bookmark with an incident.

No matter how you want to associate the bookmark with an incident, the first step is using the context menu. The context menu for each bookmark appears as follows:

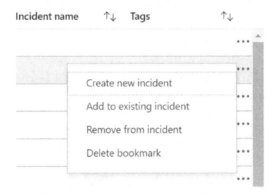

Figure 10.16 – Bookmark context menu

Let's now take a look at the different fields under the context menu in detail:

- If you select **Create new incident**, the new incident blade will open as follows. This will allow you to create a new incident based on the selected bookmark:

Figure 10.17 – Creating an incident from bookmark

These fields are the same as any other incident, so they will not be covered here. Refer to *Chapter 9, Incident Management,* for more information on incidents. Click **Create** to create a new incident from this bookmark.

- Clicking on **Add to existing incident** will open a new blade allowing you to choose one or more incidents with which to associate this bookmark, as shown in the following screenshot. Select the incident with which you wish to associate this bookmark, and then click **Add**:

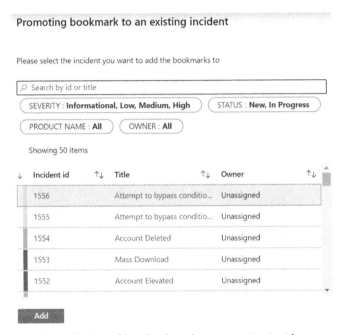

Figure 10.18 – Adding bookmark to an existing incident

- Clicking on **Remove from incident** will cause a pop-up box to show, asking you to verify that you do want to remove the bookmark from the incident. If you confirm the choice, the bookmark will be unassociated with the incident.

- Clicking on **Delete bookmark** will cause a pop-up box to show, asking you to verify that you do want to delete the bookmark. If you confirm the choice, the bookmark will be deleted.

That is all there is to the **Azure Sentinel - Hunting** page. As you have read, it is quite useful, with a large number of built-in queries, and the ability to add your own queries and add a bookmark of results in order to help the investigation.

However, there may be times when this is not enough. Perhaps you need information that is only available outside of Azure Sentinel, or you want to use a graph that is not part of Azure Sentinel. In cases like this, you can use Jupyter Notebooks, which is the topic of our next section.

Using Azure Sentinel Notebooks

Sometimes, just using KQL queries against logs does not give enough information to assist with properly performing hunting activities. In cases such as this, you can use Jupyter Notebooks, hosted in the Azure Notebooks service, to perform additional work. Jupyter Notebooks combine text with code and outputs to provide an overall view of your threat-hunting activities. The code can be written in Python, F#, and other languages, so threat hunters can work with a language they are most likely already familiar with.

> **Note**
>
> The full scope of Jupyter Notebooks is beyond the scope of this book. For more information, go to `https://jupyter.org/`.

Click on **Notebooks** in the **Azure Sentinel** navigation area to go to the **Notebooks** page, which will look like the following screenshot:

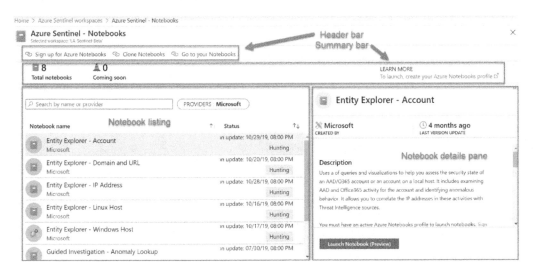

Figure 10.19 – Notebooks page overview

Each of the sections on this page is described in more detail in the following sections.

The header bar

The header bar allows you to work with the notebooks and is shown in the following screenshot:

Sign up for Azure Notebooks   Clone Notebooks   Go to your Notebooks

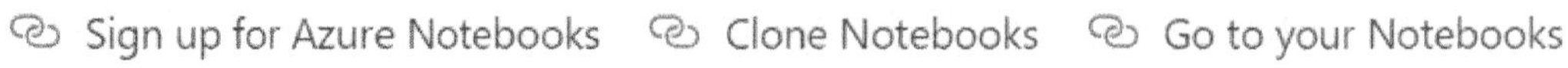

Figure 10.20 – Notebooks' header bar

On the left side is a button allowing you to sign up for Azure Notebooks. Although the notebooks are hosted in Azure, you will need to sign up for this feature separately. This action will only need to be performed once. When you click on it, you will be taken to another page where you can sign up for this service.

To the right of that is the **Clone Notebooks** button. This will allow you to create a new project inside notebooks, with a copy of the existing notebooks that are stored in GitHub.

On the right of that is the **Go to your Notebooks** button, which will take you to your instance of Azure Notebooks.

The summary bar

The summary bar shows the number of existing notebooks, the number of any coming soon, and a link to learn more information about Azure Notebooks, as illustrated in the following screenshot:

8   **0**   LEARN MORE
Total notebooks   Coming soon   To launch, create your Azure Notebooks profile

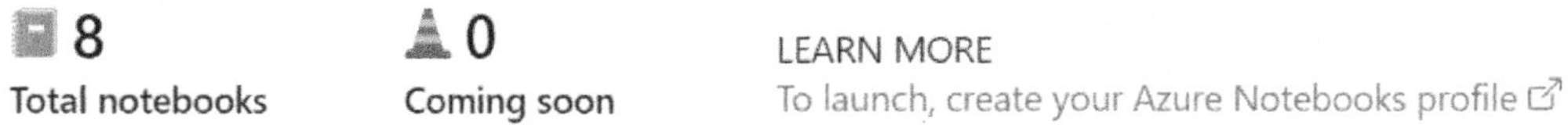

Figure 10.21 – Notebooks' summary bar

This summary bar is useful to see whether there are any new notebooks that have been added to Azure Sentinel. You can view these new notebooks to see whether they may be something you can use.

The notebook list

Looking at the page, you will see that all the available Jupyter Notebook templates are shown. These notebooks are provided by the Azure Sentinel GitHub repository, maintained by Microsoft and updated regularly.

> **Note**
>
> While the majority of the Azure Sentinel information is stored in the Azure Sentinel GitHub repository, located at `https://github.com/Azure/Azure-Sentinel`, these notebooks are stored in the Azure Sentinel Notebook GitHub repository, located at `https://github.com/Azure/Azure-Sentinel-Notebooks`.

For each notebook, the name of the notebook will be shown with the authoring company underneath it. The last update time, as well as the type—either **Hunting** or **Investigation**—will be shown to the right.

The notebook details pane

Selecting a notebook will show the notebook details blade, as shown in the following screenshot. This will show the notebook's name at the top of the page. Under that is the name of the company that created it, and the last time it was updated.

Beneath that is the description of the notebook, which will tell you what the notebook is trying to find. Under that is the **Required data types** field, which refers to the Azure Sentinel logs that it will be querying. Below that is a listing of the data sources (not shown) that are used to populate the data types, and finally, one or more images pertaining to the notebooks:

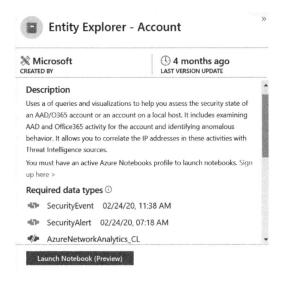

Figure 10.22 – Notebook details pane

At the bottom of this blade is the **Launch Notebook (Preview)** button. This will clone the selected notebook, even if you already have the same one present, and will then take you into the notebook.

It is recommended that you only use this button once or use the **Clone Notebooks** button in the header to create a copy of the notebooks. From that point on, click the **Go to your Notebooks** button in the header to access your notebooks.

> **Note**
>
> At the time this book was written, the button was called **Launch Notebook (Preview)**. It is possible that when you are reading this chapter, the Notebook feature will be out of preview, and the button will be called **Launch Notebook**, or something similar to this.

As stated previously, the best way to get to your notebooks is to use the **Go to your Notebooks** button in the header. Clicking that will take you to a page similar to the following:

Figure 10.23 – Azure Notebooks home page

Click on the **My Projects** link in the header to continue. This will take you to the **My Projects** page, as shown in the following screenshot. This will vary depending on how many projects you have:

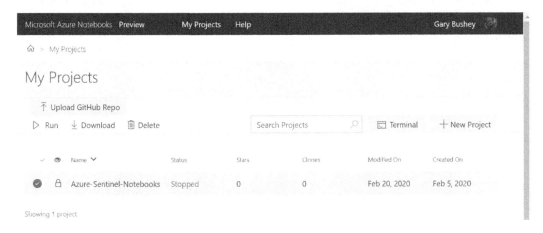

Figure 10.24 – My project page

From here, you can select your notebook and start working with it. The actual usage of the notebooks is outside the scope of this book.

Azure Notebooks will allow you to perform queries outside Azure Sentinel. They can incorporate text and code and can include data inside and external to Azure Sentinel. They can also make use of graphics packages that are not available to Azure Sentinel, to create graphs that you would not be able to create in Azure Sentinel.

Next, we will look at the mechanics of how to perform a threat hunt. This is going to focus on the tasks you will perform, and not on how to do it inside Azure Sentinel.

Performing a hunt

While there are no real set rules on how to run a hunt, there are some steps that you can take to focus your work: develop premise, determine data, plan hunt, execute investigation, respond, monitor, and improve.

As shown in the following diagram, this is a never-ending process. As new logs are added or new threats are recognized, this will be done over and over again. Even something as simple as checking for a malicious IP address will most likely be done many times and, based on previous findings, can be improved upon. You can find the logs that are most likely to contain the IP address and check those first, rather than blindly searching across all logs:

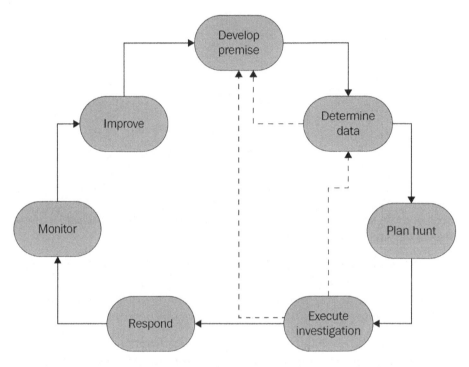

Figure 10.25 – Threat-hunting life cycle

As you can see from the preceding diagram, there are various steps to performing an investigation. Each step is described in further detail, next.

Develop premise

In this step, you need to determine what it is you are trying to find or prove. What is it you are trying to find out? Is it to determine whether a malicious IP address has been found in your environment? Did a new user account perform actions it should not have? Is someone from a foreign entity trying to gain access to your system?

When you develop a premise, you are specifying what it is you are trying to find. It may be that you are told what it is you are looking for, or it may be that you are looking for something that you think may have happened.

Determine data

In this step, you determine which data you need to start your investigation. Which data will you need to look at to work your hypotheses? Is it all in Log Analytics, or will it be found elsewhere? What do you already know about your environment and what do you need to learn?

It may be that during your investigation, you determine that there is additional information that you may need, so do not feel that you are locked into just the data you have acquired in this step.

You may also find that you do not have all the data needed to work on your premise. It may be that there is data you need that is not being logged, in which case you will need to see whether you can start gathering that information. In any event, if you cannot obtain the needed data, you may need to go back and revise your premise.

Once you start finding specific types of activities in the various logs you have, it will make sense to keep track of these to make it easier to find the data in the future. The following screenshot shows the beginning of one method to track information: using Microsoft Excel to keep track of the log name, the type of data being queried, and whether the data is found in the log. If the data is found, the name of the column holding the data is entered:

Data Type	Domain	Host Name	IP Address	Account
AuditLogs	TargetResources*	TargetResources*	TargetResources*	InitiatedBy
AzureActivity	HTTPRequest		CallerIPAddress	Caller
AzureDiagnostics				
AzureMetrics				
Event	EventData	Computer	EventData	UserName
SigninLogs	ResourceDisplayName		IPAddress	UserPrincipalName
Not available				
Sometimes available				
Always Available				
* Compound Column				

Figure 10.26 – Data field tracker

Notice that the TargetResources column is entered for multiple data types for the AuditLogs log type. This is due to this column being comprised of other fields, so the actual information will need to be extracted from it. This is designated by having an asterisk, *, at the end of the column name.

Another point to note is that your data diagram may be different from the one shown here, even for the same logs. This is due to the type of data coming in and what resources you have in your subscription. For instance, in the preceding Excel sheet data, the AzureMetrics row does not find any of the data types in question, but that may be due to not having any Azure resources saving their diagnostic information to this Log Analytics workspace.

Plan hunt

How will the hunt be performed? Can it all be done in Azure Sentinel or will you need a notebook?

In this step, you will look at the data you gathered from the previous step and determine how you need to access it. It may be that you can access all required data via Azure Sentinel queries; however, many times, you will need to look at additional information outside of Azure Sentinel, in which case you will need to use a notebook. You will also write the queries and additional code that may be needed, or use queries that were already written if those work.

Execute investigation

In this step, you will execute your queries that you obtained in the previous step, whether you wrote them or found ones that were already written that will work. You may be performing queries in Azure Sentinel as well as, or instead of, in a notebook. Wherever you run the queries, once you start looking at the results, you may find that you need to revise your premise or determine that you need more data, so you may need to go back to a previous step (refer to Figure 10.24).

Respond

Now that you have the information you need, you can respond to the results of the investigation. You may just have to plug the security gap you found, or you may need to escalate to another team and present what you found. This may be just your team or, in the event of a major breach, it could be the **Chief Information Security Officer (CISO)**, **Chief Information Officer (CIO)**, or even the board.

If the response is simple, such as blocking a port in a firewall or blocking an IP address range, most likely it is just a matter of notifying the appropriate people, updating the ticket, and moving on.

However, there will most likely be cases where you need to do a full presentation on your findings. This could be just to your team, but it could also be to a different audience. How you do the presentation is up to your company and its corporate culture; just keep thinking while you are doing your work *Would this information be useful in a presentation?* and think about how you would present it. A table of information may be enough when presenting to your team, but others who are not as familiar with the data may need graphs and charts.

At the very least, your findings and how you got to your results should be presented within your team if it is new information, so that everyone is kept up to date with the latest findings and can take the most appropriate actions.

Monitor

Develop new analytic queries if possible; otherwise, continue to periodically run the investigation to validate findings. Refer back to *Chapter 7, Creating Analytic Rules,* for a refresher on creating analytic queries.

In this step, you will determine how you can perform continuous monitoring to help safeguard against the situation you were investigating or improve the ability to investigate again next time. Can you add more information to the log? Is there a change in the operating procedures that can be performed to help avoid this situation in the future? Is there a change to your network that can be performed?

One of the best outcomes would be to create an analytics query so that this situation can be found automatically and perhaps handled via a playbook. Refer to *Chapter 11, Creating Playbooks and Logic Apps*, for more information on creating playbooks.

Improve

Based on any learnings that came from the investigation, improve the investigation code and techniques, if possible.

In this step, you— and most likely, others—will work to determine how to improve the queries used in this hunt, as well as how to avoid needing this hunt in the future. It may be that the queries you used could be rewritten to be more efficient; changes could be made to operating procedures to avoid the situation altogether; or other recommendations may be made based on the skills and experience of your team, partners, and domain-specific experts.

Those are the steps that can be taken to start your threat-hunting investigation. Again, none of these are set in stone, and the steps are only provided for guidance. You may find that your company has their own steps or that you want to add your own. The real take-away from this is that you should have a repeatable process that is always improving, enabling you to share your results at least with your co-workers and with the threat-hunting community at large, if allowed.

Summary

Now, you have learned about how to start doing threat hunting in Azure Sentinel. You learned about the **Hunting** page, the **Notebooks** page with its Jupyter notebooks, and got a brief introduction on how to perform a threat-hunting investigation.

We looked at the tools that Azure Sentinel provides to assist with threat hunting. This includes queries that only get run periodically, either due to factors such as needing to look for a specific piece of information, or the fact that they would return too many results to be useful on a scheduled basis.

Another tool that can be used is the hosted instances of Jupyter Notebooks. These notebooks allow you to combine text, code, and output into one location to make hunting easier and repeatable. In addition, notebooks can query not only Azure Sentinel logs but also third-party information through the use of programming languages, including F# and Python.

In the next chapter, we will look at using Azure Sentinel Playbooks to help automate reactions to incidents.

Questions

1. How do I run a single hunting query?
2. How do I run all the hunting queries at one time?
3. How can I view the results of a single hunting query?
4. How do I create a new bookmark?
5. What are two ways in which I can associate a bookmark with an incident?

Further reading

You can refer to the following links for more information on topics covered in
this chapter:

- Hunt for threats with Azure Sentinel (`https://docs.microsoft.com/
en-us/azure/sentinel/hunting`)

- Quickstart: Sign up and set a user ID for Azure Notebooks Preview (`https://
docs.microsoft.com/en-us/azure/notebooks/quickstart-sign-
in-azure-notebooks`)

- Security Investigation with Azure Sentinel and Jupyter Notebooks – Part 1
(`https://techcommunity.microsoft.com/t5/azure-sentinel/
security-investigation-with-azure-sentinel-and-jupyter-
notebooks/ba-p/432921`)

- Security Investigation with Azure Sentinel and Jupyter Notebooks – Part 2
(`https://techcommunity.microsoft.com/t5/azure-sentinel/
security-investigation-with-azure-sentinel-and-jupyter-
notebooks/ba-p/483466`)

- Security Investigation with Azure Sentinel and Jupyter Notebooks – Part 3
(`https://techcommunity.microsoft.com/t5/azure-sentinel/
security-investigation-with-azure-sentinel-and-jupyter-
notebooks/ba-p/561413`)

Section 4: Integration and Automation

In this section, you will learn how to create solutions that automate the responses required to handle security incidents and integrate them with a ticketing system.

The following chapters are included in this section:

- *Chapter 11, Creating Playbooks and Logic Apps*
- *Chapter 12, ServiceNow Integration*

11
Creating Playbooks and Logic Apps

In the previous chapters, you learned about the **Security Information and Event Management (SIEM)** side of Azure Sentinel. Now it is time to learn about the **Security Orchestration, Automation, and Response (SOAR)** capabilities.

Azure Sentinel's SOAR features allow for automated, or semi-automated, responses to the creation of alerts. This allows you to develop workflows that can perform tasks such as blocking an IP address from getting through a firewall, blocking a suspicious username, or something simple such as sending an email to the security team letting them know a new high-severity alert was generated. When you combine the automation capabilities offered by Azure Sentinel with the protection capabilities of the many other security products you deploy, the sky is the limit!

In this chapter, you will learn about Azure Sentinel playbooks, including how to write and edit them, configuring their workflow, and managing them. At the end of the chapter, we will walk through the process of creating a simple playbook. By the end of the chapter, you should feel comfortable getting started writing your own playbooks.

We will cover the following topics in this chapter:

- Introduction to Azure Sentinel playbooks
- Playbook pricing
- Overview of the Azure Sentinel connector
- Exploring the Playbooks page
- Logic Apps settings page
- Creating a new playbook
- Using the Logic App Designer page
- Creating a simple Azure Sentinel playbook

Introduction to Azure Sentinel playbooks

Azure Sentinel uses Azure Logic Apps for its workflow automation. In fact, an Azure Sentinel playbook is a logic app that uses the Azure Sentinel connector to trigger the workflow. As we go through this chapter, many of the screens we will be looking at are logic app pages, which reinforces this concept. The full extent of how to use logic apps is beyond this book, so we will just cover the Azure Sentinel connector, which contains a logic app trigger and actions.

> **Note**
>
> For this chapter, the terms playbook and logic app will be used interchangeably. For more information on Azure Logic Apps, go to `https://azure.microsoft.com/en-us/services/logic-apps/`.

Logic apps use connectors (not to be confused with Azure Sentinel data connectors) and actions to perform a workflow's activities. A logic app connector provides access to events and data. Actions will perform a specific task, such as sending an email, posting a message on Microsoft Teams, extracting **JavaScript Object Notation** (**JSON**) objects, and so much more.

By using Azure Logic Apps as the backend technology, Azure Sentinel playbooks already have a rich ecosystem of connectors and actions that they can call upon to perform their activities. Now, let's look at the pricing considerations when using playbooks.

Playbook pricing

As mentioned in *Chapter 1, Getting Started with Azure Sentinel*, running an Azure Sentinel playbook is not included in the ingestion costs of Azure Sentinel or Log Analytics. It has its own separate charges that, though they may be considered small, can add up quickly.

For example, in the East US region, each logic app action that is run (and this includes things such as looking up information, extracting JSON, and sending emails) will cost $0.000025 each time it is used. There is also an additional $0.000125 for each standard connector. Granted, this seems pretty small, but if you write a logic app that has 100 actions with 1 connector that gets run each second of every day for a month, that one logic app would cost $3,564 each month!

> **Note**
>
> For more on Azure Logic Apps pricing, go to `https://azure.microsoft.com/en-us/pricing/details/logic-apps/`.

Now, this is a pretty extreme example, but it serves to remind you that when designing playbooks, you need to keep them as simple as needed and you should not do a lot of extraneous work. Next, we will discuss the Azure Sentinel connector, which you will need to use in all Azure Sentinel playbooks.

Overview of the Azure Sentinel connector

While there are many logic app connectors, and more are being added all the time, the one we are concerned with is the Azure Sentinel connector. It provides us with the trigger that can kick off our playbook. It also contains various actions that can perform tasks such as obtaining information about a specific incident, getting information about the entities associated with an alert, updating an incident, and more.

> **Note**
>
> It should be noted that at the time this chapter was written, all the features of the Azure Sentinel connector were in preview, so they could have changed from what is shown and discussed here.

The connector currently has one trigger called **When a response to an Azure Sentinel alert is triggered**. This means that the trigger will fire whenever an alert is triggered. It is worth noting that while the trigger returns a lot of information, it does not return the actual incident that gets created, if one gets created at all. In order to get the incident information, you need to use one of the actions to obtain the details.

The following table lists all the current actions for the Azure Sentinel connector:

Name	Description
Add comment to incident (V2)	Adds a comment to the selected incident.
Add labels to incident	Adds a label to the selected incident.
Alert – Get accounts	Returns a list of all the accounts associated with the alert. This is the account entity of the incident. Use a for each action to loop through all the individual accounts.
Alert – Get hosts	Returns a list of all the hosts associated with the alert. This is the host entity of the incident. Use a For each action to loop through all the individual hosts.
Alert – Get incident	Returns the incident associated with the selected alert.
Alert – Get Ips	Returns a list of all the IP addresses associated with the alert. This is the IP entity of the incident. Use a for each action to loop through all the individual IP addresses.
Change incident description (V2)	Changes the description of the selected incident.
Change incident severity	Changes the severity of the selected incident.
Change incident status	Changes the status of the selected incident.
Change incident title (V2)	Changes the title of the selected incident.
Remove labels from incident	Removes the labels from the selected incident.

> **Note**
>
> Some actions may have **(V2)** or a higher number after the title. Those are newer versions of the action and may break old functionality, so you want to check periodically to make sure there is not a new version of an action you are using.

As stated before, all Azure Sentinel playbooks will need to use this Azure Sentinel connector for the logic app to be considered a playbook. It also provides a lot of actions that you can use to get more information about, and update information in, incidents. You will be using this connector a lot and you should familiarize yourself with its actions. Next, we will start the journey of creating your own playbooks by looking at the Playbooks page.

Exploring the Playbooks page

To access the list of playbooks, from the Azure Sentinel page select **Playbooks** in the navigation pane. This will take you to the Azure Sentinel **Playbooks** page.

This page will actually list all the logic apps in the subscription(s) you have selected to show in the Azure portal. You will need to look at the **Trigger kind** column at the far right to see whether the logic app can be used as a playbook. If it states **Azure Sentinel**, you can use this logic app as a playbook:

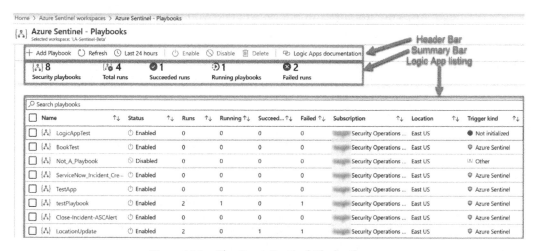

Figure 11.1 – The Azure Sentinel Playbooks page

Tip

You can also access your playbooks by going to the logic app screen. However, it will not present the same amount of information as shown in the preceding screenshot.

If you have used logic apps before, you will notice that this page is similar, but not identical, to the Azure Logic Apps page. There are some differences that make it a bit easier to use. Let's take a look at the different fields of this page.

The header bar

The header bar, shown in the following figure, contains the following buttons:

Figure 11.2 – The Azure Sentinel Playbooks page's header bar

Let's discuss each field in detail:

- The **Add Playbook** button allows you to add a new playbook (which is described in the *Adding a new playbook* section).
- The **Refresh** button will refresh the display.
- There is the time dropdown.
- The **Enable**, **Disable**, and **Delete** buttons are only available if one or more logic apps are selected.
- The **Logic Apps documentation** button will take you to a page with more information on logic apps and how to create them.

The header bar will be used to create new playbooks, as well as change the time frame that you are looking at, and give you more documentation on how to work with logic apps.

The summary bar

Under the header is the status bar:

Figure 11.3 – The Azure Sentinel Playbooks page's summary bar

All the information presented here, other than the number of security playbooks, will use the time dropdown to determine how far back in time to show the results:

- On the left side is the **Security playbooks** number. While this is called **Security playbooks**, it is the number of all the logic apps in your selected subscriptions.
- To the right of that is **Total runs**, which is the total number of times all the logic apps have run. This is the sum of **Succeeded runs** + **Running playbooks** + **Failed runs**.
- After that is **Succeeded runs**, which states out of all the number of times the various logic apps have run, how many of them were successful.

- To the right of that is **Running playbooks**, which can be slightly confusing as it really shows how many logic apps are running, not just playbooks.
- At the end is **Failed runs**, which shows how many times a running logic app failed.

Let's look at the logic app listing.

Logic app listing

Under the summary bar is the listing of all the logic apps, as shown in the following figure. For each logic app listed, there is a selection checkbox, followed by **Name**, **Status** (**Enabled** or **Disabled**), the number of total runs (which is the sum of the **Running**, **Succeeded**, and **Failed** columns), how many instances of the logic app are running, how many times the logic app succeeded, how many times it failed, which subscription it belongs to, which location the logic app resides in, and the trigger kind, of which we only care about **Azure Sentinel**.

As with the status bar, the numbers shown in the **Runs**, **Running**, **Succeeded**, and **Failed** columns are based on the time selected in the time dropdown, as shown in the following figure:

Name		Status		Runs		Running	Succeed...	Failed	Subscription		Location		Trigger kind	
☐ 👥 LogicAppTest		⏱ Enabled		0		0	0	0	Security Operations ...	East US		● Not initialized	
☐ 👥 BookTest		⏱ Enabled		0		0	0	0	Security Operations ...	East US		♡ Azure Sentinel	
☐ 👥 Not_A_Playbook		◎ Disabled		0		0	0	0	Security Operations ...	East US		ᴎ Other	
☐ 👥 ServiceNow_Incident_Cre...		⏱ Enabled		0		0	0	0	Security Operations ...	East US		♡ Azure Sentinel	
☐ 👥 TestApp		⏱ Enabled		0		0	0	0	Security Operations ...	East US		♡ Azure Sentinel	
☐ 👥 testPlaybook		⏱ Enabled		2		1	0	1	Security Operations ...	East US		♡ Azure Sentinel	
☐ 👥 Close-Incident-ASCAlert		⏱ Enabled		0		0	0	0	Security Operations ...	East US		♡ Azure Sentinel	
☐ 👥 LocationUpdate		⏱ Enabled		2		0	1	1	Security Operations ...	East US		♡ Azure Sentinel	

Figure 11.4 – Logic apps list

That is the makeup of the playbook overview page. Next, we will look at a specific playbook using the logic app settings page.

Logic app settings page

You've just seen the overview section. What if you want to look at a specific item? We'll discuss that now.

Clicking on the name of the logic app, shown in figure 11.4, will bring you into the logic app settings page. This is where you can create, edit, or delete an individual logic app, and see more information regarding your logic app, as well as see the history of your logic app's runs, as shown in the following screenshot:

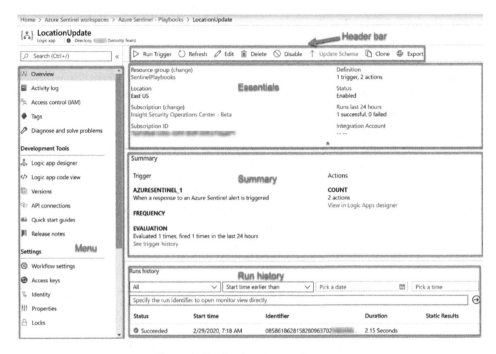

Figure 11.5 – Logic app overview page

Each section will be discussed in more detail in the following sections.

The menu bar

This is where you perform more actions against this logic app. We will not discuss all the options available in the left-hand navigation menu as they are out of the scope of this book; however, we encourage you to take some time to study the full capabilities of logic apps.

The header bar

The header bar contains the following buttons, which allow you to quickly manage the logic app:

▷ Run Trigger   ◯ Refresh   ✎ Edit   🗑 Delete   ⊘ Disable   ↑ Update Schema   ⧉ Clone   ⊕ Export

Figure 11.6 – The logic app overview page's header

Each field is as follows:

- The **Run Trigger** button will cause the logic app to run. This is not very useful with most playbooks as they will require an alert trigger's information to run.

- The **Refresh** button will refresh the page. This can be useful when running a playbook to tell you when it is finished running, as the results of the run would show up in the **Runs history** section.

- The **Edit** button will allow you to edit the logic app's workflow. Refer to the *Using the Logic App Designer page* section for more information.

- The **Delete** button will allow you to delete this logic app after confirming you want to perform the action.

- The **Disable** button will disable this logic app so that it will not run, even if the connector is triggered. If the logic app is disabled, then this button will be called **Enable**.

- The **Update Schema** button will only rarely be enabled and only if there is some change to a logic app that requires you to update the underlying schema.

- The **Clone** button will allow you to make a copy of this logic app. This can be useful if you want to try out some changes without losing the original.

- The **Export** button will allow you to export the logic app to Power Automate and Power Apps. As playbooks cannot be exported, this feature will not be covered here.

Let's take a look at the next field.

The essentials section

This section shows the most essential information for the logic app. Most of the fields are shown with all other types of Azure resources and are self-explanatory, so they will not be covered, with two exceptions:

Resource group (change)
SentinelPlaybooks

Location
East US

Subscription (change)
Insight Security Operations Center - Beta

Subscription ID
7ed1d5e8-b30e-4205-8b0f-629cb7daa671

Definition
1 trigger, 2 actions

Status
Enabled

Runs last 24 hours
1 successful, 0 failed

Integration Account
-- --

Figure 11.7 – The logic app overview page's essentials section

Each field is as follows:

- The **Definition** field will show the number of triggers and actions that make up this Logic App.

- The **Integration Account** field will show you the integration account you are using if you use enterprise integrations.

> **Tip**
>
> For more information on using **Integration Account** with logic apps, go to https://docs.microsoft.com/en-us/azure/logic-apps/logic-apps-enterprise-integration-create-integration-account.

The summary section

This section, as follows, displays information that is specific to logic apps. The fields are broken down into two sections: **Trigger** and **Actions**:

Summary

Trigger

AZURESENTINEL_1
When a response to an Azure Sentinel alert is triggered

FREQUENCY

EVALUATION
Evaluated 1 times, fired 1 times in the last 24 hours
See trigger history

Actions

COUNT
2 actions
View in Logic Apps designer

Figure 11.8 – The logic app overview page's summary section

Each field is as follows:

- The **Trigger** field will show the name and the description of the trigger that the logic app uses.

- The **FREQUENCY** field will show how often this logic app will run if it is set to run on a timer. It will be empty for playbooks as they get triggered based on when an alert is created.

- The **EVALUATION** field will show you what has happened if and when the logic app has run in the last 24 hours.

- The **COUNT** field will show you the number of actions that make up the workflow of this logic app, much like the **Definition** field described earlier.

Let's take a look at the next one.

The Runs history section

This section will provide you with information on all the times this logic app has run:

Runs history

All ⌄	Start time earlier than ⌄	Pick a date 📅	Pick a time

Specify the run identifier to open monitor view directly   ⊙

Status	Start time	Identifier	Duration	Static Results
▷ Running	2/28/2020, 9:08 AM	08586187079601445097697406115...	--	
❶ Failed	2/28/2020, 9:05 AM	08586187081299801860970022871...	737 Milliseconds	
◎ Succeeded	2/26/2020, 2:12 PM	08586188625626606183880618787...	2.94 Seconds	
◎ Succeeded	2/25/2020, 2:53 PM	08586189464724709471560635203...	970 Milliseconds	

Figure 11.9 – The logic app overview page's Runs history section

Each field is as follows:

- The **Status** field will show if this instance of the logic app is running, has failed, or has succeeded.

- The **Start time** field will show the date and time that the logic app instance started.

- The **Identifier** field will show a unique ID that represents this logic app. You may need to provide this if you are ever debugging a logic app issue with Microsoft.

- The **Duration** field will show how long it took this instance to run.

- The **Static Results** field will show any static results you have set up in order to test this logic app.

The main items on this page that we will focus on are the **Edit** button in the header, so that we can make changes to our playbook, and **Runs history** at the bottom of the page, which lets us know which instance of the logic app succeeded or failed, and if it failed, why.

> **Tip**
> For more information on debugging logic apps, go to `https://docs.microsoft.com/en-us/azure/logic-apps/logic-apps-diagnosing-failures`.

Now that you know how to look at existing playbooks, how do you go about adding one? This next section will cover adding a new playbook.

Creating a new playbook

You are going to want to create your own playbooks, so now it is time to investigate how to do that.

In the Azure Sentinel playbooks page (see figure 11.1), click on the **Add Playbook** link in the header. This will open a new tab in your browser that will open the **Logic App** screen, as shown in the following figure:

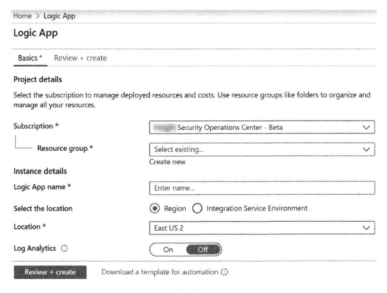

Figure 11.10 – Adding a new playbook

Let's discuss the different fields:

- In the **Logic App name** field, enter a descriptive name. No blanks are allowed but you can use underscores. Make the name descriptive enough so that other users will know what the playbook is intended to do.

- In the **Subscription** dropdown, select the appropriate subscription. This should be the same subscription as where your Log Analytics (and Azure Sentinel) workspace is located.

- In the **Resource group** field, select an existing resource group or create a new one. It does not matter whether your playbooks are in the same resource group as your Log Analytics or not. However, you should follow your organization's Azure architecture design policies, if there are any.

- In the **Location** dropdown, select the appropriate location. This should be the same location as where your Log Analytics workspace is located to avoid egress charges.

- In the **Log Analytics** field, if you want information about this playbook's runtime events to be stored in Log Analytics, turn this on. This will be useful if you need to allow another system, such as Azure Sentinel, to perform queries against this information.

Once all your information is filled in, click the **Review + create** button. This will validate that the information you entered is correct and, if it is, it will allow you to create the logic app. If not, it will inform you of what is wrong and allow you to go back to the main page to fix the issues.

It may take a little while for your logic app to get created. You will be taken back to the main playbook page while this happens.

That is how you create the basis for your playbook. As it stands right now, it does nothing as there is no workflow steps in it. Next, we will explore how to add the workflow components to make your playbook useful.

Using the Logic Apps Designer page

Once the playbook has been created, you will be taken to the **Logic Apps Designer** page. There are actually two different views for this page.

The first view, shown in the following figure, will be shown if your workflow is empty. It provides a quick introduction video, some common triggers, and predefined templates that can be used to help you get started building your workflow. Note that the view shown in the following figure will only show up the first time you edit the workflow for a specific logic app. After that, if there is no workflow, you will be shown a listing of templates and the **Blank Logic App** button, which will allow you to create an empty workflow that you can add into:

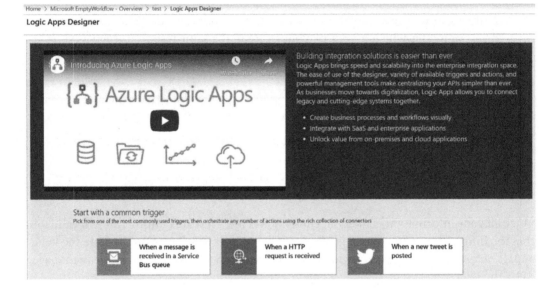

Figure 11.11 – Logic Apps Designer first view

> **Note**
> At the time of writing, there are no Azure Sentinel playbook templates on this page, but, hopefully, there will be soon.

Scroll down the page and then click on the **Blank Logic App** button to start building your playbook.

Once you click on the button, the second view will be shown, which will look similar to what is shown in the following figure. Depending on what connectors and actions you have used recently, the listing under **Recent** in the workflow editor section will be different, or it could be empty:

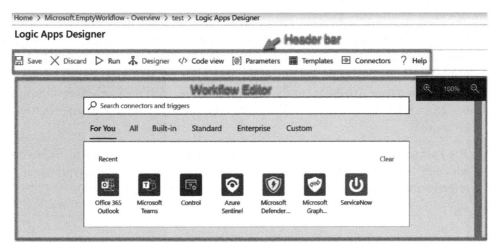

Figure 11.12 – Logic Apps Designer second view

Each section of this page is described in more detail in the next section.

The Logic Apps Designer header bar

The header bar, shown in the following screenshot, contains all the buttons to work with this workflow. Here, you can save or discard your changes, switch between the GUI and the code views, add parameters, and more:

Figure 11.13 – Logic Apps Designer page's header bar

The details of each button are as follows:

- The **Save** button will allow you to save your changes. It will only be active if you have made any changes to the workflow.

- The **Discard** button will discard all the changes you have made and revert the workflow back to the last saved instance. It will only be active if you have made any changes to the workflow.

- The **Run** button will run the workflow you are currently viewing.

- The **Designer** and **Code view** buttons work together to either show you the designer view or the code view. If you press the **Code view** button, the JSON code that makes up this playbook will be shown. If you press the **Designer** button, you will be taken to the GUI view. You can work in either view; however, only one of the buttons will be active at a time. If you are in the **Designer** mode, then the **Code view** button will be active. Likewise, if you are in the **Code view** mode, then the **Designer** button will be active.

- The **Parameters** button will bring up the **Parameters** blade, which will allow you to add, edit, or delete parameters for this playbook. Parameters are a way of passing in information to your logic app, mainly during automated deployments.

> **Note**
>
> Go to `https://docs.microsoft.com/en-us/azure/logic-apps/logic-apps-azure-resource-manager-templates-overview` to get more information on using parameters in logic app deployments.

- **Templates** will bring up a list of pre-existing templates that you can use to base your playbook on. Note that when you click this button and select a template from the list, your existing playbook's design will be overwritten by the template.

- The **Connectors** button will open a new page that will discuss logic app connectors, as well as provide a list of existing, non-preview connectors and actions. This is a good place to start if you need information on your connector.

> **Note**
>
> Go to `https://docs.microsoft.com/en-us/connectors/` to see all the available connectors under the *Connector Reference* section.

Let's discuss the workflow editor section.

The Logic App Designer workflow editor section

The Logic App Designer page's workflow editor section, shown in the following figure, is where you will do most of the work creating your workflow. It is where you will build your workflow:

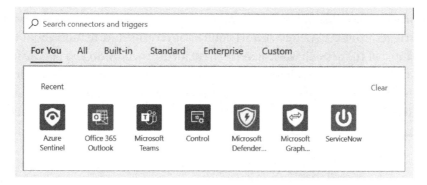

Figure 11.14 – The Logic Apps Designer page's workflow editor section

This is where you will select the trigger that you want to use and then add the various actions that you need to use.

Now you know how to create an Azure Sentinel playbook. While the process itself is fairly simple, the workflows you can create can be as complex as you want. In the next section, we will take all that we have learned in this chapter and create a simple playbook.

Creating a simple Azure Sentinel playbook

This example will take you step by step through the process of creating a new Azure Sentinel playbook. The scenario we are solving is notifying our security analysts using Microsoft Teams that a new, high-severity incident was created.

The first step is to create a new playbook that Azure Sentinel can use. Remember that for Azure Sentinel to be able to use a playbook, it *must* use the Azure Sentinel connector:

1. Go to the Azure Sentinel playbook screen and click the **Add Playbook** button in the header. Follow the *Creating a new playbook* section to add a new playbook. For this playbook, I am calling it *BookDemo*. Select the appropriate resource group and location. For this example, you do not need to store information in Log Analytics.

2. Once your playbook has been created, click on the **Blank Logic App** button to create a new logic app that has nothing in it.

3. In the Logic App Designer page, find and select the Azure Sentinel connector. If you do not see this connector listed in the **Recent** connector listing, enter Azure Sentinel in the search box and select the connector when it shows.

4. Connect to your Azure Sentinel if the connector requires it: as stated previously, the trigger from the Azure Sentinel connector returns information about the alert and most of the actions work against an incident. So, how do you get the incident? Use the **Alert – Get incident** action. Click on the **New step** link, select the **Azure Sentinel** entry in the **Recent** section, or search for it if need be. The connector will be added again and this time it will show the actions as shown in the following screenshot:

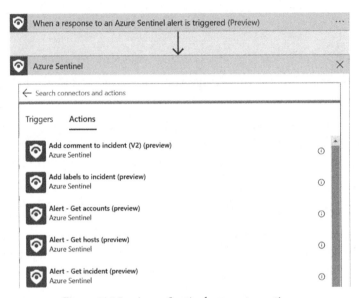

Figure 11.15 – Azure Sentinel connector actions

> **Note**
>
> There is a functionality for Azure Sentinel that allows you to create analytic rules that will raise an alert without generating an incident. For this example, we are assuming that the analytic rule(s) using this workflow will be creating an incident.

5. Scroll down until you find **Alert – Get incident (preview)** and select it.

6. Once the action is added, the following fields need to be filled in:

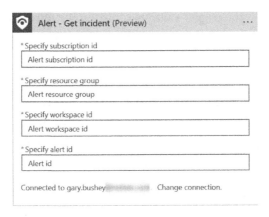

Figure 11.16 – Alert – Get incident fields

7. The great thing is that the Azure Sentinel trigger can provide all these fields for us via dynamic content. Click on the **Specify subscription id** field. A new window will pop up that has a listing of all the fields that the trigger provides, as shown in the following screenshot:

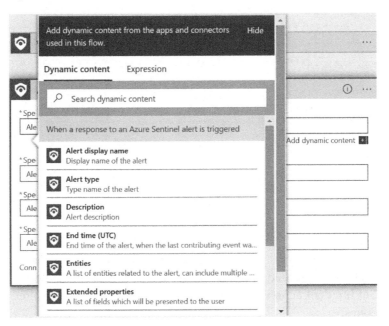

Figure 11.17 – Dynamic content

8. These fields are the dynamic content in that the variable name will be replaced with the actual value when the playbook runs. Most triggers and alerts have their own dynamic content and as new steps are added, this list will grow.

9. Map the fields with the trigger value as shown in the following table:

Action Name	Trigger value
Specify subscription id	Subscription ID
Specify resource group	Resource group
Specify workspace id	Workspace ID
Specify alert id	System alert ID

10. When you are done, your alert should look like the following:

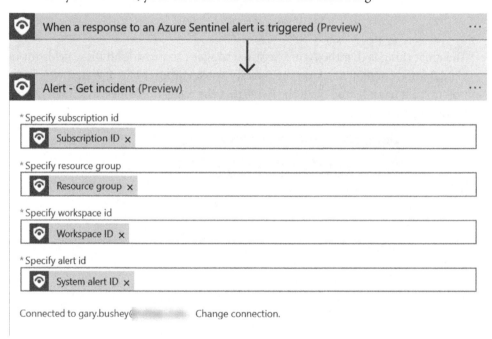

Figure 11.18 – Alert – Get incident completed

Now that we have the information from the incident, what do we do with it? The scenario states that we need to alert the analysts if a high-severity alert is raised. The **Alert – Get Incident** action returns all the incidents, so we need to filter for just the high-severity ones:

1. Click on the **New step** link and then search for **Condition**.

2. Select the **Control** connector when it shows. We are going to be using an If statement, but all the control type statements are bundled together into that one connector.

3. Select the **Condition** action and the action will be added, as shown in the following screenshot. Notice that it has three parts: the top part is where the actual condition is entered, the lower-left part is what to do if the test returns true, and the lower-right part is what to do if the test returns false:

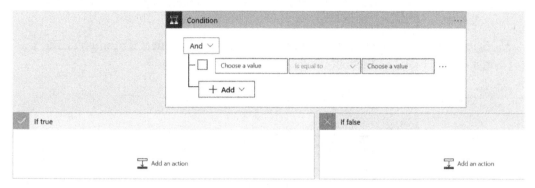

Figure 11.19 – Condition step options

4. Based on what you have learned in this section, set up the condition so that you are checking whether the **Severity** is equal to **High**.

> **Hint**
> Both the Azure Sentinel connector's trigger and the **Alert – Get incident** action both return the severity and it does not matter which one you choose.

The following figure shows you how it should look:

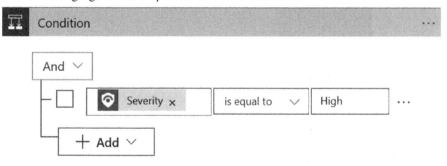

Figure 11.20 – Condition step options completed

5. You can easily add more conditions if you need to in the future.

Now we need to post the message. To do this, follow these steps:

1. Click the **Add an action** link in the **If true** box.

2. Since we don't care about any incidents that do not have a high severity, we are going to ignore the **If false** box. Search for the **Microsoft Teams** connector and select it.

3. Select the **Post a message (V3) (Preview)** action and connect if prompted. The action will look like the following:

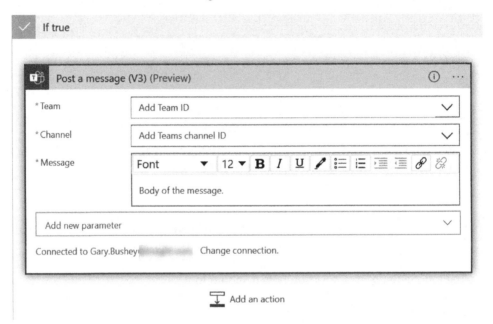

Figure 11.21 – Posting a message

4. One thing that is different in this action from the others is that both the **Team** and **Channel** fields are dropdowns. The **Team** field will be populated with all the teams you have access to and once a team is selected, the **Channel** field will be populated with all the channels in that team.

5. Once you have those filled in, you can fill in the **Message** field. This can be anything that you want. In this case, we need to tell the analysts about a new, high-severity incident, so the message should be something like *A new High severity incident has been generated. Its identification number is: ...*, followed by the incident's ID number.

6. To do this, we are going to mix regular text and a dynamic content field. First, add the hardcoded text that was just listed and then, using the dynamic content variable listing popup, select the **Number** variable. You may need to expand the **Alert – Get incident** listing in this popup to see all the available variables.

7. Once you are done, it should look like the following:

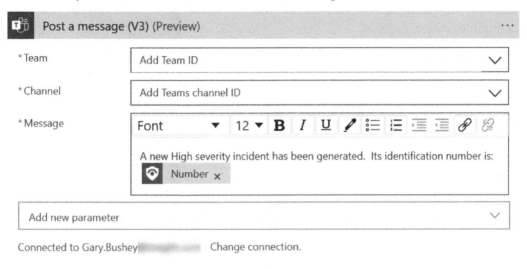

Figure 11.22 – Posting a message completed

8. Once you are all done, click on the **Save** button in the Logic App Designer page's header to save this playbook. If there are any errors, you will be informed about them. If not, the playbook will be saved. You will notice the **Save** button in the header is grayed out until new changes are made.

9. As a final step, you need to attach this playbook to an alert to verify the code is working as designed. Refer back to *Chapter 7, Creating Analytic Rules*, for instructions on how to do this.

There you have it! A fully functional and incredibly useful Azure Sentinel playbook with no coding required. It just took some figuring out of which fields to use where. This is a very simple example but, hopefully, it will at least give you some ideas of what to use playbooks for.

Summary

In this chapter, you learned how to create a playbook that you can use in your analytic query rules to perform SOAR actions. Playbooks are based on Azure Logic Apps, with the only difference being that the Azure Sentinel connector must be used for a logic app to be a playbook.

With what you have learned, you can now create playbooks to automate a lot of actions that had to be performed manually before. You read about one such example, but there is no limit to what you can do!

In the next chapter, we will use what we learned in this chapter to build a playbook that will create a new ServiceNow ticket and update the incident with the ticket number.

Questions

Use these questions to test your knowledge of this chapter:

1. What needs to be done before a logic app can be used as an Azure Sentinel playbook?

2. What needs to be done before a logic app can be used as an Azure Sentinel playbook?

3. How can I tell whether a specific playbook was successful the last time it ran?

4. In a playbook's workflow, how can I get information regarding an incident?

5. What is dynamic content?

6. Can I combine dynamic and static content in one field?

Further reading

- Logic Apps overview: `https://docs.microsoft.com/en-us/azure/logic-apps/logic-apps-overview`

- Connectors for Azure Logic Apps: `https://docs.microsoft.com/en-us/azure/connectors/apis-list`

- Sample Azure Logic Apps: `https://docs.microsoft.com/en-us/samples/browse/?products=azure-logic-apps`

- Sample Azure Sentinel playbooks: `https://github.com/Azure/Azure-Sentinel/tree/master/Playbooks`

- Testing logic apps with mock data but setting up static results: `https://docs.microsoft.com/en-us/azure/logic-apps/test-logic-apps-mock-data-static-results`

12
ServiceNow Integration

As you have read so far, Azure Sentinel is a powerful solution to gather logs and threat intelligence, and to discover threats across your entire environment. However, this is only part of the solution required to run a **Security Operations Center** (**SOC**). When a security alert is raised in Azure Sentinel, the SOC may need assistance from several other teams in order to investigate the issue, mitigate the threat, and remediate any impact caused.

In order to coordinate these activities, organizations utilize a service management platform, such as ServiceNow, to create cases and track the progress being made by each team. While this chapter is focused on the specifics of using the ServiceNow platform, the procedures may be modified for use on a different platform if it supports the integration with Azure Sentinel and Azure Logic Apps.

The process of case management begins by generating alerts within Azure Sentinel; then, those alerts are used to create a ticket in ServiceNow. We will walk through this process in this chapter so you can see the results from end to end.

In this chapter, we will cover the following topics:

- Overview of Azure Sentinel alerts
- Overview of IT Service Management (ITSM)
- Logging in to ServiceNow
- Creating a playbook to trigger a ticket in ServiceNow

Overview of Azure Sentinel alerts

The key benefit of using Azure Sentinel is the centralization of logs and alerts from multiple systems across your organization. By centralizing the information, and enhancing it with threat intelligence, it is possible to build a full picture of the potential malicious activities occurring in any system.

In *Chapter 7, Creating Analytic Rules*, we covered the ability to create analytic rules and queries, using **Kusto Query Language** (**KQL**), to monitor and detect activities across a wide range of data sources gathered by Azure Sentinel, and generate alerts based on these detections. The rules may be created manually to detect known activities and behaviors, or they may include machine learning algorithms to enhance detection capabilities.

To prevent overloading the IT and security teams with too much irrelevant information, the alerting rules can be configured to ensure a high degree of confidence that the issue is both relevant and important. It is imperative that a balance is found to reduce the number and frequency of alerts generated, while avoiding the potential of suppressing useful alerts that may indicate an early warning of a threat or successful compromise.

Once an alert is triggered, it needs to be assessed for prioritization and criticality; ideally, this is an automated process, otherwise, an analyst will need to do this manually. An incident is then created and sent to the individuals and teams who can assist. Appropriate notifications need to be sent to ensure awareness and enable them to take appropriate actions. Their responses need to be coordinated and clearly communicated to show progress and correlate any additional information as it is discovered through the investigations.

As soon as possible, mitigation actions need to be implemented to limit the impact and begin the resolution of the threat. Finally, there needs to be a comprehensive report of the incident, actions taken, lessons learned, and recommendations for improvement to prevent reoccurrence in the future.

All of this is made possible by sending accurate information from Azure Sentinel to the IT Service Management (ITSM) platform. In the next section, we will cover how this processis enabled, as part of the wider incident management framework, using an

ITSM platform.

Overview of IT Service Management (ITSM)

In the security context, the ability to quickly identify and respond to threats is critical to reducing the risk of exposing valuable data and confidential information. However, in the day-to-day running of any large-scale IT environment, security isn't the only concern. Demands from the business result in high-priority requests for modifications or new technology implementations. The IT department is usually made up of many different roles, which each have a part to play in the implementation and ongoing management of multiple complex systems, and, without their assistance, the security team will struggle to respond to threats at the speed required to prevent a major impact.

So, how then do we ensure everyone is made aware of requests and issues, and can quickly and effectively respond? The role of a service management platform is primarily to log, track, and communicate the coordination of efforts required by each of the solution areas and experts to resolve IT requests, issues, and, especially, security incidents. Each platform will offer a variety of additional services to assist with this goal, including workflow automation, and, potentially, the ability to act as a **security, orchestration, automation and response** (**SOAR**) platform (see *Chapter 1, Getting Started with Azure Sentinel*, for more information about the need for SOAR capabilities).

Security alerts generated in Azure Sentinel trigger the creation of a new security incident. Through the direct integration with an ITSM platform, Azure Sentinel can directly generate a new ticket – in this chapter, we use ServiceNow as the ITSM platform of choice. Once received, the **Security Operations** (**SecOps**) module of ServiceNow will take the appropriate actions, which may include sending notifications to inform key personnel and start to involve other teams as necessary. All actions and responses are then tracked as part of the evidence for investigation and remediation.

The workflow that follows is specific to the needs of your business. Ideally, it will enable the tier one personnel to perform the initial analysis and response actions before they need to escalate to tier two or tier three. For simple tasks, and if configured to do so, some automatic remediation will take place.

The SecOps module provides built-in flows, based on standards and recommendations from organizations such as the **SysAdmin, Audit, Network and Security** (**SANS**) Technology Institute and the **National Institute of Standards and Technology** (**NIST**), which are universally accepted as a great starting point.

If your procedures require modification to these flows, there is great flexibility with the options available, but do consider the potential impact of complex changes when the platforms are upgraded in the future. Record details of any modifications so they can be recreated if necessary.

In the next section, we will explore the basics you need to know about the ServiceNow platform to begin using it as the integrated ITSM platform for Azure Sentinel.

Logging in to ServiceNow

ServiceNow is offered as a fully customizable ITSM platform, running as a cloud-based **Service as a Service** (**SaaS**) platform (that is, there is no infrastructure to deploy in order to get started). As an extensive platform, many additional modules are offered via the ServiceNow store (`https://store.servicenow.com`), allowing you to choose solutions from first-and third-party solutions to fully expand the capabilities and integrations across your technology landscape.

While there are a lot of options to cover with ServiceNow, we are going to focus on the specific areas that we need in order to create the integration with Azure Sentinel, and confirm the incidents are correctly triggered.

When you first sign in to the ServiceNow portal (`https://www.servicenow.com/products/service-portal.html`), you will be presented with the following home screen:

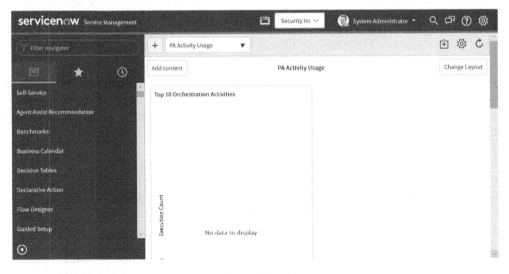

Figure 12.1 – ServiceNow home screen

You can use the menu on the left-hand side of the screen to navigate the various components. For this chapter, you will need to go to the **Incidents** page to view new incidents created by Azure Sentinel. You can find incidents by scrolling through the list, or you can search for it using the **Filter navigator** option at the top of the left-hand side menu.

Creating a playbook to trigger a ticket in ServiceNow

We have already covered what an Azure Sentinel playbook is, and how to create one, in *Chapter 11, Creating Playbooks and Logic Apps*. As a quick refresher, a playbook is a set of logical steps that are taken to perform an action. These are also called workflows in other applications. Playbooks use Azure Logic Apps technology; the only difference is that a playbook *must* use the Azure Sentinel connector's trigger. After that, you are able to use any of the many actions that are provided by Azure Logic Apps.

We are going to take this one step further in this section and explain how to use a playbook to create a ServiceNow **Security Incident Response** (**SIR**) incident. If you do not already have the SIR module loaded in your ServiceNow environment, follow the instructions located at `https://docs.servicenow.com/bundle/kingston-security-management/page/product/security-incident-response/task/t_ActivateSecurityIncidentResponse.html`.

> **Note**
> While this section is dealing specifically with ServiceNow SIR incidents, the logic app connector for ServiceNow will create most, if not all, of the incidents that ServiceNow can handle.

Now that you are aware of what we are going to accomplish, let's start looking at how we are going to do this.

Cloning an existing logic app

At the end of *Chapter 11, Creating Playbooks and Logic Apps*, you will find a step-by-step guide on creating a playbook that took the information from an incident and then wrote the incident's number back as a comment (see the *Creating a simple Azure Sentinel playbook* section for more details). We are going to take that same playbook, clone it, add a ServiceNow action, and update the comment that is being written to the incident to show what the incident number is, from ServiceNow.

We will start by cloning that playbook. If you did not create it while reading *Chapter 11, Creating Playbooks and Logic Apps*, go back and follow the steps to create it now. Follow these steps to create a new playbook by cloning the existing one, which we can then modify:

1. Go to Azure Sentinel's playbook overview page. It should look something similar to what is shown in the following screenshot. Note that the Azure Sentinel menu has been minimized so that more of the screen can be shown:

Figure 12.2 – Playbook listings

Select the playbook you want to clone. If you followed the instructions from the previous chapter, it will be called **BookTest**.

2. On the playbook's logic app overview page, in the header, select the **Clone** button:

Figure 12.3 – Playbook's logic app overview header

3. This will open a new pane, as shown in the following screenshot. Give the new logic app a descriptive name. For this example, we will be using `ServiceNow_Incident_Creation`. Leave the **Logic App Status** dropdown as **Enabled**, and click the **Create** button:

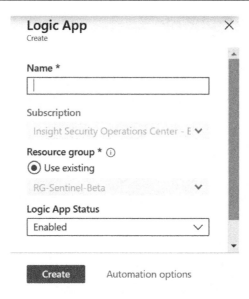

Figure 12.4 – Azure Logic Apps clone page

4.   Azure will then take you back to your Azure portal home page. Periodically check
     the status of your new playbook's deployment. When it is complete, go back into
     your Azure Sentinel environment's playbook page. You will now see the new
     playbook, as shown in the following screenshot:

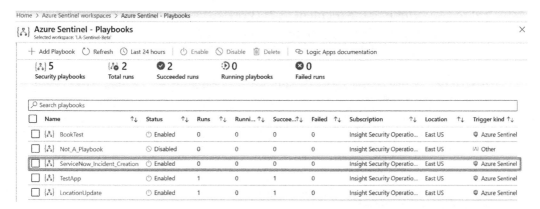

Figure 12.5 – Playbook listing with new playbook

Now that we have cloned an existing playbook, we can start to make the changes that
we need to it. We will be changing it to add the actions needed to create the
ServiceNow ticket.

Modifying the playbook

Now you have the new playbook, which is identical to the one you created earlier. Select it, and then, from the logic app overview, click the **Edit** button in the header to edit the playbook. When it opens, it will look as in the following screenshot. You can expand the various sections to ensure it is identical to the one you created earlier:

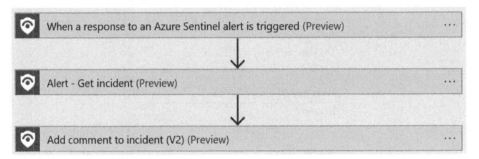

Figure 12.6 – Playbook workflow

What we are going to do now is to add a new step. This is the step that will create the ServiceNow incident. It will be added after the **Alert – Get incident (Preview)** and before the **Add comment to incident (V2) (Preview)** steps. Perform the following steps to add the new action:

1. Move your mouse to the down arrow between the **Alert – Get incident (Preview)** and the **Add comment to incident (V2) (Preview)** steps. There will be a plus icon that shows up. Click it to see the drop-down list, as shown in the following screenshot, and select **Add an action**:

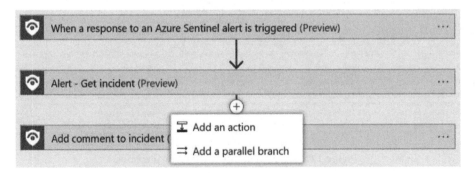

Figure 12.7 – Add a new step to the playbook

2. The **Choose an action** window will show up, as shown in the following screenshot. If the **ServiceNow** connector is not listed under the **Recent** header, enter ServiceNow in the **Search connectors and actions** search box:

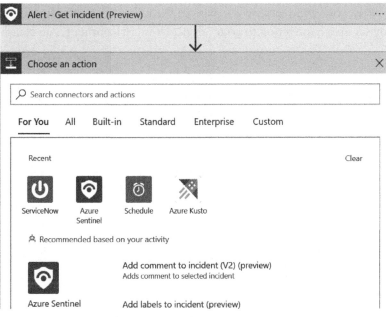

Figure 12.8 – Choose an action

3.   Select the **ServiceNow** entry from all of those shown. From the list of **Actions**, select **Create Record**:

Figure 12.9 – ServiceNow connector

4. Most likely, your connector will look as in the following screenshot. If you have already set up a connection to your ServiceNow environment, you can skip to step 6:

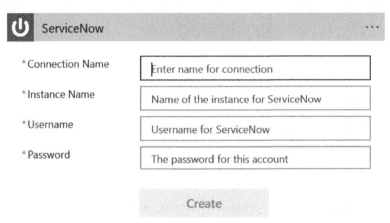

Figure 12.10 – ServiceNow needs a connection

Add the following information:

Field	Description
Connection Name	This is the name of the connection. We will be using ServiceNow.
Instance Name	This is the name of the instance. If you are not sure what to put here, contact your ServiceNow administrator.
Username	This is the username that will be used to connect to ServiceNow. It will need the rights to create a new ServiceNow ticket. If you are not sure what to put here, contact your ServiceNow administrator.
Password	This is the username's password. If you are not sure what to put here, contact your ServiceNow administrator.

Click **Create** to create the new connection to ServiceNow.

5. Now your logic app action should look like this:

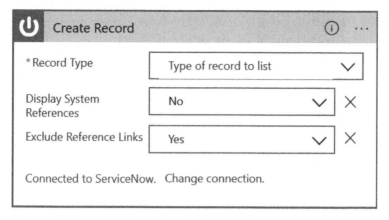

Figure 12.11 – Connected ServiceNow action

6. In the **Record Type** dropdown, scroll to locate and select **Security Incident**. Leave the other two fields as they are. Once you are done, your action should look as in the following screenshot:

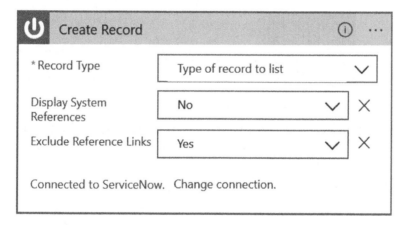

Figure 12.12 – ServiceNow security incident action

Now we have made the necessary modifications and we could, in theory, create the ticket. However, it would be better if we had more information, which is what we will add in the next section.

Additional incident information

This is actually enough to create a ServiceNow **SIR** incident, but it will not have enough information to be very useful. For the incident to be useful, there needs to be more specific information. How much detail and context is provided is up to you and your company standards. We will fill out several additional fields here.

In the following screenshot, we show some of the fields that we are going to be filling in in ServiceNow. These are the basic fields that define the ticket:

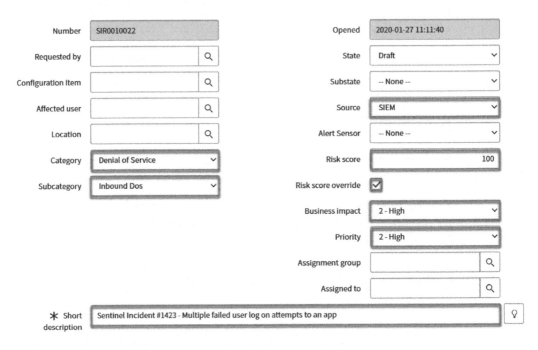

Figure 12.13 – ServiceNow updated fields

If you scroll down the page in ServiceNow, there are a couple more fields that make sense to fill in as well. We will be providing values for them, too:

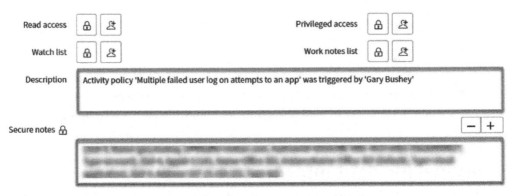

Figure 12.14 – ServiceNow updated fields continued

In order to provide ServiceNow with the information for the selected fields, follow these steps:

1. If you do not still have the **Create Record** action open so that you can edit it, click on it so that you can edit it, as shown in figure 12.11.

2. Change the **Display System References** dropdown to **Yes** so that all the parameters will be displayed in the next step.

3. In order to minimize the number of times you need to access the **Add new** parameter dropdown, since there are a large number of entries in it, use the following table of parameter names to select all the items at once. Just use the checkbox to select the entries you want, then click anywhere outside of the dropdown for the entries to be added. Note that the items will be listed in the order that they show up in the list. Don't worry about adding values to these fields yet, which is taken care of in the following steps:

Parameter Name
Priority
Short description
Business impact
Subcategory
Risk score override
Description
Source
Secure notes
Risk score
Category

Category options

The listing of parameters has two entries called **Category** in it. Make sure to select the correct one. The one we want is almost at the bottom of the list of parameters.

4. Once all the parameters have been added, your action should look as shown in the following screenshot:

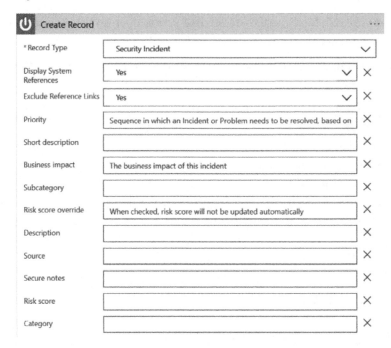

Figure 12.15 – ServiceNow action with parameters

Now you have all the fields that we are going to use to populate the ServiceNow ticket ready to go. The next sections will show you how to add the information.

Adding dynamic content

Now comes the fun part: what values to put into the fields. We will handle this in stages. In this first stage, we will add the dynamic content that the previous actions give us. We will be using this for the **Short description** (more or less), **Description**, and **Secure notes** fields. Use the following table to fill out these fields:

Field	Value
Short description	• Text: `Sentinel Incident #` • Dynamic content: Number from the incident • Text: - • Dynamic content: Title from the incident
Description	Description from the incident
Secure notes	Entities from the alert

When those fields are filled in, your action should look like this:

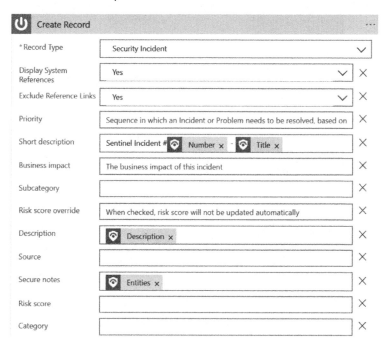

Figure 12.16 – ServiceNow action with dynamic content

That is all the dynamic content we will be adding. The next section will show you how to add the static content we will be using.

Adding static content

Now we will fill in the drop-down entries in ServiceNow. These are fairly easy to do as all it takes is the correct text to be passed through. The text matches a value in the respective drop-down list. In a production environment, these would vary depending on the incident's value, but for now, we are hardcoding in the values. Use the following table to fill in those values. Make sure the text you enter matches exactly:

Field	Value
Priority	2 – High
Business impact	2 – High
Subcategory	Inbound Dos
Risk score override	True
Source	SIEM
Category	Denial of Service

Text values

It does not matter what you enter for the actual text values as long as the text matches an entry in the respective drop-down list exactly. If you wish to use different values than what is listed here, look at the other entries in the drop-down list in question and choose one.

When these fields are filled in, and assuming you used the preceding listed values, your action should look like this:

Figure 12.17 – ServiceNow action with textual content

So, we have the dynamic and static content ready to go. There is just one more thing we need to add, and that is an expression for **Risk score**.

Adding an expression

That just leaves the **Risk score** field. While you can just enter text into that field, we are going to do something a little different to show you some more the power that a playbook can offer.

We are going to enter an expression to determine what gets entered. If you have worked with Microsoft Excel formulas, you will be familiar with logic app expressions, as they are very similar.

The code we will be entering looks like the following. In a nutshell, it is checking the severity field of the incident. If the severity is **High**, it will pass in **100**, if it is **Medium**, it will pass in **50**, otherwise, it will pass in **0**:

```
if (equals(body('Alert_-_Get_
incident')?['properties']?['Severity'],'High'),100,
if (equals(body('Alert_-_Get_
incident')?['properties']?['Severity']),'Medium',50,0))
```

Azure Logic Apps provides an easy way to create these formulas. Use the following steps to complete this process:

1. Click on the field, **Risk score**, in this case, and when the **Dynamic content** popup shows, click on the **Expression** tab. This will appear as shown in the following screenshot:

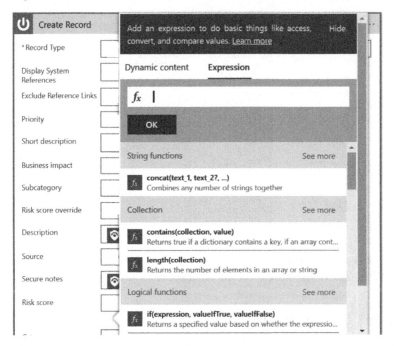

Figure 12.18 – Logic app expression tab

2. From here, you can select the expressions you want. To enter a dynamic value, such as the incident's severity, switch back to the **Dynamic content** tab to find and select the value, and then you can switch back to the **Expression** tab to add more expressions.

> **Warning**
>
> The **Dynamic content** pop-up window cannot be resized so you cannot see much of the expression at once, making it very easy for errors to occur. It may be easier to use an external program, such as Notepad, to see the entire expression at once.

3. We will not be taking you through the steps to add the expression, but we will tell you that there is an `if` statement nested inside another `if` statement, and two `equal` expressions used. The rest should be easy enough to figure out.

4. The last step is to modify the **Add comment to incident (V2) (Preview)** rule to add the ServiceNow number to your Azure Sentinel incident. Rather than telling you how to do this, look at the following screenshot to see what it should look like, and modify your action accordingly:

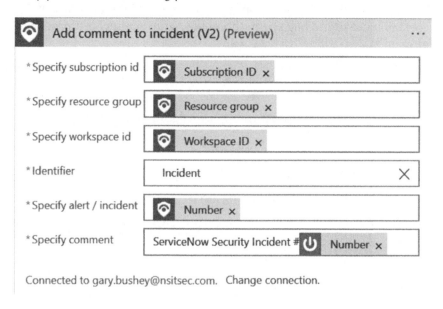

Figure 12.19 – Add comment action

That is it, your playbook is complete! Now you can assign it to an Azure Sentinel analytics scheduled rule. Remember only scheduled rules can run playbooks, to be run automatically whenever that rule generates an alert, or you can run it from the incident's full details page (see *Chapter 9, Incident Management,* for more details).

As stated earlier, this is just the basis for a full-blown ServiceNow incident creation playbook. You will probably want to change at least some of the hardcoded values into items that make sense based on the incident, most likely using more expressions.

Summary

In this chapter, we explored the need to integrate Azure Sentinel with an ITSM platform to coordinate the response to threats detected across your organization.

The example used was the ServiceNow platform, due to its broad adoption; however, you can use this information to integrate with other ITSM platforms, if it can support the connectivity with Azure Sentinel and Azure Logic Apps.

In the next chapter, we will discuss the operational tasks required to ensure the appropriate maintenance and ongoing health of the Azure Sentinel platform and dependent solutions.

Questions

Answer the following questions to test your knowledge of this subject:

1. What is the purpose of an ITSM platform?

2. Why do we need to tune alerts?

3. What is the risk associated with tuning alerts?

4. What is the main requirement when populating a ServiceNow drop-down field with text?

5. What is it called when you perform some computation on a value before using it in a logic app field?

Further reading

- ServiceNow main page: https://www.servicenow.com/

- Get a free developer instance of ServiceNow: https://developer.servicenow.com/app.do#!/home

- Logic apps overview: https://docs.microsoft.com/en-us/azure/logic-apps/logic-apps-overview

- Logic apps ServiceNow connector: https://docs.microsoft.com/en-us/connectors/service-now/

Section 5:
Operational
Guidance

In this section, you will learn how to ensure that your system remains at peak operational efficiency and how to keep up to date with solution improvements.

The following chapters are included in this section:

- *Chapter 13, Operational Tasks for Azure Sentinel*
- *Chapter 14, Constant Learning and Community Contributions*

13
Operational Tasks for Azure Sentinel

As with any service or solution, an ongoing maintenance routine is a critical process to ensure timely service improvements, maintain operational efficiency and cost control, and —most importantly— ensure the service remains highly effective in detecting and responding to security issues.

In general, **Security Operations Center (SOC)** operations are performed by two distinct roles: SOC engineers and SOC analysts. In a small organization, this may be a single person carrying out both roles; in larger organizations, these roles will span many teams and will be carried out by dedicated professionals. In this chapter, we will provide details of the daily, weekly, and monthly tasks required for each role, and any ad hoc tasks that should be carried out as required.

The information in this chapter is meant to provide a starting point for your own planning and ongoing improvement, so you can carry out the necessary processes to produce a high-performing team and a well-managed Azure Sentinel solution.

In this chapter, we will cover the following topics:

- Dividing SOC duties
- Operational tasks for SOC engineers
- Operational tasks for SOC analysts

Dividing SOC duties

A well-developed SOC will be made up of multiple roles, to divide responsibilities and ensure that each individual can focus on their specific tasks. Depending on the size of the team, there could be many roles and many layers of management, leadership, and expertise, or it could be a smaller team in which two or three individuals carry out all the roles between them.

At a high level, the operation of an SOC will require experts that know how to install and maintain the technology solutions required to run the SOC (SOC engineers), and another set of experts that are able to use the solutions to hunt for threats and respond to security incidents (SOC analysts). These two roles work together to provide constant feedback on what works well, and where improvements are required.

Let's review the primary differences between the two main roles, to understand the type of operational tasks they might need to carry out.

SOC engineers

SOC engineers are responsible for the initial design and configuration of Azure Sentinel, including the connection of data sources, configuring any **threat intelligence (TI)** feeds, and securing access to the platform and the data contained within.

Once the service is operational, SOC engineers are then responsible for ongoing improvements, creating analytic rules for threat detection, and fine-tuning to ensure the service remains operationally cost-effective and efficient.

SOC engineers will implement new features made available by Microsoft, and develop automations and other improvements based on feedback from SOC analysts.

SOC analysts

SOC analysts focus on using the tools and data available to respond to alerts and hunt for other threats that may not have been automatically detected.

This role relies on the continuous development of new detection methods, the advancement and integration of machine learning algorithms, and the automation of threat responses to ensure SOC analysts can react quickly to new alerts.

To ensure they can focus on threat detection, SOC analysts offload the tooling and rule configuration to SOC engineers, allowing them to create and maintain their playbooks, and define their standard operating procedures for identifying and responding to suspicious events and behaviors.

Operational tasks for SOC engineers

In this section, we will provide an initial list of tasks that have been identified as engineering tasks. You can use this list as a starting point, and then add your own tasks based on what works for your specific requirements. Each component that is added to the SOC architecture will have its own task requirements—for example, if you integrate a **Cloud Access Security Broker (CASB)** solution, you will need to carry out similar tasks within that platform to ensure it is well maintained and sending the appropriate information to Azure Sentinel.

Daily tasks

A list of daily tasks is as follows:

- Monitor the service health of all core components such as the Azure platform, **Azure Active Directory (AD)** for **identity and access management (IAM)**, and any data collection servers (syslog), ensuring dashboards are available and alerts are triggering
  as expected.

- Review the planned maintenance, service health, and availability monitoring of the Microsoft Azure platform, using the following resources:

  Publicly viewable information: `https://status.azure.com/en-us/status`

  Signing in to your Azure portal and viewing specific details: `https://portal.azure.com/#blade/Microsoft_Azure_Health/AzureHealthBrowseBlade/serviceIssues`

Weekly tasks

A list of weekly tasks is as follows:

- Review the **Data connectors** page for any new or preview connectors, and updates to existing connectors. Ensure each connector that is enabled is still functioning correctly.

- Review the **Workbooks** page for new workbook templates and any new updates, and ensure existing workbooks are functioning correctly.

Monthly tasks

A list of monthly tasks is as follows:

- Review the trends for data ingestion to carry out projected cost analysis; adjust the pricing tier to reflect the most cost-effective option (see the *Service pricing for Azure Sentinel* section in *Chapter 1, Getting Started with Azure Sentinel* for more details).

- Validate the quality of the logs ingested and carry out noise-reduction tuning, especially after the introduction of new data sources.

- Carry out a scenario-mapping exercise with SOC analysts to identify additional detection and response requirements (see the *Scenario mapping* section in *Chapter 1, Getting Started with Azure Sentinel* for more details). Transfer this knowledge to key stakeholders across business and technology teams.

Ad hoc tasks

A list of ad hoc tasks is as follows:

- Review any changes made to the IT infrastructure; look for opportunities to integrate additional log data to gain key insights; and configure automated responses based on attack scenarios.

- Review announcements from Microsoft for potential changes to the Azure Sentinel platform, and any integrated services and solutions. If you have them, also check third-party announcements.

- Update the Azure Sentinel architecture documentation to reflect changes made.

- Engage with external services that offer advanced security practices to further test and train your SOC capabilities, including penetration testing, social engineering, and define? activities.

Operational tasks for SOC analysts

In this section, we will provide an initial list of tasks that have been identified as operational requirements for SOC analysts. These tasks focus on the work required to create, maintain, and organize Azure Sentinel components to ensure operational efficiency.

Daily tasks

A list of daily tasks is as follows:

- Check the **Incidents** page to ensure any new incidents are assigned to an owner, and all open or in-progress incidents are actively investigated until completion.

- Go to the **Hunting** page and select **Run all queries**:

  Review the results for each query that returns at least one result.

  If any queries return a result of **N/A**, then investigate why results are not available (you should return at least 0 as a result).

Review TI sources for current activities and new findings; apply findings to your threat-hunting procedures.

Weekly tasks

A list of weekly tasks is as follows:

- Go to the **Hunting** page and review all bookmarks that have been created, ensuring they are still associated with an active incident. Aim to keep this list short by deleting those that are no longer relevant.

- Review TI feeds to ensure they are still active; look for recommended new TI feeds relevant to the specific industry and region.

- Review all existing analytics queries; check those that are disabled, and decide whether they should be removed or enabled. For all active queries, review the following:

  When possible, each rule should be associated with an appropriate automated task to ensure notifications are sent, a case is raised in the ticketing system, or other runbooks are triggered to carry out remediation activities.

  Work with SOC engineers to implement any changes, to further automate detection and response capabilities.

Review tuning metrics to ensure rules are not overly suppressed, which may cause important events to be missed: rule period and frequency, rule threshold, and suppression.

Monthly tasks

A list of monthly tasks is as follows:

- Carry out a scenario-mapping exercise with SOC engineers to identify additional detection and response requirements (see the *Scenario mapping* section in *Chapter 1, Getting Started with Azure Sentinel* for more details). Transfer this knowledge to key stakeholders across business and technology teams.

- Review all Azure Sentinel workbooks to ensure they are relevant and run correctly (execute them using test cases).

- Review the tag taxonomy.

Ad hoc tasks

A list of ad hoc tasks is as follows:

- Check naming conventions that are being used for various components that are created manually. Keeping strict governance over naming conventions and other standards ensures easier communication across the team when handing over incidents for review.

- Engage with external services that offer advanced security practices to further test and train your SOC capabilities, including penetration testing, social engineering, and Purple Team activities.

Summary

While this is one of the shorter chapters in this book, it has covered the importance of ongoing maintenance that will ensure SOC teams remain vigilant with respect to ongoing changes in the threat landscape, and will also keep Azure Sentinel tuned for efficient and effective security operations.

In the final chapter of this book, we will introduce some resources you can use to continue gaining the knowledge required to implement and operate Azure Sentinel and related solutions.

Questions

Review the following questions to test your knowledge of this subject:

1. What are the two main types of role within an SOC?

2. Which role carries out the scenario-mapping exercise?

3. How frequently should you check the log ingestion rate and pricing tier?

4. How often should an SOC analyst check the **Incidents** page?

5. If you, as an SOC engineer, are told that a new project using an Azure SQL instance is just starting, when should you start looking at ingesting its logs?

14

Constant Learning and Community Contribution

Thank you for taking the time to read this book and gain a thorough understanding of this new solution. In this final chapter, we want to provide some useful resources that you can use to continue your learning journey and get involved with community-based efforts to share knowledge. You can also find resources to directly provide feedback to Microsoft, ensuring the continual improvement of this solution.

This chapter will explore the official resources from Microsoft, additional resources for **Security Operations Center (SOC)** operations, and other resources made available by GitHub.

In this chapter, we will cover the following topics:

- Official resources from Microsoft
- Resources for SOC operations
- Using GitHub
- Specific components and supporting technologies

Official resources from Microsoft

In this section, we will cover resources that are made available by Microsoft to support the design, implementation, and operation of Azure Sentinel as a core security platform. This will include links to official documentation, blogs and technical forums, feature requests, and groups on LinkedIn.

Official documentation

Microsoft Docs (`https://docs.microsoft.com/en-us/`) is a great resource for documentation on every Microsoft solution. The following list provides some specific links to relevant documents you should start with:

- There is a comprehensive section on Azure Sentinel that will provide the latest official release of information about products, and product-specific guidance for the design and implementation of solutions: `https://docs.microsoft.com/en-us/azure/sentinel/`.

- Azure Monitor, and Log Analytics specifically, has a separate section that can be used to further study the information we provided in *Chapter 2, Azure Monitor – Log Analytics*. Visit this site for more details: `https://docs.microsoft.com/en-us/azure/azure-monitor/`.

- **Azure Active Directory (AD)** is another key component that is worth studying in more depth to ensure you can properly secure access to the Azure Sentinel subscription and critical resources. Guidance for Azure AD can be found here: `https://docs.microsoft.com/en-us/azure/active-directory/`.

Tech community – blogs

Microsoft has built a tech community for many different areas of its solutions offerings, each offering a blog to allow expert articles to be shared via specific focused blog posts. The one dedicated to Azure Sentinel can be found here: `https://techcommunity.microsoft.com/t5/azure-sentinel/bg-p/AzureSentinelBlog`.

You can join this site to keep up to date on announcements and new product features, or to ask questions that will be answered by members of the community and experts from Microsoft. The Microsoft team provides links to future training and webinars, and to previously recorded sessions and their associated resources, such as presentation slides.

You may also want to subscribe to the **Really Simple Syndication (RSS)** feed to ensure the latest information is instantly available and easy to find.

Here are some additional blogs and related material available:

- Microsoft blog for **Chief Information Security Officers (CISOs)**: `https://www.microsoft.com/security/blog/ciso-series`

- Blog for all Microsoft security initiatives: `https://www.microsoft.com/security/blog`

- Microsoft Azure security blog: `https://azure.microsoft.com/en-us/blog/topics/security`

- Microsoft Graph Security API blog: `https://www.microsoft.com/security/blog/microsoft-graph-security-api-4`

- Azure Sentinel questions on Reddit: `https://www.reddit.com/r/AzureSentinel/`

Tech community – forum

As with blogs, there are many forums available to cover each Microsoft product. Forums allow you to read questions from other members, learn more about potential challenges and resolutions, then raise your own questions if you can't find answers elsewhere. Some of them are as follows:

- Forum for Azure Sentinel: `https://techcommunity.microsoft.com/t5/azure-sentinel/bd-p/AzureSentinel`

- Forum for Azure Log Analytics: `https://techcommunity.microsoft.com/t5/azure-log-analytics/bd-p/AzureLogAnalytics`

- Forum for Azure Security community: `https://techcommunity.microsoft.com/t5/security-identity/bd-p/Azure-Security`

Feature requests

If you have a good idea to improve Azure Sentinel, or you find a gap in any of the Microsoft security solutions that needs to be addressed, you can provide your ideas via the feedback option within the Azure portal. The feedback option appears in the top right-hand corner of the screen, and looks like the following screenshot. You can select the smiley face to provide positive feedback, or the sad face to explain any issues you may have with the functionality, as shown in the following screenshot:

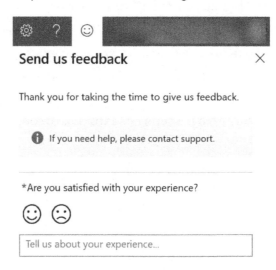

Figure 14.1 – Azure feedback options

While blogs and forums are a good resource for research and to ask questions, you should not rely on them for problems that are having an immediate effect and may need specific technical expertise to resolve. If you need immediate assistance with your implementation of Azure Sentinel, you should reach out to Microsoft Support, using one of the official channels:

If you do not have a support plan, you can sign up for one here: `https://azure.microsoft.com/en-us/support/plans`.

If you have a **PREMIER** agreement, you will be provided with direct contact details for your dedicated support team.

In the Azure portal, navigate to the Azure Sentinel home page, then select the question mark icon from the menu at the top right of the screen, as shown in the following screenshot:

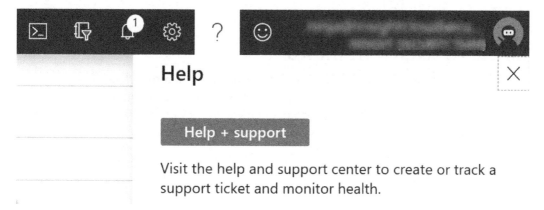

Figure 14.2 – Help and support

Select the **Help + support** button, then follow the instructions to create a new support request.

LinkedIn groups

LinkedIn can be used to build your professional network and gain access to other experts in your field. Groups are for general discussion on topics of interest and usually anyone can join. Microsoft moderates its own LinkedIn group dedicated to the security community. To join, use the following link to get to the group, then ask to join:

```
https://aka.ms/AzureSentinelLinkedIn.
```

Other resources

Microsoft also provides resources on Facebook and Twitter. The following links are shortcut links you can use to get directly to these resources:

- **Facebook**: `https://aka.ms/AzureSentinelFacebook`
- **Twitter**: `https://aka.ms/AzureSentinelTwitter`

Resources for SOC operations

The following study resources are available for improving SOC capabilities, such as advanced threat-hunting procedures, incident response tactics, and adopting a strategic *Zero Trust* approach to implementing technology:

MITRE ATT&CK® framework

ATT&CK stands for **Adversarial Tactics, Techniques, and Common Knowledge**. The MITRE ATT&CK® framework was developed to ensure documentation of these behaviors and that they are applicable to real environments. The framework provides a common taxonomy to promote comparison across different types of adversary groups using the same terminology.

The MITRE ATT&CK® framework contains four common use cases:

- Detections and Analytics
- Threat Intelligence
- Adversary Emulation and Red Teaming
- Assessment and Engineering

This framework has been embedded across Azure Sentinel to ensure ease of reference. To learn more about this framework, and to gain access to relevant resources, start by reading the guide to the MITRE ATT&CK® framework at: `https://attack.mitre.org/resources/getting-started`.

National Institute of Standards for Technology (NIST)

NIST provides a rich source of materials that have been developed for the advancement of security across a range of industries, government, and critical infrastructure. If you are not based in the US, you can still use this information as a guide to secure your own operations and infrastructure.

One of the key articles to review is the **Cybersecurity Framework (CSF)**, aimed primarily at private sector organizations to assess and improve their ability to prevent, detect, and respond to cyberattacks. You can view this here: `https://www.nist.gov/cyberframework`.

If you are working in government, or looking for the strongest guidance for security controls, we recommend reviewing the information provided by NIST specifically for risk management in government, *NIST 800-53* – Security and Privacy Controls for Federal Information Systems and Organizations: `https://csrc.nist.gov/publications/detail/sp/800-53/rev-4/final`.

Using GitHub

GitHub is the largest, and one of the best, platforms for sharing content and securely storing your code. The platform is primarily used for software development version control, using a distributed version control system called **Git**. When you start to use GitHub, you create a new project. This contains the code repository and allows for secure collaboration between different authors and contributors. The repository can be set to **Private**, ensuring only specific people can view the contents, or you can allow others to view and contribute by making it **Public**.

GitHub is available for free and offers plans for professional and enterprise accounts. To learn how to get started with GitHub, sign up for the tutorial. If you get stuck at any time, there is also a help site dedicated to getting the most out of this unique solution. You can choose between the Learning Lab or the Help site, which can be accessed at the following links:

- GitHub Learning Lab: `https://lab.github.com`

- GitHub Help site: `https://help.github.com`

GitHub for Azure Sentinel

Microsoft created and maintains a specific GitHub repository for Azure Sentinel. You can use this repo to find sample queries for Hunting to aid in the development of techniques for threat hunting, by leveraging logs from multiple sources. With these sample queries, you can get a head start in learning the **Kusto Query Language** (**KQL**) and understanding different data sources. To get started, simply paste a sample query into the user interface and run the query. To view Azure Sentinel Hunting queries on GitHub, go to the following link: `https://github.com/Azure/Azure-Sentinel/tree/master/Hunting%20Queries`.

GitHub for community contribution

One of the great benefits of adopting Azure Sentinel as your SOC platform is access to a community of like-minded security professionals who want to help make the world a more secure place. If you have a great idea for a hunting, investigation, or detection query that can be shared with the Sentinel community, you can submit it to the repository and it will be brought directly into the Azure Sentinel service for direct customer use. To learn how to do this, use one of the following resources:

- Azure Sentinel Wiki pages: `https://github.com/Azure/Azure-Sentinel /wiki`

- Send an email with questions or feedback to: `AzureSentinel@microsoft.com`

Specific components and supporting technologies

As we have covered in this book, Azure Sentinel is built upon the Log Analytics platform, as part of Azure Monitor, which uses KQL for queries; Jupyter Notebook; Flow; and Logic Apps, and has machine learning capabilities. Mastering Azure Sentinel requires growing your skills in each of these areas. The following are some of our top picks for resources available today. You may find many more by joining the communities or developing your own groups of special interests.

Kusto Query Language (KQL)

In *Chapter 5*, *Using Kusto Query Language (KQL)*, we introduced KQL, and in *Chapter 6*, *Azure Sentinel Logs and Writing Queries*, we showed how to use it to query logs within Azure Sentinel. However, you will likely need to continue learning this technology in order to write more useful queries and use advanced techniques to fine-tune the results.

For the official KCL documentation, go to the following link: `https://docs. microsoft.com/en-us/azure/kusto/`.

Pluralsight (`https://pluralsight.com`) is another great resource for many types of training course across the IT landscape. Specifically, we found the Pluralsight KQL course, which may be of interest to you: `https://www.pluralsight.com/courses/ kusto-query-language-kql-from-scratch`.

Jupyter Notebook

Jupyter Notebook is an open source application used to create and share documents that contain notes, visualizations, live code, and other resources you can share between SOC analysts to improve threat-hunting and response capabilities.

Find more resources for Jupyter Notebook at the following link: `https://jupyter.org/`.

Machine learning with Fusion

Fusion is a Microsoft technology based on machine learning that helps Azure Sentinel automatically detect multistage attacks. By encasing two or more alert activities, such as anomalous behavior and suspicious activities, Azure Sentinel can produce accurate high-fidelity incidents, reducing false positives and detecting attacks that may otherwise go unseen.

This feature is enabled by default and currently supports several scenarios:

- Impossible travel to atypical location, followed by anomalous Office 365 activity

- Sign-in activity for unfamiliar location, followed by anomalous Office 365 activity

- Sign-in activity from infected device, followed by anomalous Office 365 activity

- Sign-in activity from anonymous IP address, followed by anomalous Office 365 activity

- Sign-in activity from a user with leaked credentials, followed by anomalous Office 365 activity

To learn more about this technology and keep up with the latest developments, visit the following site: `https://docs.microsoft.com/en-us/azure/sentinel/fusion`.

Azure Logic Apps

Azure Logic Apps can be used for a wide variety of automation tasks, including the following:

- **Schedule-based workflow**: Creating a task to automatically carry out actions on a frequent basis, such as gathering data, then comparing that value to the last time it was gathered, and raising an alert if the value exceeds a threshold.

- **Approval-based workflow**: Creating a task to monitor for a given trigger, then sending an approval request (such as an email), and continuing the requested action once the approval is received.

- **Azure Functions**: This can be integrated with Azure Logic Apps to carry out additional tasks and integrations, such as:

- Running code based on HTTP requests
- Scheduling code to run at predefined times
- Processing new and modified Azure Cosmos DB documents
- Processing new and modified Azure Storage blobs
- Responding to Azure Storage queue messages
- Responding to Azure Event Grid events via subscriptions and filters
- Responding to high volumes of Azure Event Hubs events
- Connecting to other Azure, on-premise, or other cloud services by responding to Service Bus queue or topic messages

- **Storage workflow**: Enables integration with Azure Storage to enable the automated collection and retrieval of data.

To enable this automation, Azure Logic Apps is able to use connectors to provide quick access to events, data, and actions across other apps, services, systems, protocols, and platforms. This integration works for on-premise workloads, Azure, and other cloud platforms. Learn more about connectors at the following link: `https://docs.microsoft.com/en-us/connectors/`.

We recommend studying these capabilities further, to ensure you can automatically trigger actions when alerts and incidents are raised in Azure Sentinel:

Azure Logic Apps: `https://azure.microsoft.com/en-us/services/logic-apps/`

Summary

As you can see, there are plenty of opportunities for extended learning and contributing your own expertise to benefit others. As Microsoft adds new features to Azure Sentinel, read about the improvements from their blogs and official documentation, then apply the most appropriate changes to your own implementation.

We encourage you to engage and pass on your experience and expertise with others, as we have learned from writing this book; it is only by sharing your knowledge and listening to others' feedback that you will truly master the topic and appreciate how much more there is to learn!

Assessments

Chapter 1

1. It is used to assist with the discovery and mapping of current security solutions, and to plan for the future state.

2. The three main components are Azure Monitor, Azure Sentinel, and Logic Apps.

3. The main platforms include **Identity and Access Management (IAM)**, **Endpoint Detection and Response (EDR)**, **Cloud Access Security Broker (CASB)**, **Cloud Workload Protection Platform (CWPP)**, and the **Next Generation Firewall (NGFW)**.

4. Third-party solution providers include AWS, Cisco, Palo Alto Networks, Fortinet, and Symantec.

5. There are seven steps in the scenario mapping exercise.

Chapter 2

1. The name of the query language is the **Kusto query language (KQL)**.

2. Azure Lighthouse enables the central management of multiple Azure tenants, usually deployed by managed service providers, but may also be used in complex environments.

3. A few of the different layers of protection for securing data are: Microsoft-managed incident management process, data retention and deletion policies, per data source type, and data segregation and isolation, with geographic sovereignty.

4. Log Analytics workspaces can be created via the web portal, PowerShell, and the command-line interface.

5. Engineers should be provided with the role of Azure Sentinel Contributor and Log Analytics Reader.

Chapter 3

1. The seven Vs of big data are Volume, Velocity, Variety, Variability, Veracity, Visualization, Value.

2. The four types of connectors are native, direct, API, agent-based.

3. The Syslog server acts as a central collector for logs that support Syslog or CEF data types, and forwards them on to the SIEM solution.

4. Azure Sentinel will store data for 90 days as part of the service. If longer retention is required, a charge is applied based on the volume of data retained and the length of time (which can be up to 2 years).

5. Alternative storage options include Azure Blob storage, Azure SQL, and Azure Data Lake Storage Gen 2.

Chapter 4

1. Threat indicators may include IP Addresses, URLs, or specific files.

2. ATT&CK stands for Adversarial Tactics, Techniques, and Common Knowledge.

3. The following Azure Sentinel components can utilize Threat Intelligence feeds:

    -   Analytics

    -   Workbooks

    -   Hunting queries

    -   Notebooks

4. STIX and TAXII were developed as an open community effort, sponsored by the U.S. Department of Homeland Security, in partnership with the MITRE Corporation.

Chapter 5

1. You need to filter the StormEvents table by all the states that are set to California (remember the case-sensitive versus not case-sensitive filters) and then get a count of those rows. You could cheat and look at the output of the first two lines of the following code in the ADE, but that isn't really the best way to get the answer, which is 898:

```
StormEvents
| where State =~ "California"
| summarize count()
```

2. This entails looking at the StormEvents table and getting just one instance of each State. Use the distinct operator for this:

```
StormEvents
| distinct State
```

3. You will need to look at the **DamageProperty** field in the StormEvents table and make sure it is greater than 10,000 and less than 15,000:

```
StormEvents
| where DamageProperty >10000 and DamageProperty <15000
```

4. You have three out of the four columns needed in the StormEvents table already. The fourth column, the one for the total amount of damage, can be created by adding the DamageProperty column and the DamageCrop property. In the following answer, it is called TotalDamage but it really does not matter what you call it as long as you use the same name in the extend and the project commands. Bonus points if you combined extend and project into one. While this is perfectly legal in KQL, if you want to use the variable again, then extend will be needed as the project just outputs the results:

```
StormEvents
| extend TotalDamage = DamageCrops + DamageProperty
| project State, DamageProperty, DamageCrops, TotalDamage
```

Chapter 6

1. You can see pre-made queries by using the sample queries and the query explorer.

2. Use the filter icon at the top of the result pane to show specific computers without changing the query.

3. To see a preview of the log entries; go to the **Tables** pane, mouse over the desired log, and click on the eye icon.

4. To change the number of results on a page when viewing all results pages, go to the page settings and change the **Set # of rows per page** dropdown to **200**.

5. To change the number of results on a page when viewing a single results page, go to the results footer and change the **Items per page** dropdown to **200**.

Chapter 7

1. The four different rule types are Scheduled, Fusion, Microsoft Security, and ML Behavior Analytics.

2. To run a rule on a set interval, use the Scheduled rule type.

3. Yes, you can have alerts from other Azure security systems create incidents in Azure Sentinel.

4. To have a playbook run automatically, select a playbook from the **Automated response** page.

5. To delete a rule that's no longer required, you can hover your mouse over the rule and select **Delete** from the context menu or select the rule and click **Delete** in the header.

Chapter 8

1. To create a new workbook, you either use a template or create one from scratch.

2. To show user instructions on how to use the workbook, use the **Text** step type.

3. To change how far back in time a query in a workbook will search, create a `time` parameter and change all the query steps to use the new parameter.

4. Yes, you can have a workbook step only show when certain conditions are met. Enable the **Make this item conditionally visible** in the step's advanced settings and then add a condition.

5. To show two steps side by side, go to each step's advanced settings and under the **Style** tab, enable **Make this item a custom width** and set each to **50%**.

Chapter 9

1. To change the incidents view to show **In Progress** only, go to the **Search and Filtering** section and under the **Status** dropdown, select **In Progress**.

2. An incident's severity can be viewed in two ways: the first way is by looking at the colored strip at the top of the page and the second is by looking at the **Severity** dropdown.

3. In the **Incident Detail** pane, if the **Investigate** button is grayed out, this indicates this incident has no **entities**.

4. To get the full details of an alert, follow these steps:

   • Find the incident in the incident list.

   • Click on the **View full details** link.

   • In the **Alerts** tab, click on the alert's ID.

5. To check for malicious URLs, go to the **Investigation** page, click on the **Info** button and then select the entity. Look at the **DETONATIONVERDICT** field.

Chapter 10

1. To run a single hunting query, select the query and, in the details pane, click the **Run Query** button.

2. To run all hunting queries, click the **Run all queries** button in the hunting page's header.

3. To view the results of a single hunting query, select the query and in the details pane, click the **View query results** link.

4. To create a new bookmark, run the query on the **Logs** page, select the result(s) to add to a bookmark and then click the **Add bookmark** button.

5. To associate a bookmark with an incident, you can use one of two methods:

   • Create a new incident from a bookmark.

   • Add a bookmark to an existing incident.

Chapter 11

1. To use a Logic App as an Azure Sentinel playbook, it must use the **Azure Sentinel connector**.

2. To tell if a playbook ran successfully, select the playbook from the playbook's page and then look at the **Run History** section.

3. When using a playbook's workflow to get information about an incident, use the **Alert | Get Incident** action and pass in the necessary parameters.

4. Dynamic content is information provided by either a connector or action that can change for each instance of the playbook; for example, the **System Alert ID** field that was used to get the incident in the *Creating a simple Azure Sentinel playbook* section.

5. Yes, you can combine dynamic and static content in one field.

Chapter 12

1. The purpose of an ITSM platform is to log, track, and communicate the coordination of efforts required by each of the solution areas and experts to resolve IT requests, issues, and especially security incidents.

2. The tuning of alerts is necessary to ensure they are relevant, reduce noise, are still valid, and are not returning false positives.

3. The risk of tuning alerts is the potential of missing true positives.

4. When populating a **ServiceNow** dropdown field, the text being passed in has to exactly match what is in **ServiceNow**.

5. An **Expression** is used when a computation is performed on a value before using it in a Logic App field.

Chapter 13

1. The two roles are the SOC Engineer and the SOC Analyst.

2. Both roles need to be involved in carrying out the scenario mapping exercise.

3. The log ingestion rate and pricing tier should be checked at least once per month, carried out by the SOC Engineer.

4. The SOC Analyst should check the **Incidents** page every day.

5. You should look at ingesting logs the moment the instance is created. This will provide maximum visibility of security events.

Other Books You May Enjoy

If you enjoyed this book, you may be interested in these other books by Packt:

Azure Networking Cookbook

Mustafa Toroman

ISBN: 978-1-78980-022-7

- Learn to create Azure networking services
- Understand how to create and work on hybrid connections
- Configure and manage Azure network services
- Learn ways to design high availability network solutions in Azure
- Discover how to monitor and troubleshoot Azure network resources
- Learn different methods of connecting local networks to Azure virtual networks

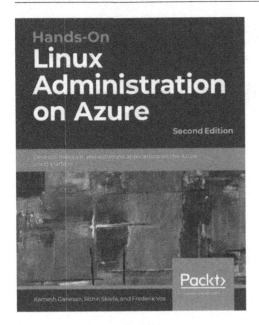

Hands-On Linux Administration on Azure - Second Edition

Kamesh Ganesan, Rithin Skaria, Et al

ISBN: 978-1-83921-552-0

- Grasp the fundamentals of virtualization and cloud computing

- Understand file hierarchy and mount new filesystems

- Maintain the life cycle of your application in Azure Kubernetes Service

- Manage resources with the Azure CLI and PowerShell

- Manage users, groups, and filesystem permissions

- Use Azure Resource Manager to redeploy virtual machines

- Implement configuration management to configure a VM correctly

- Build a container using Docker

Leave a review - let other readers know what you think

Please share your thoughts on this book with others by leaving a review on the site that you bought it from. If you purchased the book from Amazon, please leave us an honest review on this book's Amazon page. This is vital so that other potential readers can see and use your unbiased opinion to make purchasing decisions, we can understand what our customers think about our products, and our authors can see your feedback on the title that they have worked with Packt to create. It will only take a few minutes of your time, but is valuable to other potential customers, our authors, and Packt. Thank you!

Index

Z

Made in the USA
Coppell, TX
02 June 2020